CW01497262

Merlin

The Gordon Hill Autobiography

Merlin

The Gordon Hill Autobiography

Gordon Hill with Wayne Barton

Vertical Editions

www.verticaleditions.com

Copyright © Gordon Hill and Wayne Barton 2014

The right of Gordon Hill and Wayne Barton to be identified as the authors of this work has been asserted in accordance with the Copyright, Designs and Patents Act, 1988

First published in the United Kingdom in 2014 by Vertical Editions, Unit 4a, Snaygill Industrial Estate, Skipton, North Yorkshire BD23 2QR
www.verticaleditions.com

ISBN 978-1-904091-85-1

A CIP catalogue record for this book is available from the British Library

Cover design by HBA, York

Printed and bound by Jellyfish Print, Hampshire

This book is dedicated to my wife and my family who I love dearly and also to the many people who helped me on my way throughout my career. I thank you all.

Gordon Hill

Contents

Acknowledgements

In addition to my dedications I would like to say thank you to Tommy Docherty, Sammy McIlroy and Lou Macari for their contributions. Thanks also to Wayne Barton for helping me put my story down and the various people who helped him, and a big thank you to my sister-in-law Colette Copeland who assisted during the editing process. Thanks also to my dog Cleo for keeping me up all night and finally, thanks to my brothers and sisters for all their support.

Gordon Hill

Thanks to Gordon and his family for their time and help, and for the enriching journey and experience we went on whilst putting this together. Gordon – thank you so much for your fantastic hospitality throughout the road trip of a lifetime across North America. There are many, many funny stories and great memories of that trip which we will never forget, including bingo, gourmet worms, Corbin, and never reaching Amish country. Also the never-ending journey through Georgia, and that sunset.

Thanks to Tommy Docherty, Lou Macari and Sammy McIlroy for their assistance and also to Chris Bethell and Gordon Macey for their help.

Special thanks to Dan Burdett for his consistent help, to Oyvind Enger for being there at any time, and also to Mikiel and Phil Gatt. Extra thanks to Elfyn and Hayley Roberts for their unwavering support.

Huge thanks also to my wonderful mother for her profound contribution for which I will be eternally grateful, to my beautiful wife for her enduring support, and to my brother, Nana, and in-laws for always believing, encouraging and having faith in me.

Heartfelt thanks to Brian Greenhoff who introduced me to Gordon.

Wayne Barton

Foreword

I first became aware of Gordon after watching him play for Millwall around the same time that we noticed Steve Coppell playing for Tranmere Rovers. As it happened I couldn't attend the game I wanted to watch Gordon in, which was some time after we signed Stevie, so Jimmy Murphy, who was our chief scout at the time and a wonderful man, went in my absence. He took a report as he always would do but I got a phone call at midnight that very evening and it was Jimmy who said 'Sign him.' I was slightly confused and asked him who he wanted me to sign. When he answered Hilly, Gordon Hill, I told him he would have to fill in the report. I won't repeat what he replied but it was basically to forget the report, because he insisted that by the time we'd gone through it someone else would have signed him.

We talked to Millwall and agreed a deal but I wanted to confirm Jimmy's opinion so I went to watch Gordon play for Millwall at Walsall. He was playing centre forward and after about twenty minutes I knew he was a stone-wall certainty. I wanted to confirm the signing there and then as I daren't wait any longer as someone else might have been in for him at half time. A great talent and a left foot to die for, it really was like a wand. He had great vision and was cheeky, a real character. I was a big believer in trusting a player's ability regardless of their age and Gordon fitted the bill. Jimmy was an unbelievable judge of talent and so we pushed through a deal with Millwall.

The fee was around £70,000 and a percentage of that was to be paid up front with another payment after a dozen matches. When

Gordon had played a couple of games for United I went to Les Olive, the club secretary, and told him he might as well send the cheque. Gordon was the biggest certainty ever. I've always loved wingers and Gordon was a revelation. He was a good trainer who just loved to play. You couldn't exactly sit down and work through a pattern of play with him, you'd just have to let him go out and perform. There was no point giving him instructions to beat the full back on a certain side, he was his own man and had so much talent that some of the other players were envious of him. He could infuriate his team-mates as I can remember in a game against Coventry at Old Trafford which I missed because I had flu. I listened on the radio and could barely believe my ears when I heard that Martin Buchan had slapped Gordon in the face. I think it was because he hadn't defended in a way that Martin wanted. But that was Hilly, he could do nothing for eighty minutes and then he'd win you the game because he had so much skill.

He proved that with his fantastic goals in the 1976 FA Cup semi-final, although people remember that he was brought off in the final. It wasn't an easy decision that day because you knew that if you were going to bring him off you could lose the potential match winner. Gordon being Gordon, he always responded to that kind of motivation. He wanted to be the best and liked to be told that he was the best.

There's no question that if I had remained manager of Manchester United, Gordon would have stayed at Old Trafford until his playing days were over. Of course, when he did leave United, I was the one who signed him for Derby County, and again after that for Queens Park Rangers. Unfortunately he suffered an injury at Derby in a freak accident and following that he was never quite the same. I had hoped that being back in London would have suited him but it never really worked out. Despite that, he was a wonderful signing for me and he was an absolute joy to watch. He was a crowd pleaser, a great attraction for the supporters and a great goalscorer. As soon as he crossed the line at three o'clock on a Saturday he was his own man, impossible to coach, but I wouldn't have had him any other way.

Tommy Docherty, March 2014

Introduction 1

When Gordon arrived at Old Trafford from Millwall in November 1976 he was a cheeky, chirpy Cockney but as soon as we saw him training his ability really stood out. He had a fantastic left foot, incredible power in his shot and great ability on the ball.

He was definitely a great character and you certainly knew when Gordon Hill was around. He was a jovial bloke, always happy-go-lucky, and always one to tell a joke and keep the spirits up. A few of the lads would try and wind him up but he played along with it and would have a laugh and a joke about everything. He really fitted in well with the team.

Gordon was a winger; but he was not only a scorer of great goals, but a great goalscorer. In fairness, his goal tally for a wide man was incredible. The number of goals he scored in our team was something that really stood out. We had a great wing pairing with Stevie Coppell and Gordon, both with their strengths, and as soon as Gordon came in his goals were a great help to us. He gave such an extra dimension. Stevie was more of an all-rounder but Gordon wasn't, but he gave us something different and we accepted that. At the end of the season one of our wingers was in double figures for goals and it was always Gordon Hill. He fitted in to the side perfectly and excited the crowd every time he was on the pitch.

As a midfielder I had the job of getting the ball and giving it to Hilly. He was great to play with, and a good provider, but I really can't stress how incredible his goal return was. He was unique, there just weren't players about like him, and in his last season for us he got over twenty goals which was remarkable. The amount of those goals that were from outside the box is also worth mentioning. There were two great goals against Derby County in the semi-final which everyone remembers, but he scored plenty of goals just as good at Old Trafford and it was easy to see why he was a favourite of the fans.

Once Tommy Docherty left the club a few players also left and Gordon was one of them. I thought he was let go too soon. Even though the new manager had different ideas I felt there was always room in our team for Gordon. It was his goals that played such a big part in our success.

Manchester United have always had a fine tradition of fantastic wingers going back to the Sixties, right through the Seventies. The Old Trafford crowd and flying wingers go together. People still talk about the team we played in with a large degree of fondness, and there is no question about it, Gordon Hill deserves to be mentioned alongside the greats.

Sammy McIlroy, April 2014

Introduction 2

Nobody had heard a great deal about Gordon before he signed from Millwall so we were in the dark a little bit. It's fair to say that over the years, players have come to Old Trafford from any club with both big and small reputations, and so often it's been a bit too much for them, but Gordon took it in his stride and it was no problem to him whatsoever.

He was a confident lad and he was able to settle in easily. I think the main reason for that was because he was a young player trying to make his way in the game and there just wasn't a bad bone in his body. He was happy-go-lucky and determined to make the most of his opportunity and be a success at Manchester United. He managed to do that and we were all delighted that he became such a big favourite with supporters.

He was naturally left footed and there weren't too many of them about, certainly not at United, but he could play on either flank and play well. Alongside Steve Coppell, who'd done exceptionally well, Gordon really shone. There weren't many wingers around and to get a pair from the lower leagues who were both top class was pretty lucky. It was a real achievement by the Doc. Hilly was one of the best strikers of a ball that I'd seen in my time at Old Trafford. Volleys, awkward situations, he could cope with all of it, and as a result of that he scored some memorable goals at times when goals probably didn't seem possible.

He was different to Stevie. You had to accept that Gordon was a flair player who wanted to do his own thing and I couldn't find a fault in him. He took his fair share of jokes and pranks, but for what he did on the pitch, even if he sometimes made the wrong pass or shot, you would accept it because of what you knew he was capable of. Even if he did make the wrong choice then maybe, because he'd had such a meteoric rise, he was entitled to do so and could be forgiven.

As for pranks, there were a couple I was part of but I think he deserved it. If I had ten pounds for every time he mentioned Mr Grimsdale at Old Trafford, then I'm in no doubt that today I'd be a millionaire. Gordon loved Norman Wisdom and would do the impression up to twenty times a day so it deserved a little bit of a backlash. Gordon loved his tennis, in fairness he was very good, but sometimes we'd set up mythical tennis matches with him in the hotel and he'd never ever win one. Me and Sammy McIlroy, or one of the others, would do the commentary and shout 'Out' or 'double fault' – no racquets or balls, but every service from Gordon would be out. On occasion, we'd shout that it was out and he'd reply that it wasn't out. I'm not a tennis player but I think the other lads preferred the mythical games because in all fairness he would have beaten them at the real thing.

We played at Middlesbrough on one of the first trips after he joined and I got somebody to ring up pretending to be from Tyne Tees Television offering £500 for an interview with Gordon. Of course there was no such interview but we arranged a taxi to come and pick him up, take him a couple of miles, and then drop him off in the middle of the country in no-man's land. We were all anxiously waiting for his return from this 'television' appearance and a couple of hours later he came back. Alex Stepney asked him how it went and quick as a flash he said, 'Bit of a mix up. It wasn't television, it was radio.' That wasn't arranged either but Gordon took it in his stride and it was just part of the good team spirit we had.

Dave Sexton wasn't a fan of his and that was the end. Some managers have their own views and Dave had a different view than Tommy Docherty, but one thing no one could say was that Gordon hadn't been a success at United. He was clinical and looked at home at United. Some would say he wasn't a team player but I wasn't interested in that, I was only interested in the ability he had and what he brought to us. I could forgive him for not being as hard working because of the imagination and youthfulness that he brought to the table.

I would go as far as saying that Gordon truly summed up the United team under Tommy Docherty. He wasn't full of himself and had so much flair, creativity and technique that he was a pleasure to play alongside. I'm sure Gordon would say the same and the only downside to his time at Manchester United was when he had to leave.

Lou Macari, April 2014

Prologue

There are so many things I'm asked about my time at Manchester United and it's very difficult to give answers to what was my favourite goal, my favourite game, and who was the best player I played with. I enjoyed every game of football I ever had but especially for Manchester United, the biggest club in the world. I mean this sincerely when I say that every time I walked out for that club with the badge on my chest it was the best time I've had in the game. Every moment I put the ball in the net was as thrilling as the one before and I would not have changed a player from my team at United. They were my team, my friends, and I believed we could have conquered the world and achieved it all.

To some that may seem like an easy way out of answering. Of course it was special to score those semi-final goals against Derby County in 1976, and of course it was special to play alongside the likes of Lou Macari and Stuart Pearson. But if I'm asked to single one out I simply can't because of the respect and esteem in which I hold all of my old team-mates and the pride with which I was filled when I represented United. It goes back further, to my education in the game at Millwall when I was given some fantastic guidance from the late Brian Clark, and my time in North America where I had what was a fateful meeting with the legendary Bill Foulkes.

I decided it was the right time to set down my autobiography in late 2012, and it is fitting that the journey of writing it reflected my life and career so far. I played my football in Europe and I played all over the USA, and what an experience. In the process of putting my life into this record, the book has been written and put together in North America and the UK. I hope you enjoy the story.

1

So, You Wanna Be a Pro?

Well, where do we start? I never even had my own pair of boots until I was eleven!

We had very little when I was growing up. I had five brothers and three sisters, eleven of us living in a three bedroom council house down Laytons Lane in Sunbury-on-Thames, Middlesex, on the west side of London. Today it's classed as being in Surrey. Mum and Dad had their room, the girls had their own room and that meant the boys would have to sleep head to toe and queue up to wait for someone to leave the house to get their own bed. We'd argue and fight like all brothers and sisters, particularly the boys. The love was there, that was for sure, and we were a very close family who made do with what we had. The chicken would have to serve us all on a Sunday dinner, it never had anything left on it after we had finished eating.

My mum did really well though. She was so generous and kind that she would give you the sweater off her back if you needed it. My dad helped look after the gardens at Hampton Court Palace and he was always working. He'd also been a car sprayer but gave it up because it had affected his lungs. He was a Labour man through and through and he loved a pint or two, or ten.

Our parents brought us up with good values and we were taught never to steal, tell lies, or cheat. Mum always used to say that she never wanted to see a policeman knock on the door. As well as teaching us those values they were very proud and strict, and we were always told we had to be in bed by seven at night because of school the next day. Dad didn't drive, though he could drive a tractor, so we never had a car but he did have a bike and it was like a Rolls Royce to him. He'd strap his spade and fork on there and ride all the way from Sunbury to Hampton Court, which was about three miles. He would get on his bike some evenings and try to find us if we were out late. I can remember when he used to come up to the 'Rec' to get me, and the boys I was playing with would shout out that your Dad's here, so I would leg it and run out of the other gate and try to get home before he got hold of me.

We were brought up to be streetwise and we needed to be. But I felt that if I'd cheated someone then I had to tell them the truth. I would never feel right taking something that wasn't mine or I hadn't earned, and those are the values and principles that Mum and Dad gave us. When I was very young there was a threepenny bit on the table. I asked Mum if I could take it and she said no. But I did, and I felt so awful that I put it back. Mum would go to the Women's Voluntary Service, to get us clothes. There was a nurse there called Nurse Plant and she was a diamond. She would always tell my mum that her kids were the best behaved, which made Mum really proud, and then Nurse Plant would give us all a penny.

On our street we knew everyone. One side was private, but the other was council. There was Mrs Taylor with her son Johnny, Mrs Smith with Jack, David and Kevin, Mrs Brant with Neddy, Mrs Hogg, who had twins Barry and Garry and their younger brother Harry and eldest brother Derek, and also Mrs Bale with Peter and Dickie. We knew everybody and lived right in the heart of the street. Just up the road was Mrs Edwards with Paul and Johnny, Mrs Howell with a son called Kenny, and Charlie and Ray Moore were on the Lane too as well as a guy called Zigmont Liszt who was a good lad but a bit strange. I could go on and on and on as most of the families had girls as well, but I would only really know the boys. When you came from 'the Lane' everybody knew you.

Up the road was a pub called the Jolly Gardeners which was run by landlord Jack Woods. My dad's favourite place was 'up the Jolly's.' Sometimes Mum would join him for a gin and tonic as it was only fifty yards up the road. He'd have a game of darts there and enter the competition on a Sunday to win a chicken which would be a bonus to the chicken or beef we already had, but we weren't allowed in apart from the off licence area in the middle. It was great as that was where we'd buy Arrowroot biscuits for a penny, usually the penny we'd got from Nurse Plant, and they would last for ages. Sometimes we'd buy toffee bars, but only if we fancied a trip to the dentist because those things back then took your teeth out. Because Mum rarely had treats, when we were older and earning money, with mine coming from football, we used to give her some hoping she would get something or do something nice for herself. Typical Mum though, if we'd given her £20 we'd find out she'd passed on £10 to Dad. With the £10 she had left she'd go straight up the shop and buy food to feed us. It drove us mad. We'd tell her to go to bingo at the Sunbury Conservative Club and sit with her friends.

At Primary School, which was Nursery Road Primary School right at the top of the lane, I met a boy called Jon Barnett who would turn out to be my best friend, and who I've kept in touch with ever since. He lives in Swansea now but he's only ever a phone call away. Despite a reputation that would follow me in later years, at school I wasn't exactly stupid. I got B's and C's, but I was always concentrating more on playing football. I'd be doing that morning, noon and night. I'd take on the teachers in five-a-sides during breaks and I'd try to roast them. I just wanted to play. I'd do normal things as a kid like 'Penny for the Guy,' which is an English tradition that takes place around Bonfire Night on November 5th where children make effigies of Guy Fawkes and ask for money, but I was always just so obsessed with football. If I had a girlfriend I'd leave her at home with my mum and I'd go and play football. When I got home my mum would let me know that she had been waiting there for two hours and I would reply by saying, 'Yeah ... but I had a good game of football though Mum!'

My brothers and I were very competitive with each other. My big brother Sid was a good footballer but also a fine cricketer too. He was also interested in gardening and went to college to study agriculture. He worked with his friend Chris Mews in his father's nursery where you would get your flowers or tomatoes.

After doing all that work he decided he wanted to be a postman and did that for about thirty years or more. He was also a long distance runner and he ran the Boston and London Marathons.

My brother Graham was a good defender who was in the youth set-up at Chelsea as a kid. My brother David didn't play football too much but was very tough and he was in the army. I can remember him coming home one day into a tiny little road in one of the big army lorries. All of a sudden out of the back jumped twelve big army boys. I turned to Mum to tell her that David was here and he had brought the army home with him. They were based in Aldershot which wasn't too far away, but were from all over the country. Mum made tea for every single one of them, she made friends with them all, and after they left the forces half of them came back at one time or another. That was Mum. David was a cross country runner who had won a few medals and yet he was discharged from the Army for having flat feet. Can you believe that?

I thought about maybe joining the army or the navy but it just wasn't for me in the end. My brother Tony was an electrical engineer who was an electrical genius for the band 'The Who' for about twenty years. Adrian is another brother who works in car sales, and Cyril is my other brother. My brothers and I entered a football tournament as a team when we were kids though I can't remember much about it. We won and I scored most of the goals ... like I say, my memory is hazy on that, but it's been brought up that many times that I don't doubt it happened. It's a shame because I'd love to remember that clearly!

My sister Dawn now lives in our old house on Layton's Lane. My sister Sue lives in Bracknell and she had a boy named Paul who had spina bifida when he was born and also fell ill with leukemia. He wasn't supposed to see four years of age, but is now well in to his thirties. The illness took away his toes, ankles, and eventually both of his legs but he is such a lovable, laughable fella despite his troubles. He had a permanent bed in Great Ormond Street and later on in my career when I used to travel to London for a game I'd always make time to be sure I went and saw him. I'd take him little bits and pieces from United but then it turned out he supported Liverpool. He'd tell the doctors and nurses that his uncle Gordon was coming to see him, but he didn't care because he supported Liverpool. He played a five-a-side once and his legs fell off so he went in goal!

Sue has had a tough, tough time bringing him up. She's had to fight so hard to get help from the council. When I consider all they've been through, it really brings reality back to me. I love him so much, he's so funny. One time I received a phone call from Sue to ask for a favour. She said Paul had been trying to get a signed shirt from Liverpool for years. I had many nice friends at Liverpool and got in touch with Phil Thompson telling him that I don't know how this happened, but I've got a nephew and he supports Liverpool. I explained what had been happening and Thommo did a great thing. He got a shirt and had all the players sign it. Sue contacted me after Paul received it for his birthday and told me that I should have seen his face. He told his mum that he knew Uncle Gordon had got it for him but thought I didn't like Liverpool. That really made my day. Sue and her husband Rob have done so well. I have another sister, Caroline, who lives in Southampton, and she is a nurse. It's difficult because I don't know so much of the family as I haven't had chance to meet them but I would still do anything for them, and I'm always concerned about all my brothers and sisters. If I had played in an era where I was earning the money that players earned in today's game then I would help them all out.

Mum and Dad's house was very much the hub of the family. Apart from me, everyone lived within a ten mile radius and would always pop in to see them. Mum loved to be the nursery for everyone to bring their kids and stay for a few hours. It wasn't just our close family that was big, our extended family was large too as my Dad had seven brothers as well. It was tough, but we never did get in any trouble though we knew people who did and had a holiday with Her Majesty. But we were always more involved with sports and that kept us away from the things that might have led us into trouble. Sometimes we'd get on the train and go to Waterloo and back just for the train ride, though to do that we'd have to get to the station at a certain time when the ticket conductor wasn't there.

With our family being so big, Mum and Dad never got the

chance to take us on proper holidays, but we managed to have plenty of adventures. The holidays we did have would be a trip down to Brighton beach for the day and sitting on the rocks was fun. It was the closest beach, so if anyone was going to Brighton we'd go along. So we'd see the sea, but my favourite past-time near the water was fishing. Dad would go down the River Thames and as we grew older I'd go down there night fishing with my mates, where we'd mainly catch eels or carp. We couldn't afford a tent but it was great.

I also used to love going apple picking in the orchard. We'd do anything for an extra shilling, selling blackberries we'd picked, or shovelling snow for the neighbours. We'd even go on building sites and help unload the bricks off the lorries and get a couple of shillings from the driver for helping. I once saved up the money to go to Butlins purely on my own. I paid for it and everything but then, in the end, I never went. I thought it would have been a good way to go and meet some girls as one of my brothers had worked at Butlins in Skegness and met his wife Ann there so it sounded like a good place to go. I thought I could make friends anywhere and a friend of the family called Steve Armitage, who I'd do some odd jobs for, encouraged me saying it would do me the world of good. In the end I just decided not to go.

I'd play football with my brother Sid and his friend Johnny Taylor who was our neighbour, and we would always pretend we were players like Ferenc Puskas, Alfredo Di Stefano, George Best or Denis Law. Coming from such a big family it was easy to settle in playing football, particularly as a young boy. We used to play up on Cedars Recreational Ground, nicknamed the 'Rec,' in Sunbury-on-Thames. Even in those very early days I was learning my skills. There was a field down the bottom of Laytons Lane which was an old farmer's field where he grew everything. The man was named George Roots and it was called Roots Farm. He'd turn the soil over with his plough. I could get a shortcut to the 'Rec' if I went across the field, so I'd run over, chipping my ball over the little ridges in the soil and seeing how quickly I could get to it. Playing in the rough I was able to learn some early ball control.

Our next door neighbour, bless her soul, was called Mrs

Harding. If we were playing on the street and kicked the ball into her garden she'd stick a knife through it if she got to it first and we'd lose the ball. Despite this she was ever so nice, but just didn't like us kicking the ball into her garden. Whenever the ball went in there I'd always try and jump over the fence and retrieve it before she came out. She would say that she would get me the next time but I would tell her that she had no chance. But if the ball was too near her front door I'd have to think twice.

If we didn't have a ball we had to try and get one from someone else, or use a plastic Frido ball. If that got punctured, then you could repair it with a red hot poker, melting it back together, but half the time you'd put a great big hole in it! We'd always let the kid who couldn't play the best but who had a ball be captain to make sure he'd play. Then when he went home we'd have a problem so we'd ask him if we could borrow the ball and if he wouldn't let us then we'd be back to square one.

Not only did we not have a ball very often, I didn't even have a pair of boots until QPR bought me a pair when I was eleven. They were Power-Points, a black pair of boots with a number one fixed on at the front, a number two at the side and a number three at the back. One for shooting, two for inside and three for back-heels. They were a good pair of boots once I took the numbers off. It made a change from wearing boots that were either too small for me or so big that I had to stuff paper in. We used to play the game called Wembley where everyone plays against each other and you have to score a goal to go through to the next round. My mates used to make me score three goals instead of the one, but I'd still end up winning.

Sometimes they wouldn't let me play at all because they said they could never get the ball off me, so I would give in and tell them that I wouldn't be allowed to score, only pass. Then I'd be setting everyone up and they'd all be happy because they were all scoring goals. The Rec was my second home, I had some fantastic memories with Jon who was goalkeeper when we played for the Cubs. When it came to playing games everyone would want me on their side, that was just how it was. Playing for my school, Kenyngton Manor, I was a first year and I was playing for the first, second, third and fourth year every night they had a game.

I loved it and just couldn't get enough of playing.

I was twelve when England won the World Cup on July 30th, 1966. I remember the day very vividly. I was sitting in the lounge, or the front room as we called it, watching a tension filled game on television. Germany went in front, Geoff Hurst equalised, and when Martin Peters scored with less than a quarter of an hour to go we thought we'd won it. Wolfgang Weber took it to extra time with a last minute equaliser. Franz Beckenbauer had taken control of the game in that stylish manner he had to get them back into it, but I still say we had a player just as good in Bobby Moore – man that guy was cool. Geoff scored his second, that controversial goal that would have the whole of England saying it crossed the line and the whole of West Germany saying it didn't.

Little did he know it but he'd also caused some argument in the Hill household. As he scored I jumped up off the sofa and back down on it breaking a spring. Well, my mum went absolutely potty at me, shouting, 'Get out of this house you little sod.' I just about managed to see Geoff complete his hat-trick as the fans invaded the Wembley pitch. What an incredible memory.

Of course, as soon as the whistle went I was the first to run out to the park where all the other boys had come out to play the World Cup Final with everyone wanting to be Bobby Charlton or Geoff and Martin who'd scored the goals. The World Cup is the biggest and most prestigious tournament there is and to represent your national team and win the trophy must be the most fantastic feeling. I've sometimes suggested there should be two World Cups, one for the bigger countries and one for the smaller ones who don't really have the chance to win it, just so that they get the opportunity. It'd never happen, but it'd be great to see.

I'd been playing football all over the place in and around the West London area when all of a sudden I started to get spotted by clubs. A guy who worked for West Ham called Wilf Chitty wanted me to join them at an early age, maybe when I was nine or ten. My parents wouldn't let me sign because I lived on the other side of London. Tottenham got in touch in October 1967 and sent me six programmes and a signed photograph sheet with a letter asking if I'd like to start training with them. I've still got the letter

27

to this day. My dad turned Spurs down for the same reason he turned down West Ham, it was just too far. He wasn't much at writing letters so he basically just said no to them. Despite that, I wasn't upset. It was nice that clubs were interested in me and it wasn't the end of the world that I didn't get to go though I'd have liked it. Both Tottenham and West Ham were fantastic clubs but honestly, my reaction was 'never mind'.

I wouldn't say it was only a matter of time until I was noticed by a club that my parents felt I could go to, but it was a great feeling to know that Football League clubs were aware of who I was, and there were so many in London that I just felt I could keep playing the way I was and hopefully I'd get offered a place by a club that my mum and dad were happy for me to go to. They just didn't want me travelling across London, my mum was definitely against that, and I could understand it.

In the meanwhile, I was playing for the football team of the 1st Halliford Cubs, as they played in the only league that was structured and the Cubs were the only team who had a decent strip – full shirts, shorts and socks. I wore the number ten because I wanted to be an out and out forward. I played five games for the Cubs and scored forty nine goals, it was great. I never went to the Scouts. I did enjoy the Cubs but was mostly there for the football. I was selected for the Cubs county team in a game where we won 6-4. About 20 minutes into the game this little kid kicked me, so I turned around and whacked him. The referee grabbed me by the scruff of the neck, lifted me up and told me to get off the field for ten minutes. Sent off for the Cubs. That was the first time I'd been sent off and I was only nine. So off I went and I was really ticked off because they were winning 4-3. When the ten minutes were up, I came back on and scored three. We played in a cup final against 1st Sunbury Cubs and won 9-2, and I scored eight of them. When I was a bit older I played for a club called Sunbury Celtic, a local select side who gave me a great big club handbook which I've still got. In two seasons there I scored 176 goals. We played in a final against a team much bigger than us and I got a hat-trick.

The only time we ever had a policeman at the door was during my spell at Sunbury Celtic, and that was because Bill Robinson, the local policeman, was the coach. He was a brilliant man who would regularly come and pick me up. I just wanted to play, and they wanted me on their team because I would help them win. The reason I really loved playing for them was that they had a brilliant new green uniform. Growing up, I never really followed a particular team.

I was good at tennis, which made a change from football, and I took it up at a local boys club when I was thirteen with a coach called John Moyle. I had one racquet and I broke it quite early on as I tended to get frustrated quite a lot. I entered about half a dozen tournaments and John used to tell the local county people that if you gave this boy a racquet he would be your next champion. It was too snotty for me, though but I played in a tournament against the likes of Buster Mottram and Linda Mottram, and the Lloyds, Tony, David and John, were there. I played against John and he did me 6-1, 6-1 but funnily enough, we became friends after that. He's a Wolves fan, but I never held that against him. I couldn't afford the proper kit and they were walking around with their Dunlop racquets and bags. I can remember playing a match in the Surbiton Open. My opponent kept calling my shots out when they were in. I walked up to the net and used a little bit of football banter on him. I told him that if he called out one more time I was going to put this racquet through his head. I knew that maybe my etiquette for tennis wasn't quite right because I'd have killed McEnroe. John knew how good I was at football, John Moyle that is, not John McEnroe!

One Christmas, Mum bought us football kits that cost ten shillings and sixpence, and we had a choice of red and white, or blue and white. I was always for red and white because I used to admire a big poster above my brother's bed of the Manchester United European Cup Final team with Bill Foulkes, Denis Law and Bobby Charlton. I could never travel up to Manchester to watch them play at Old Trafford, but my tennis coach had a season ticket at Chelsea in the West Stand. When I wasn't playing, I'd go there and watch players like Peter Osgood, Charlie Cook and the great Jimmy Greaves in a superb team managed by Tommy Docherty. When Man United came to town all I wanted was to be like the players I was watching. The mid-sixties really were a golden era for English football and I can remember watching that 1968 European Cup Final and being on the edge of my seat as Bobby Charlton and Brian Kidd scored. How could anyone not be excited by George Best's goal, the way he moved around the goalkeeper with such confidence to put the ball in the net. I couldn't say 'this was my team' about any club, I was a lover of all football and took in as much as I could, but as my life went on there would be one club above all that would have that hold on me, and the magic of United was with me as early as the 1960s.

Despite being good at tennis it was pretty much destined that I would go on to play football. My brothers were very good players too, one of them played for Walton and Hersham and turned down Brentford, while another played for Chelsea as a right back. I was the only one who signed for a club as a schoolboy and that was for Queens Park Rangers when I was ten because the club was the most local to us. As a young boy there I was introduced to professionals like Terry Venables and Rodney Marsh. It was quite strange considering that I would go on to play for Terry later on, while in my opinion Rodney had his best spell at QPR.

As a boy I was no height at all, so QPR went to the expense of sending me to hospital for an x-ray on my back to try and determine what my height would be when I was eleven. They said five foot seven which turned out to be right. The doctors said I would be very strong and would benefit from a low centre of gravity, not that I'd ever worry about fighting as I'd never want to fight on the field anyway. I might get in someone's face but if I was to start a fight I'd probably have got a clip on the ear. I would go training there two nights a week with a view to hopefully signing as an apprentice in the future. As it turned out, I never served my apprenticeship in the game. When I was thirteen, Derek Healy, the scout, told me I should get my hair cut. I told him I don't play with my hair. I wanted to leave but they wouldn't release me until I was fifteen.

Around the same time, friends of my brothers wanted me to play for their Sunday team. Anyone familiar with playing football at a local level will know that Sunday is the rough football because the good players are playing in the semi-pro divisions that normally play on a Saturday. The Sunday team was called

Sunbury Casuals and it was made up of all those good players who would also play on a Saturday, and the team would pay my two shillings and sixpence which was my subs. I loved going to the games early on a Sunday afternoon to help putting the nets on the goals, and even getting the goals from the war bunkers and putting them in the holes in the ground.

The only thing I wanted when I was a kid was to play on a pitch where the goals had nets on. When you played without nets and scored a goal you might have to run a mile to get the ball back. My mum would be the tea-lady for the team but my dad would never come and watch me play. Sid and his mates would protect me which was great but playing in those leagues really helped toughen me up after sometimes getting kicked, bruised and battered. It didn't bother me, I knew they were doing it because I was scoring goals. I wasn't cocky or arrogant, I was just confident in what I did. I suppose you could say I was a greedy little bugger, but I just wanted to put the ball in the net and to do that as quickly as I could. My confidence had come from being in a big family and not being taken seriously, having brothers who would always tell me to get out of it. That competitive nature was really bedded into me. I would hate losing a game of football, sometimes it would upset me so much I would cry, and it would make me so determined to go back and take it out on the next team. These were parts of my personality that would always stay with me.

As well as the ball games which I loved, I was also enthusiastic about woodwork at school. I loved the smell of it when you shaved it with a plane, and I'd miss classes and lessons to go and do extra woodwork. I also started missing lessons when I got selected to play for the various school teams. There were three sports teachers: Mr Denslow, Mr Thomas and Mr Bremner, as well as the history teacher Mr Atkinson who loved his football. They watched me play football all the way through school and would always want me to play. They would tell me that the fifth form needed a player and as it meant I could get out of lessons early I would say yes. I was only twelve but the school were really great with me.

I left school quite early, not so much because the family

needed it, but it was always nice to earn money. So I got a job at a local foundry in the woodwork shop to train as an apprentice pattern maker where I was paid five pounds a week, and three pounds of it I gave to Mum. I would go without, I was happy just to have my family around. It's amazing that when you haven't got anything, you really don't worry. You haven't got it, so what can they take? I loved being around the wood, the precision that went into working with it. It helped that my mate Jon was in the foundry as his dad was the manager there, plus the shop would let me have Saturdays off to play football if I had a game. At the time I went to an England schoolboys trial but was rejected as they said I was too small and that really upset me.

When I turned fifteen and finally managed to leave QPR, Bill Robinson and Mr Treddigo who had been looking after me at Sunbury Celtic sorted me out with a trial up at Nottingham Forest and I went up there for a week. I was in digs with Duncan McKenzie and John Robinson. John and I were both left wingers. Tommy Cavanagh, who I would come across later in my life and career, was a coach at Forest. It was a good week. I played in a game against the police and I scored. In the end the choice was between Robbo and me and they decided to take John who went on to play with Forest and Scotland, with some distinction.

I began to play for a really good local side called Hanworth United. The coach was a guy called Bill Latter who worked at an airport. He was football mad and really into our team. We had a very senior team for our age group which included schoolboys who played for different clubs, and we got to the County Finals where I once again managed to score.

My brother Sid was playing for Southall FC who were an amateur club in the Athenian League. He played under a coach called Tom Tranter who was also a PE instructor at Borough Road College in West London, which was a famous college for developing teachers. I asked my brother if I could go with him and they allowed me and then also let me train.

After a pre-season of training my brother left, but they said they wanted to sign me. I was eager to play at the next level and to sign as a semi-professional at the age of sixteen, and I started really well there, scoring twenty two goals in twelve games.

After a game a scout from Millwall, Dave Phillips, came over and said they'd like to take me for a trial. I played one full reserve game there and half of another in front of the manager Benny Fenton who said straight away that they would sign me. I signed without hesitation, meaning I'd become a professional without having to go through an apprenticeship – in football anyway. The move meant I left my job where I'd started to earn a bit of money. The contract I started on was twenty five pounds a week, and I gave my mum ten pounds of it. The transfer fee Millwall paid to Southall was a bag of balls, so make your own joke ...

After being so obsessed with football while growing up, I suppose it seemed a natural progression that I would get a career in the game, but my family were still surprised when I signed terms with Millwall and I certainly never took it for granted. I could quite easily have been turned down and at times I had doubts that it would ever happen. My brothers would tell me I was dreaming, and it seemed like my chance had gone as not many people would sign professional terms without serving an apprenticeship. I just kept hoping and working hard and believed one day it would happen. I know my brothers and sisters were very proud, though nobody expected that I would go on and play as high as I did. In West London and Middlesex there were so many good players who fell by the wayside or simply lost their way. There were countless stories of young men who could have made it but didn't have the right attitude or application. I never gave in when faced with concerns about my height. I never smoked – though I tried it once and hated it – I rarely went out or drank when I was young, I've never seen or touched a drug and I really looked after myself. I was so grateful that Benny Fenton gave me a chance at a club where I would go on to share some wonderful times.

2

Becoming Merlin

It was February 1973 when I joined Millwall. I signed for the club as they travelled to Goodison Park on the third of the month to defeat Everton with a Harry Cripps goal. The club had taken me up there, and my good friend Jon was with me. He sorted out a message on the scoreboard at half time, a congratulations message to me for signing for the club. As someone who absolutely loved being around the game so much that even putting the nets up was a thrill for me, to travel to one of the most renowned stadiums in England knowing that I was signing for one of the most famous – or should that be infamous – clubs in the country was a strange, but wonderful feeling.

As I mentioned earlier, I had been to games before and sat on the terraces at Stamford Bridge, but to be there as someone who had just signed as a professional, someone who was hopefully about to participate in games just like this, it really showed me what it was all about. It was a real day out for Millwall as it was the fourth round of the FA Cup, and though we would get knocked out in the next round it gave me a taste of what to expect, what to aspire to. What a dream come true.

I started training with Millwall on a Tuesday and gave my notice in at work on the Wednesday or Thursday. My manager at work, John, was a close friend of the family and a big supporter of mine. When I told him I was going to go have a trial with Millwall he said he had no problem at all with it. He was so accommodating and when I eventually signed he told me that he had been watching me all my life and that he would go over the

Rec to see me play. He also said that he was pleased for me and knew that it was what I wanted.

My training and trial matches hadn't been with the senior professionals at the club so when I first went there I had to go and earn their respect. The squad wasn't very big when I joined so I was training with the first and reserve sides. In a way, that was the apprenticeship I'd missed out on, especially considering I was around the team for a couple of months and it wasn't until I turned nineteen that I would actually go on to make my debut. There were legends at the club such as Harry Cripps, Barry Kitchener and Gordon Bolland who were all players who had established themselves at the Den. Harry, who was a Jack Jones fanatic, had a Jaguar which he would have the young players clean on a Friday.

Millwall was a club that had players like Alex Stepney who had since left to win a European Cup. Keith Weller, too, who was a great player. It was a club that wouldn't stand on sentiment, a famous club, and of course I'd now gone from playing amateur football to playing in the Second Division. There was a guy called Jack Blackman who was the kitman-cum-physio-cum-waterboy. He was a diamond and in his playing days was a centre forward for Charlton. Benny Fenton was the manager and he would come to the training ground with silver and black hair looking like one of the Kray brothers. It was a strange world. The players were all characters in their own right, Harry was for sure. I can remember playing in Barry Kitchener's testimonial against Tottenham Hotspur in 1975. It was Kitchie's night, but Harry, who had his testimonial some time before, was running around shaking everybody's hand as if it was his own. I asked him what he was doing as it was big Kitch's testimonial but all he could say was that it was a great night.

Kitchie's brother had his own stall at the Covent Garden market selling flowers. Down at Millwall everyone seemed to have access to everything, everyone knew someone who could get something from the back of a lorry. Some players would come in with trousers, some would come in with shirts and some could even get jewellery. Big Kitch lived in Essex but was so revered by everyone that when there was a petrol and sugar shortage, there was always somewhere we could go to make sure we filled up. That was the kindness that he showed but that was what it was like living in the Millwall world. Sugar shortage? There was never a sugar shortage in the back of Kitchie's car!

I don't think it's changed and I don't think it ever will. It's the tradition of the club that existed before and went on for so long after. Maybe it's difficult to understand for someone who doesn't quite get Millwall, and maybe it was different back then to how it is today. The club was the hub of the community, the Millwall people loved their football and their team and the players and club understood that. Of course, with the rascal side of it as I've mentioned, there was a unique relationship there and I can't help but feel that we had a greater connection as a consequence.

For me and for all those reasons, Millwall could not have been a more perfect club for me to learn the ropes. It signified everything that I loved about the game, the down to earth relationships, the camaraderie between the players and the players and supporters, the way that everyone pulled in to make the best for each other. I wouldn't say it was daunting and I knew I had a challenge on my hands to establish and prove myself, but I felt that with Millwall I would be given every chance as long as I tried my hardest for the shirt and it was my intention to do just that.

My debut for the club, my first ever senior appearance, was in the second to last game of the 1972/73 season away at Carlisle when I came on as a substitute for Dougie Allder. I did very well, setting up the winner in a 1-0 victory. It was quite an adventure. There was a rail strike on the weekend of the game, meaning that we had a nine hour bus journey from Millwall to Carlisle. What a feeling, to make your professional debut and make a contribution as well in front of 6,000 fans. Brunton Park wasn't exactly Goodison Park but it was a very special moment for me.

The club are very proud, as I said it means a lot to the supporters. If you're born a Millwall person, you are a Millwall person, the club meant so much to those on the Docklands. It was one of the toughest clubs as well, not only to play, but to establish yourself in the hearts of the fans. These were fans who knew their football, and they did all walks of trades too – good businessmen and rogues – but their hearts were in the football club and everything came down to the game on a weekend. I would go and watch the reserve games and mingle among some of the supporters who would go on to form some of the most loyal support in the club for many, many years.

We'd get 8,000 fans at Millwall but sometimes it would sound like 80,000. As well as giving us their support they were also renowned for their passion too. There was one game against Luton in the winter of 1973 where I came up against their full back Don Shanks, who was perhaps better known as Stan Bowles' betting partner. He upended me in the first half down one side of the field. A supporter jumped on to the pitch and chased him, yelling that if he kicked me again he was going to kill him. I laughed and agreed with Don when he said that the supporters were mad, but in the second half he did exactly the same, thinking he would get away with it because it was on the Directors' side. But there was a low wall and someone else ran on to the pitch and chased him. This time Don said that he thought the supporters were fucking mad. Then the referee told him to stop kicking me and said that if he did it again he would cause a riot. Welcome to Millwall, Don ...

The Cold Blow Lane End of the old Den holds so many memories for me, and it really was cold. On a Saturday that place used to rock. Supporters wouldn't come down to try and 'take over' the Cold Blow Lane unless they had a death wish. When it did happen, it was crazy. In one game the away fans stormed the stadium and tried to take the Cold Blow Lane End. It was the worst thing they ever did as the supporters at the Millwall end jumped over the stand and ran to meet the away fans on the pitch. There were police on horseback there, and I was just stood on the wing. A guy ran past me with a chair he'd ripped from the stand and shouted to me as he passed that they would get those bastards out of there, just you watch. He was really worked up and couldn't understand why they dared to try and take over the stadium.

I was at the club for two and a half years and fortunate enough to be around many of the supporters who took me to their hearts. I loved entertaining them on the pitch. I liked to score good goals and do tricks and because I was doing things they hadn't seen before, they nicknamed me Merlin, after the magician. I never called it myself but it has stuck with me ever since.

Even though the supporters had taken to me, I still had to earn the respect of my team-mates, players who were part of the fabric of Millwall. They could win and lose games but they had a remarkable camaraderie and team spirit. It was funny because the training ground was on a cinder pitch in Deptford Park and it was absolutely terrible. The goals were metal and if you hit them you'd have to spend three weeks in hospital! Jack would bring the washing down and throw it on a table and we'd have to get our slip, shirt, shorts and socks before all the good stuff was taken. The senior professionals would get their stuff first, of course, and it was tough for the younger players. One of them had just signed pro so the older players got hold of him and shaved his bollocks and put black boot polish on him. That was part of his initiation. I avoided that, but I was to get an initiation of my own in my first pre-season with the club. I can tell anyone who wants to get into the game and stay grounded, Millwall is the right club to be at. A fork is a fork and a spade is a spade.

Millwall would sometimes stay in hotels for away trips but never for a long time, and we went away to play a friendly and do some training down on the south coast in Bournemouth. They had a good team with the likes of Harry Redknapp as a player and the flamboyant John Bond senior as their manager. We were down there for three or four days and stayed at the Norfolk Hotel. I'd been at the club for a few months so the other guys had the chance to get to know me.

I was rooming with our centre forward, the late Brian Clark, who became a very dear friend of mine. He came from Bristol, and we used to call him the Country Boy as he spoke with a strong West Country accent. All the lads would rib him by going 'ow arr ya, Clarky' in an over-the-top accent. He was a gentle giant, so mild mannered and such a nice guy. We would travel to training together and we got on so well that he eventually became godfather to my daughter. He was so supportive of me that in the end he kept telling me that it was only a matter of time before a bigger club signed me. He had been my room-mate for the trip to Carlisle on my debut and had kept me calm, telling me stories about when he had scored for Cardiff a couple of years previously to beat Real Madrid in the European Cup Winners Cup. I really looked up to him. Anyway, Clarky went along with a prank the lads set up.

I got a phone call in my room from the *Bournemouth Echo*. It was a reporter who wanted me to be on a programme as they had heard I was good at tennis. It appeared that they wanted to talk to me about football as well. It was arranged to meet in the hotel lobby and they wanted me to be wearing all the gear. I just happened to have a pair of training shoes so I agreed. I went down all prepared but nobody was about, then Harry Cripps and the rest of the players turned up. Harry wanted to know what I was doing so I told him and then he asked if I played tennis. I was greener than the grass on the hills because then he asked me what would I do if I played a ball like this. I thought they were interested, I didn't realise they were taking the piss. So I went through all the strokes with Harry and we were having an imaginary game in the foyer of this lovely, prestigious hotel. Finally the penny dropped and I've never lived it down. It's been written about many times after and the story was even included in a movie about Millwall. I felt like a right idiot and asked Clarky if he knew about it. He replied in his funny accent that he did, but thought it was a right good laugh.

My fun and games in the pre-season didn't end there. We went to Jersey, and it was the first time I'd ever been on an aeroplane. We went there for a couple of days, had some training, played a couple of games and then we went out and let our hair down. That was my real baptism into Millwall Football Club. God rest Harry, but I still swear I won that game of tennis!

I wasn't the only one to fall victim to the pranks of the group. Dougie Allder also had his own tale afterwards. Stevie Brown and some of the boys went into his bedroom and carried his bed down to the foyer. On the way they bumped into Dougie and he asked them what they were doing, so Steve told him that they had one of the lad's beds and were taking it downstairs. Dougie even helped them and when he got down into the foyer he wanted to know whose bed it was. Then they told him it was his. The jokes were good and that summer felt like an apprenticeship in itself.

Millwall finished the 1972/73 season in eleventh place. The

aim for the following season was to push on and try and get promotion to the First Division. They had narrowly missed out on promotion in 1971. In fact, they thought they had been promoted at that time, but the wrong result came through. As well as the great professionals we had, there were also some decent young players like Mickey Kelly, Steve Brown, and we signed David Donaldson in the summer of 1973 from Arsenal.

That pre-season optimism didn't translate into results. Three losses and a draw from our first four league games meant we were going to be up against it. Now I'd made my debut I was itching to get back in the team and I was called into the side for my first start in our third game, which was a loss to Blackpool. I would only miss one game for the rest of the season. As great as it was for me, it wasn't always easy as I had to replace Dougie Allder in the side. He was a smashing bloke but that was football. He would obviously have been disappointed but he never showed it and was as good as gold.

All of the players were great with me, apart from Eamon Dunphy who I never got on with. He was very opinionated and against having me in the side. He would say to Benny Fenton that I shouldn't be put on a pedestal as that's what he thought was happening. He was entitled to his opinion but I was also entitled to play the way I wanted.

I didn't feel I had anything to prove to anyone, I just loved the fact I was getting games. Following that difficult opening we won three league games on the bounce but then registered four consecutive losses to underline just how difficult it was going to be. In October we faced Nottingham Forest three times in the space of eleven days. We were defeated in the league fixture, which was that other game I missed, but gained some revenge in the League Cup. After drawing at the Den we got an impressive win at the City Ground where I scored my first professional goal in a 3-1 win. Every goal was special for me, whether they were simple or spectacular, I just loved the ball going in the net. Nottingham was clearly a good place for me to find my goalscoring form as less than a month later we played at Notts County and I scored my first league goal in a 3-3 draw.

We managed to sort our form out and became tougher to beat

until February. At one stage, we went on an eight match unbeaten run in the league, the last game of which was a thumping 3-0 win at Oxford where I scored twice to take my season's tally to six. Joining me on the scoresheet was Brian Clark. Our main scorer that season was Alfie Wood, but I was happy to be chipping in with a decent amount for a young guy in his first season. In the game before that we had played Fulham.

To anyone reading this, Millwall versus Fulham might not seem like the most significant fixture, but it was in the context of British football history as it was the first ever Football League game to be played on a Sunday. Incredible isn't it, to think that normally the standout game is now kept back for Sunday at 4pm. My old pal Brian scored the only goal of the game to go down in history – and I was delighted for him. Good on ya, Clarky. There's no doubt that Brian has probably gone down in trivia books as the first player to score a Football League goal on a Sunday but he was much, much more than the footnote to a quiz question to me. Incidentally, a week later, Geoff Hurst scored the only goal for Stoke against Chelsea in the first ever Division One game to be played on a Sunday. So there you are, I've given you one for free, and even the trick question too. It was an early kick off and I remember having to go to the ground soon after waking up. It showed how much our fans wanted to be there as it was one of our highest gates of the season. So much for going to church, but then the club was almost like a religion to them as well.

It's always good to have your name in history for whatever reason and so it was nice to be a part of that occasion but it didn't really matter to me what day of the week we played on. Sure, there's something special about the tradition of a 3pm kick off on a Saturday but so long as I was playing I was happy. There was a brilliant sub-plot to the story that English football still had to follow the Sunday Observance Act from 1780. That meant that on the sabbath, businesses were forbidden from charging an entry fee, and this extended to football. To get around it Millwall charged for the match programme but made that the match ticket – typical. It's just as well they had fifteen thousand programmes as the previous home game in the league had not even seen nine thousand in the ground.

The league win against Oxford put us in tenth position, a season high, but we remained in mid- table with mixed form from then until the end of the campaign. The 1973/74 season ended with some disappointment as a twelfth place finish didn't really do justice to our home form which was comparable with Luton Town who had finished second and were promoted. Our away form had been our downfall and when the league season was over we had won, lost, and drawn fourteen matches apiece. My first full season had been okay. Eight goals, and I was third top scorer at the club. I'd really been accepted by the fans and had a great relationship with them.

I would travel to some of the games with my brother David, and on the way back we would stop at the pub and have a couple of drinks. The fans would be great in there though they'd call me 'Hilly', but I would never answer to that as that was what other players called me. I didn't like answering to Merlin, but I know that if someone refers to me as Gordon, I know it's serious. I think it's just a familiarity thing.

The supporters took me to their hearts and it was the same for me. If I hadn't had gone to United I would have spent my entire career at Millwall as I was very happy there and so eager to do well. A first season as a professional had been magic. When you play as a kid with jumpers as your goals, and then go on to the next stage and play where it's a little bit more organised with good pitches and goalposts, moving into the professional game is something completely different. Here was Millwall, a club who had stood for so long and had so much pride, and it meant so much. I talked about enjoying scoring goals and nothing gave me greater pleasure after scoring a goal than to look up and see supporters smiling.

When they speak to me now and describe goals they saw me score, it means so much. I don't want to sound big-headed but I appreciate a good goal when I see one and I know when one is good if I have scored it. It was just something in my make up that gave me the ability to score good goals. I think it's a shame that every league game wasn't recorded as it is today. It's difficult to go back and analyse every goal that I did score. I know, more or less, every game and goal that I scored but sometimes I'm told about doing certain things and it can be difficult to recall who I was playing against. That's the thing with instinct, you act on impulse and it goes from you as quickly as it comes. Again without sounding big-headed, I could do something and immediately wonder how I did it. Maybe that's why I was given the nickname Merlin. That it was magic, something that came around unexpected and can't really be explained because you don't have video evidence, just the eye-witness accounts of a few thousand people. I don't call myself Merlin, I don't insist on anyone calling me it and I never have, and I get embarrassed when people do refer to me by that name, but it has stuck with me for forty years and it is absolutely flattering. How can it not be?

I can reject various descriptions of myself and shrug off things that I don't think are accurate but I cannot reject a nickname given to me by supporters that I lived and loved to impress, because it makes me very proud to know that people held me in such high regard for what I was doing. I knew, writing my autobiography, that the subject of the nickname would come up so I have to embrace it. You can probably tell how awkward it makes me feel by the fact I'm trying to justify mentioning it.

My life had changed a lot in just over a year. I also got married in early August, just before the kick-off to the 1974/75 campaign, to a girl named Jackie who I had been seeing on and off since school. One of the times we got back together everything just clicked, and so we decided to get married in a Catholic church at the age of twenty. It wasn't something I'd been advised to do or convinced into doing, but I suppose it was an age where I felt like a man, grown up and about to embark on my second full season in the Football League. I bought my first house in Lightwater, which cost me £7,000. Can you believe that? I'd achieved an ambition of playing professional football, and then became a regular in the team.

Soon after we got married, I was off playing pre-season games with Millwall, preparing for another long year. For the 1974/75 season, Division Two was joined by the most famous name in football. Manchester United had been relegated from Division One and they were our first away game of the season. We lost our opening match at home to Sunderland but then had a good 3-0 win over Forest where I scored twice before we went to Old Trafford. Now Millwall are known as the Lions, but being at Old Trafford we were more like lambs to the slaughter in a setting like a Roman Colosseum. We were the bait and there were 41,000 there but it seemed more like 60,000. I loved the stage, I'd never been anywhere like it and 'frickin eck', I thought it was fantastic

I was trying as hard as I could, and doing quite well against Alex Forsyth who was marking me but it didn't help as we lost 4-0. Being the Lions didn't help as we were the ones who were mauled! Our form and our pride, didn't have much of an opportunity to recover before we were to face United again as they travelled to the Den in September for an early reverse fixture. United had brought so much support that they had to keep about 10,000 fans out and it was no surprise that it was comfortably our biggest gate of the season. They closed the Old Kent Road down and shut all the shops because they were worried there was going to be a massacre.

The Second Division didn't want United to leave as they brought so much money to the clubs who weren't used to filling their grounds. Gerry Daly scored a penalty to win the game for them 1-0, adding to the hat-trick he'd scored in the first game, and they went on to walk the division. I did well again. I hit a shot from the left hand side of the box about twenty five yards out, with the outside of my foot as the ball came to me. The ball bent in the air and seemed destined to go in the top corner but it hit the crossbar and came back out. The defeat was one of four we suffered in our seven games in September. We didn't score in five of those games, winning only one against Bristol City, and drawing 1-1 with Hull City where I scored. Travelling with the team to Everton as I signed was an eye-opening experience but playing against United just about opened my eyes up to superstardom. They were one of the biggest draws around and to play in a stadium like Old Trafford was unbelievable. It was an arena I knew I wanted to play in again and the best way to do that was to do as well as I could to help Millwall get into a position where they could play there every year.

Perhaps the lack of goals and the difficult start to the season were simply too much for the board to take and Benny was sacked and replaced by Gordon Jago. Gordon introduced running to training – the boys had never seen spikes before. One of Gordon's new coaches, Ron Jones, came in to training one day with a box that had about fifty pairs of spiked running shoes in it telling us that Tuesday morning we were going around the park. We were wondering if we were in training for the Olympics. At the end of the training session where we'd been throwing the spikes at each other, we said thank you very much to Ron and never saw another spike again.

Jago began to tinker with the side and as a result I started to miss some games. When a new manager comes in you're automatically fighting for your position again. Where Benny believed in me, Jago came in and for whatever reason just didn't have the same faith. He played Dougie Allder in front of me, and towards the end of the season my appearances were few and far between. My relationship with Benny had been good. He was a shrewd manager who had great conviction in his own beliefs. He had kept Millwall running with some well-timed sales and he saw the club as a developing ground for players to establish themselves before moving on to a bigger club.

Gordon, on the other hand, was very flash. We were used to grabbing what we could to wear at training because we didn't have a pot to piss in, so Gordon brought in sparkly new tracksuits thinking he was going to change us. That wasn't going to happen. Millwall as a club had a strong identity and the responsibility of any manager at the Den was to try and accept that and, to an extent, play up to that image in order to achieve success there and win over supporters. I don't want to name anyone but you see many football clubs without prestige, without identity or personality. Some have had their soul ripped from them. Wherever a club has built up a strong identity and plays an important role in the community, that should be preserved and maintained by everyone responsible. We as players, knew what Millwall was about, and it wasn't about being flashy.

I wasn't in the side and I wasn't even playing reserve football, but I was involved with the squad most of the time if only on the bench. It was killing me to know the team were getting relegated and I could only watch on. It got to the last ten games and we knew what we had to do but when it got to the last four games it felt like we were sucking air, helpless to stop the inevitable.

Towards the end of the season when I was on the bench, I would naturally spend more time alongside Jack Blackman. He'd always sit on the end with a bucket, often shouting at the players telling them to push up. On one occasion I watched him and he was fumbling around in his pockets and then put his hand to his mouth when he was shouting. I worked out that he didn't want to give anyone a sweet so he would peel the wrapper in his pocket and put it in his mouth as he started to shout. In the next game I asked him if I could have one, but he said that I couldn't as I may go on any minute. Jack was lovely, strong as an ox, very down to earth and an absolutely brilliant guy.

Unfortunately we were confirmed to relegation at the end of the season. In those days of two points for a win we never thought we were out of it, even if we lost three on the bounce, but just as our away form had arguably cost us a shot at promotion the previous season, it had crippled us again in 1975. We'd be going into away games thinking that we could get 'half a loaf here', which was our slang for one point, being half of two, but then that would make the loss a real setback if and when it came. Only losing four home games all season showed that we could more than handle ourselves in the division and it was a cruel irony that one of the good results at the Den, a draw with Norwich who ended up getting promoted, ended up being fatal for our chances of staying up. It said how close we were to the good sides but unfortunately Gordon had messed around with the team too often in the second half of the season.

I came back into the side for the last few games but it seemed that was because I was more of a commodity that could bring some money in. I knew I had been playing well so it was absolutely frustrating not to be on the pitch helping my team-mates, especially when I knew I could make a positive contribution. I wouldn't say I was owed a game by the club but I felt my performances justified my place there and I'm certain I could have made at least a small difference to our fortunes if I'd been given more of a chance. Could I have saved Millwall from relegation? I don't know, I wouldn't like to say yes, but I could have done something. And when I was back in the team, when it felt like anything we did would not be enough, the feeling that I was a commodity grew. I wasn't looking for a move, if the manager had me in the shop window then it certainly wasn't my doing as I just wanted to play well for the team. I wasn't conscious of it at the time but maybe it might have looked that way to supporters because of the situation Jago had created, but it could not have been further from the truth as I considered myself one of the Millwall people.

Gordon Bolland told me that he had heard there was interest at international level and that I was to be closely watched with a view to being selected for the under 23 side, but he said I wouldn't get an international cap at Millwall. Steve Brown once said to me in the shower after a game that it was only a matter of time before I left the club. Tottenham, the club that had tried so hard to persuade me to sign as a young boy, showed an interest and Arsenal sent a scout to watch me on seven occasions, but at the time I didn't realise teams were interested in me. Suggestions of playing for England made me proud. I'd met players like Bobby Moore but I sincerely only ever had thoughts of playing for Millwall. The interest was nice, after all I was a young professional, but there was no way I was going to try and leave. The club had just been relegated and I had no idea about the completely different journey my life was about to take.

3

New Frontiers

Because I hadn't been playing regularly, towards the end of the 1974/75 season Gordon Jago asked me if I fancied doing something different for pre-season. He wanted me to get some games and he had some friends in America so asked if I wanted to go over and help with a franchise. The idea was that I could go on loan to help Chicago Sting set up in the North American Soccer League. I agreed to go and this effectively meant I would miss the entire pre-season, joining up with Millwall again at the start of the following season. I had no intention of leaving the club permanently and was looking forward to helping get Millwall back into the Second Division. It did feel a little bit like a kick in the teeth as I hadn't been played when I really wanted and needed to help my team, but now I was being sent over to America to do a favour. I was young and so desperate to play that I was never going to turn the opportunity down. The loan deal with Millwall was never with a view to a permanent transfer from their side, so it wasn't as if I was being 'put in the shop window' again. It's strange how things work out though, as going to Chicago meant I would be watched by someone who would be influential in my eventual move.

My only experiences of life outside of Sunbury-on-Thames and London had been when I'd travelled to away games with Millwall and even that was to play football, so I could hardly have been described as a globetrotter. As I've said, the only time I'd been on a plane was to go to Jersey with Millwall in a pre-season training trip for a couple of days, yet the next one was this

48

Jumbo Jet that looked like a double decker bus. It was incredible. Me and Jackie flew to Chicago where we were picked up by the general manager of the Sting. He took us to an apartment block that looked over Lake Michigan and we were told that it was near where Al Capone had lived. So I'd gone from playing for a club that had the Kray twins supporting them to one that was near Al Capone. We were told not to go diving in Lake Michigan as nobody could be sure what was in the concrete blocks – Holy Moly!

Chicago was a great city, Hugh Hefner had opened his first Playboy club there, and the likes of Frank Sinatra would always visit. And Lake Michigan, at over 300 miles in length, was vast. Thankfully Chicago Sting had a number of British players on their books which helped make me feel comfortable. Ian Storey-Moore, formerly of Manchester United but contracted to Burton Albion, was there although he was injured. Clive Griffiths, another former United player, Mervyn Causton, Johnny Webb, there were players from all over but there was a good British core. That, and the United link, was probably due to the fact that the manager was none other than Bill Foulkes, one of the most legendary names ever to play for the club. He was such a gentleman. He made me feel at home for which I was very grateful, and you could tell that he put into practice everything that he had learned at United. He was very mild-mannered and quiet but efficient. He was also a cracking golfer and if he wasn't on a training pitch you'd find him on the golf course.

Chicago played at Soldier Field on astro turf. The stadium had recently become the home of the NFL side the Chicago Bears and could hold up to 100,000 people, yet the Sting only drew attendances of about 4,000. It was odd, but one of the more pleasing aspects of my time at the Sting during 1975 was that I got to play in virtually every big NFL stadium in the United States. The soccer franchises all shared stadiums and we got to play in Dallas and Washington. I felt the NASL did very well. Franchises like the Chicago Sting were created and a manager appointed. The manager was allocated a budget where they were allowed to sign so many foreign players and so many American players. The season was scheduled to make travelling as easy as possible.

It would mean a few days travelling for a couple of away games to play say Seattle and Portland, but then we would play a couple at home to even it out.

People got to know us pretty well in Chicago and while the Bears were more popular, the soccer team had its fans. The general manager for the sports franchise which included us was a man called Mike Pyle who had represented the Bears for eight years. The guy who owned us was called Lee Stern, known around Chicago as 'the Soya Bean King'. He was great and really supported the teams and put all the players in apartments downtown around a thousand yards from Hugh Hefner's place. The apartments were fully furnished and we were well looked after. The weather was beautiful while we were out there. We could go walking on the beach every day and it really was fantastic. That said, it was probably better that we trained in the evening at Soldier Field due to how hot it did get in the days. If it's 100 degrees locally then it is about 115 degrees on the field and though I didn't mind playing on the artificial pitches the hot weather was tough.

Playing the game itself was fantastic. I'd hardly been there very long when the New York Cosmos announced they were bringing Pele, the legendary Brazilian forward, out of retirement. I was just an ordinary kid coming through but the league was made up of clubs that had one or two big name players. One of them had failed to sign George Best though he would play in the NASL in later years, as did Franz Beckenbauer and Johan Cruyff. I wasn't aware at the time but I would go on to share some pitch time with those players too but in 1975 I was just stunned to be in the same league as Pele. It was a long way to go for a kid from Sunbury playing in the semi-professional game to be on the same pitch as arguably the greatest player of all time in less than three years. Though past his prime, he was far from a shadow of his former self, and was still capable of moments of magic.

The quality of the league was top class. Yes, we were there to help get the game off the ground so to speak, but the attitude of some of the American players who were learning from all of the seasoned professionals from overseas, and even from me despite being only twenty one was commendable. I wasn't doing too badly myself. A duck out of water I may have been in America, but on the field I was flying and completely in my comfort zone. We were sponsored by Seiko, the watch manufacturer, who would give a watch as a Man of the Match prize. I was winning it so often that our entire team was kitted out in flashy new watches as I would give the prize to the player that I thought played the best. I was scoring lots of goals and maybe sometimes I was given the award because of that.

There were obvious differences in the way the Americans tried to present the games. They had bands playing or shows before matches, and to be honest they were spectacles I couldn't stand. But you get used to it and the nicest thing of course was looking at the cheerleaders. It's a good job that they didn't have them in England because no-one would keep their eyes on the game. Much of the way they tried to advertise the game or promote it was hit and miss, as were the changes to the natural format of the game. There were only wins and losses and if a game ended with a tie then it would be settled with a shoot-out. But the shoot-outs weren't conventional either. You had a few seconds to run and put the ball in the net. A point was awarded for each goal you scored, and if you managed a clean sheet, what they called a shut-out, they gave you an extra point.

One rule I did like was that you couldn't be offside up to twenty five yards and they had a line painted on the pitch to show it. I felt that really opened the game up as teams couldn't defend too high. I enjoyed playing with that rule as it was a novelty, but I don't think it is something that would benefit the game long term or in the modern day. It was just one of a number of changes they made to make the sport more appealing to the North American public. When I returned years later, as I'll explain, this philosophy would be something that I would be continually at odds with. I don't think it can be put simply down to that rule, but I was having a field day and scored sixteen goals in twenty one appearances. We played against the Polish national side at Soldier Field and I destroyed them on my own. I was so pleased with my contribution at the birth of the game in the United States.

Despite how well the spell had gone, I insisted to Gordon

Jago that I did not want to leave Millwall, I didn't want to live in America, and my desire was to help the club get back up the divisions. I was looking forward to going back there and working on a ten or fifteen-year career. And after Chicago failed to make the play offs, in a way I couldn't wait to get back home and play for Millwall. I was due to return following their pre-season anyway, but the early exit from competitive football by the Sting meant I would be on my way home a little earlier than expected.

Bill had already told people at United about me. Jimmy Murphy and Sir Matt Busby were getting feedback about my good performances. To me personally he would just say not to worry, that I was doing fine. There wasn't much I could say to respond, after all I was with a living legend. Bill had described me as the most entertaining player in the league, which was some compliment coming from him especially considering Pele was also in the league. I was named in the All Stars selection alongside Pele up front. Even the player many call the greatest ever praised me during a game. He said I was a Brazilian player that came from England. Naturally I thanked him as coming from him it meant a lot.

The United States, Pele, and cheerleaders were a world away from the reality of what was awaiting my return to England. The Third Division hadn't entered my mind since we'd been relegated but I really wanted to get stuck into it and help the club back up. I'd missed pre-season but playing in the heat had been just as intense. I'd had no rest from the end of the previous season but I was young enough to handle it. I left America match fit and was ready to play my part for Millwall. As I've said, there was talk before I even left for Chicago that the club might not be able to keep me but talk is cheap as they say, and I was honestly only concentrating on my form for the Lions. I would be told that clubs would be watching, and Arsenal sent scouts seven or eight times, and obviously I would try and do well, but I would do that anyway. It was nice to receive praise. Bill had played with the great team that had won the European Cup and also players like Duncan Edwards and Tommy Taylor who both tragically perished in the Munich Air Disaster. There's little else you can do as a player than just try and keep doing what you do, because if for one second you get above yourself, you'll soon learn how hard the game, and life for that matter, can hit. I'd had the right schooling at Millwall so I certainly wasn't about to get ideas above my station just because a few nice things were being said.

*****

The quality of football in Division Three wasn't remarkably different to how it was in Division Two. The game in those days was such that any team, with the benefit of a decent run, could get promoted back to back and it wouldn't necessarily have cost a lot of money to do so. Millwall had never played in the top flight but were easily capable of getting back up and I just wanted to play, whatever the division. It was only relatively recently that I had become a professional and I wasn't taking it for granted.

No matter the level or time in history, it's always the case that when a club is relegated, the teams in that lower division see them as a side to beat. I was able to keep up the form I had been displaying in America and was scoring lots of goals but the team as a whole had a little trouble acclimatising to Division Three. Form was patchy with a win followed by a loss and so it was difficult to get any consistency. I didn't play in the first game of the season while I became used to being back in the country. I scored five goals in my first few games in the league but to prove how tough it was, our run of games at that time went win, loss, loss, win, loss, win. A disappointing loss at high flying Bury put us in eleventh place at the end of September, underlining just how difficult we were going to find the task of promotion. We went on a little run of a win and four draws and I scored in three of the games, with a goal at the Den in the draw against Colchester on the first of November turning out to be my last for Millwall.

I didn't want to leave the proverbial sinking ship but when Jago told me that the bank said the club had to sell me, the best thing I could have done was leave to help them get the money. We were playing a game at Dulwich Hamlet on a sloping pitch on a Tuesday night preparing to play against Yeovil in the FA Cup on the weekend. At half time I was brought off and Jago said to me, 'Have a shower as we've decided to accept a bid from Manchester United and the bank say we need to sell you.' I went home and told my wife and she was elated. We hadn't long been in the new house but when it came to the house or Manchester United, United were definitely going to be my preference. The other lads told me I'd be foolish to turn it down.

Personally, my head was spinning as it was happening so fast. Little did I know that I'd go from preparing to play against Yeovil for Millwall in the world's most famous cup competition, to a few months later being forever remembered for my contribution for my new team in it. I didn't know, but United's interest had been standing for a few weeks. I later discovered I'd been watched at Walsall by Jimmy Murphy and he insisted to Tommy Docherty that they sign me. The deal with Millwall might have taken quite a while to sort out but I was none the wiser until I was told I had to travel up North the next day.

The following morning I headed to Euston Station. I had my boots and X-rays under my arm and was told that I would be met by Gordon Clayton at Manchester Piccadilly. As I sat on the train on the two and a half hour journey north, many things ran through my mind as I attempted to gather my thoughts. Would I like it and could I really be about to sign for one of the biggest clubs in the world, never mind the country? Would I buckle under or show them what I could do? Sure enough when I arrived in Manchester, Gordon was there and picked me up in Tommy Docherty's Mercedes. We went to Old Trafford and as we pulled up I thought holy shit. I can't believe I'm about to be signed by Manchester United.

I went into the ground and up to the manager's office. Louis Edwards, Tommy Docherty, Frank Blunstone, Jimmy Murphy and Sir Matt Busby were all there. Tommy said that they had been waiting for me. In those days, United only bought players who were capable of going in and making a difference to the first eleven. They'd added Stuart Pearson to their side to get promoted but generally concentrated on developing players. They had a proud tradition of doing that under Sir Matt and Jimmy, and it had been something that Tommy had tried to re-ignite. The fee for my transfer was £70,000, which even in those days wasn't a great amount.

Sammy McIlroy was a fantastic player and I had so much

admiration for the way Lou Macari played in midfield. These were players I knew of but was only used to seeing on *Match Of The Day* when United, as they always are, were the team to watch. Tommy Docherty had a tough job when he started at United and had not only answered every critic under an intense spotlight, but also rebuilt the team into an entertaining side that won football matches. He had to deal with ending the Old Trafford careers of Bobby Charlton, Denis Law and Willie Morgan, and those people might not have many kind words to say about Tommy, but he had to make some tough decisions for the good of the club in the long term.

Tommy was a man who knew what he wanted and knew how to get there. Sometimes that meant upsetting people on the way but that's what it took and he had done a superb job while at Chelsea. In fact, he could have won the league while there. In the 1964/65 season they'd won the League Cup and got to the semi-finals of the FA Cup. Chasing Manchester United at the top of the table he dropped a number of senior players for breaking a curfew and they lost a crucial game against Burnley. They were that close to winning the league, and later on he managed Scotland and did so wonderfully there that he was asked to be the man to bring success back to United.

Tommy was liked among his fellow managers such as Bill Shankly and Terry Neill and he was respected in the game. Arsenal and Tottenham had been interested in me, but once United made their move I was only going to leave Millwall for them. United represent something different to a footballer, something I'll explain in further detail a little later on, but it gave the opportunity to walk amongst legends and carve your own name in the history of the game. I wasn't particularly attached to a club while growing up but I'd seen the likes of Denis Law and Bobby Charlton and that's what I wanted to be, a great like them. I wondered if I could adjust to life in Manchester, especially with the weather as I was told it rained all the time. They weren't wrong. In later years when people asked me what my signing-on fee was, I would answer, twelve umbrellas and a pair of wellington boots!

I'd been at odds with Gordon Jago's decision not to play me

when I thought I should be on the pitch, although maybe as a kid you don't see the bigger picture. I had my thoughts on whether he was the right kind of character to lead Millwall, and I had conflicting thoughts about what was happening to my career. I wanted to stay at Millwall, I wasn't sure if I was being put up for sale, and the trip to Chicago right in the middle of it all had further confused me. I had a single-minded approach to wanting to help Millwall back to Division Two but not knowing what the manager's intentions were for me was a little difficult. Looking back I can still only guess why I was used in a certain way towards the end of that relegation season. Maybe Gordon felt that my style simply wouldn't be helpful to a team battling relegation. Maybe he was preserving me, as an asset, and knew that keeping me fresh was the best way to attract buyers, and then maybe he just felt that selling me was in the best interest of stabilising the club. Perhaps he sensed that relegation was inevitable, and as a saleable asset he wanted to make sure the club got top dollar for me. Though I was confused at the time, looking back I certainly didn't hold on to any misgivings about Gordon, if I even had any at all. Some time later, Gordon moved out to America and I lived close to him while I was in Texas. We're very close friends and I respect his views on the game, he's as passionate about the North American game as am I, so it just goes to show that a temporary difference of opinion doesn't have to mean a lifelong grudge. Had he not done what he did, or acted the way he acted, I may not have had the move to Manchester United. He once told me that I was the best player he'd ever had, so that was really nice to hear.

It was a wrench to leave Millwall. I loved the club and still do. They introduced me into proper football and I met so many wonderful people there. I have a special bond with the club and its fans, we had a strong relationship and that continues to this very day. I would like to say that I believe the move was best for everybody, even though my new manager would praise me by saying it was a bargain for him and the club, and £70,000 wasn't the greatest amount, yet it was a good deal for Millwall at the time. They were able to do what they needed with the money and they were promoted that very season back to Division Two so they achieved their goal, which I was delighted about. I was pleased to have made a meaningful contribution with eight goals in the fifteen games that I'd played for them in the league season. I will always have that special fondness for Millwall and it was a shame that I never got to play at the Den with United, or that I didn't get the opportunity to be involved with the club at some point during the rest of my career. Football is football and people move on and have careers that take them all over the place, something I was going to find out for sure, but only one team can give you your debut, your first steps in football, and Millwall was the club that did that for me.

The move happened so swiftly that I didn't get a chance to speak to my parents about it. When I finally did, Dad's response was strangely understated with the comment that I should do what I had to do, but Mum was delighted for me. Millwall were eighth in Division Three when I left but if I felt life was going to be a bed of roses at United then I was in for a shock just hours after signing. I went to see United play Manchester City in the League Cup on the Wednesday night. United were given a 4-0 beating and were eliminated.

From a personal perspective, I wouldn't have been able to play any role in United's League Cup run anyway, as I'd played against Swindon Town for Millwall and would have been cup-tied. I had no involvement and no real indication until the night before that I would be signing for United, so I don't know how much of it is true that I was being watched for a while by them. It's all about timing though, and it's just as well that I never did play for Millwall against Yeovil or I would have been cup-tied from playing in the FA Cup as well, and I would never have enjoyed what would become one of the best days of my career, the day that would really catapult me into the headlines. Yet even moving to Manchester United, I didn't feel like a star. Seeing REAL stars in the side like Martin Buchan, Sammy McIlroy and Lou Macari, I couldn't help but mutter, 'Shit – I've arrived,' under my breath.

4

United

I'd only seen and spoken to Tommy Docherty when Millwall had played Manchester United in the 1974/75 season and if I'm to be honest, he never really said that much to me then. I knew that Tommy and Frank Blunstone, his assistant, had come up to watch me at some point. I must have played alright, or good enough to convince them anyway. Less than a month after that I joined Man United. There were more and more reports about me being the next big thing though I never paid any attention to it, I just wanted to play and play well.

I was just a young pup who wanted to play, but it goes without saying that Manchester United didn't need much selling to me. There was a sense of irony about Tottenham's interest after they had pursued me so heavily when I was younger. I might have been just as happy there or at Arsenal, but Manchester United has a sound that's very much different. I'd seen the crowd and played at Old Trafford. I'm not taking anything away from Tottenham or Arsenal, but United were still the biggest club then and it meant something completely different that they were interested.

It was mentioned when I joined that I was the final piece as a goalscoring winger, but when signing for the club Tommy Docherty told me he just wanted me to go out and play my natural way, the way I had been doing for Millwall, and that gave me much encouragement. I was now at a club where supporters expected entertainment and the best football. They had seen great players before. It wasn't a case of being the next George Best and I'm sure that if Ian Storey-Moore had been fit, I wouldn't have even been signed by United. Again, it was either ironic or just a plain strange coincidence that Ian would have spent some of the summer with me in Chicago trying to get over an achilles problem. He was a fantastic player but unfortunately he was forced to retire. Incidentally, I would also play against George in later years in the United States.

Other players had come through since George and had to live up to that reputation. Willie Morgan played in the same team and was a fantastic player down the right, a brilliant Scottish international, and very flamboyant. John Aston had played on the left in the 1968 European Cup Final but that was because Denis Law had been suspended as normally George or Bobby Charlton would play on that side. So it wasn't simply following one player. There were so many talented players in the club's recent history. Storey-Moore was signed as a left winger but was so unfortunate with injuries. That was the stroke of luck that saw me arrive at the crème de la crème when I may have moved to Spurs or Arsenal.

I was a goalscorer and creator who wanted to entertain and I was joining a midfield full of talent such as Sammy McIlroy, Lou Macari and Stevie Coppell. We all had our own strengths. You would never put me down as the number one defender, I had a nose bleed when I went back into my own half. I only knew one thing and that was scoring but maybe that was naivety due to my age. When you arrive at a club like United you know all about the names that have shone in the past. You're aware of the history, of the expectation, and I knew that with my own reputation I would be walking into a direct comparison with some of the great entertainers of the past. I knew I couldn't be George, who could, but I didn't want to be George, I wanted to make my own name at the club. They were big boots to fill but this was a different team, a different time and I was a different player. With the speed in which everything had happened, I had to pinch myself to think that it was happening at all. I was put up in a hotel near Manchester Piccadilly where I could have anything I wanted. I'd never experienced anything like it at Millwall. I could even ring room service and get a cup of tea. Fortunately we weren't surrounded by media, as in those days Manchester only had three or four press men, one of whom was David Meek who has written so much on United over the years. You would only really see them on a Friday. My wife Jackie didn't make the move right away so I won't lie, it was difficult and lonely in those first few weeks living in that hotel room. It was the first time I'd ever been in such a situation and it was hard to adjust to life in a new city which is ironic given that it's something I've ended up doing many times since.

Maybe it helped that I was around the same age as many of the young players who were starting to make a name for themselves at Old Trafford as I was heartened by the welcome I received from my new colleagues. Brian Greenhoff, who had come through the club's youth system, showed me wonderful hospitality that told me they were down to earth while big Jim Holton was fabulous as well. Jim would be so encouraging by telling me that some of the things he saw me do he couldn't believe. He'd always refer to me as 'Wee Fella', he did to Lou Macari too, but then Jim was big – six foot two, eyes of blue as the song went.

Stuart Pearson was very welcoming as was Sammy McIlroy, a Busby Babe who had played with all the greats. Sammy, Brian, Dave McCreery, as well as younger players like Arthur Albiston, these were all men who knew what it meant to come through at United. To this day Arthur Albiston remains one of the best left-footed players I've ever seen. There were so many young players growing up at the biggest club in the world and now I was in there with them. As well as those, there were plenty of experienced players such as Gerry Daly, the Irish international who displayed great skill in midfield and Alex Forsyth, who had a phenomenal shot on him.

For the first time I could probably look at the situation and say I was daunted because I realised I would have to perform to the high standards set by the club and the players, of whom nearly every single one was an international. When the international matches came around the training ground only had one or two players left. Perhaps it's true that some of the players didn't take to me straight away. Lou Macari and I didn't see eye to eye many times, but it didn't take away from the fact I thought Lou was one of the best midfielders in the league. Though the team was

young and improving, I wasn't joining a team of players that
were nearly there, they already were there. There was a great
blend of youth and experience, with the European Cup winner,
goalkeeper Alex Stepney, our eldest player. Paddy Roche was
his deputy and for all his perceived faults he was an absolute
gentleman. Martin Buchan was a character in his own right and
the way he conducted himself you knew you were in the big
leagues. He was the right man for captain because he personified
the standard of what was expected of you at Manchester United.

And, oh my gosh, the difference in intensity between Millwall
and Manchester United. Everything had to be first class. Training
had to be spot on, the fields were far superior to what we had at
Millwall. The Cliff training ground had an outdoor and indoor
facility, there was a structure, and up to two hundred people
would watch us train. We had our own changing rooms where
our kit would be put out and washed for us. It was a world away
from Millwall where you would just grab whatever was available.

Observing the likes of Martin and the way he was conducting
himself pushed me to thinking I had to up my game, although
knowing that the club had signed me because they felt I could
handle such pressure put me at ease. That's not to say that
Millwall were not a professional outfit that did things wrong, far
from it, but United were another level.You could tell that you
were entering a club that prided itself on being the best, and
expected the very same from the players who represented them
at all times, not just on the pitch. But ultimately, people are just
people, and the players were just as down to earth as any I'd met
in the past. There were no airs or graces, no feeling from any
of the other players that they were better. That could have been
because they were a team who had just been promoted and they
had the collective desire to restore United to be the best again.

I mentioned it earlier but there's a lot to be said about the way
United acquired players and how they brought them through.
There were people like Sammy and Brian who, just as Martin
embodied the professional conduct of the club, showed so much
about the identity of it. These guys were United through and
through, Busby Babes, products of the famous youth system.
Players who were United fans and would give their all for the

club. I knew that the same would be expected of me and that I had been chosen as someone that the club, and the Doc, believed would complement that team well. It wasn't just Martin, or Sammy and Brian, everyone at the club knew what playing for Manchester United represented.

If you were to be completely honest you could say there was not quite the same concentration of home-grown players in the first team squad that there had been under Sir Matt Busby but Tommy was trying his best on that front. To complement that, he was making sure he was acquiring the best young talent around and had proven that with Martin Buchan and Lou Macari. To be bought as a player for United was an honour. Still, there was a little bit of getting used to everything, particularly the players I'd seen on television, or playing for their countries, and I was now one of them. Wow. It would be any player's dream to stand on the pitch at Old Trafford and realise you're one of the players now representing this famous club. I confess to have been in awe of the place, and some of the players, when I first arrived, but in all honesty that wore off pretty soon. Not because I felt any different, but because people would show that same kind of attention to you as they did the other players.

My surroundings weren't the only thing I had to get used to. Just four days after signing for the club I made my debut at Old Trafford against Aston Villa. I'd signed and knew I would be playing sooner or later, but I didn't necessarily expect to be in the team right away. In training, I got used to being around these great players very quickly because of how they helped me settle and I was just eager to get performing. I'd worn the numbers seven, nine, and eleven at Millwall, but had preferred wearing number eleven. When I walked into the dressing room at Old Trafford on the day of the match and saw that number eleven shirt hanging up it was a dream. There was just one thought in my mind and that was to keep that number and that shirt. I would have felt foreign, strange in any other number, but eleven just felt right. I didn't have any superstitions before a match but I did have routines. I would normally be last in the line-up walking out and I would put my shirt and shorts on at the last minute. Obviously, I'd wear my slip.

It was quite an experience walking out of that tunnel at Old Trafford representing Manchester United for the very first time and it hit me. The arena, the noise of fifty thousand people in the crowd, but most of all the incredible pace of the game. It was so demanding. I don't think I've ever been as knackered after a football game. That first game left me with no illusions as to how tough it was going to be playing in the First Division. United won that game 2-0, but lost the next game in the league at Arsenal. I'd been in the North Bank at Highbury with an Arsenal supporting pal of mine when I was a kid and I told him that one day I wanted to play on that pitch. And I might well have done if Arsenal had pursued me with more intent and managed to convince me to leave Millwall. I was proud and felt like I'd really achieved something big when I represented Manchester United at Old Trafford and it wasn't that different a feeling to representing the club in London.

My first away game for United, and back in an area I knew well. It was a strange but wonderful feeling returning down south with the biggest club, arriving at the palatial Highbury with its marble floors. The Premier League today is massive and there are plenty of fantastic stadiums yet there was something prestigious about playing in arenas like Highbury with all their history and tradition. Nothing excited me more than playing in these grand stadiums that held so many memories and trying to match the entertainers of the past and attempting to thrill supporters.

I don't want to sound spoiled, as I would play at Old Trafford so many times and play in so many big occasions in the future, but in those early days everything was so fresh for me that I can remember how excited I felt, even to run out of the tunnel and on to the Highbury grass. It's a shame that the hospitality ended there as the game wasn't fifteen seconds old when Alan Ball and his shiny white boots put the Gunners ahead. On one occasion I went to take a corner and I heard heckles from some supporters with one yelling out, 'Fuck off you traitor.' Welcome home, Hilly. We were battered 3-1 as Arsenal were really up for it and that gave me an immediate insight into life as a Manchester United player. We were everyone's scalp – even to Arsenal, this was their big one.

If it's a fair summary to say I was daunted by the size and history of Manchester United then it's equally fair to say I was hit straight in the face with it a few days after the trip to Highbury. The club held a testimonial for Paddy Crerand and the event was to be the current United side against the team that had won the European Cup in 1968. Sadly, Bill Foulkes wasn't in the side, but Denis Law, who, as I said, had missed the final through suspension, was there in place of Johnny Aston. Some of the biggest names in the history of the club and yes, some had come to the end of their careers and some had already retired, but I was still in awe to share the pitch with the likes of Denis, Bobby, and George Best. Wow. It was something else.

We won that game 7-2, and I scored twice. I even nicked the ball off Paddy to score one of my goals. Sorry about that Paddy! Seeing the Doc's team play their natural game and beat that side in such a style began to excite a lot of people. I was training hard and adapting to life in Manchester but I would still sometimes wonder how the lads at Millwall were getting on. After we played Newcastle on November 29th and won 1-0, the club let me go down to London for a few days. The club had bought me a first class ticket for the train and when it got to Piccadilly I could barely believe my eyes. On the platform were the Millwall players who were getting the train back to London after they'd played at Port Vale. The boys saw me and said I must join them down the train. After all, we only ever saw first class when we passed it at Millwall. I went and sat with them and it was fantastic to be with them and the supporters. I was in my suit and the boys were ribbing me about it saying I must be on a lot more money, all the usual jokes. They were so pleased for me though and were asking me questions about what it was like. I told them it was unbelievable playing in front of 50,000 fans.

I'd often make the journey back down south as my wife wouldn't come up to Manchester while I was living in hotels. She did come up for about a week but then went back home to our house in Lightwater, Surrey. We sold that house and eventually moved to a house in Buxworth in Derbyshire. On our road there was a pub on the corner which was owned by Pat Phoenix who played Elsie Tanner in Coronation Street. I liked living out in the sticks and a lot of the players lived close to each other in Sale.

Brian and Big Jim showed me their houses and they lived near each other. I can always remember Big Jim's misfortune. He broke his leg which really set him back. When he made his comeback he was injured in the warm-up of his return game. He was back in plaster and I can remember he got his foot stuck under the pedal of his Vauxhall 2000, which was a World Cup car, and put it through the back of his garage. Sammy lived in Sale, but Stevie Coppell still lived in Liverpool so he was rarely seen.

The Irish boys used to play at the snooker club in Chorlton-cum-Hardy after training. They were very good players, I can't say the same about me. I would just play my tennis, which I was still into, and I would play with David Davies who would go on to be the Chief Executive of the Football Association. I'd also play with Roger Day who was a DJ at Piccadilly Radio. Thankfully, there were no tennis-related initiations in my first few days at Old Trafford, but that was soon to change when Lou Macari got hold of the knowledge that I liked my tennis. I thought I'd escaped my initiation, but I was wrong. I think on introduction, the other lads might have thought I was a flashy Londoner but that wasn't the case.

The dressing room had another Cockney in Alex Stepney, so outsiders might have expected that he and I would get on, or that he would take me under his wing so to speak. But Alex and I were from different generations. He was about twelve years older then me and we had virtually nothing in common, but sometimes that happens in life. It wasn't as if we hated one another, we did get on and would say hello, but that was it. In the early days I roomed with Alex, though that was only once or twice. Only once or twice was enough for me as well. I guess the boss thought he might be the ideal person to help me settle, thinking along those lines of us being from the same area, but we had a completely different mentality. He was also a smoker and that wasn't me. If I'm being honest, it would be fair to say that perhaps I wasn't exactly the ideal person for Alex to room with either.

I ended up normally sharing with Chris McGrath. Chris was a decent winger who had been on loan at Millwall but was more or less always on the edge of the first team. With Stevie and myself he was second choice, and ironically only got his major run in the first team when Lou Macari was injured for a spell in the autumn of 1977, but he was unable to establish himself afterwards. Chris was a good lad to room with, as was Arthur Albiston, who was as good as gold. I didn't really mind who I roomed with, I'd come from a big family so was always used to being around people and sharing a room. My best roommate, incidentally, was Paul Mariner who I shared with while on England duty. At United the younger players would stick together whereas the older players had their card schools and loved their horse racing. I didn't gamble and I rarely drank.

I was delighted to have settled into life at United as quickly as I did. A major factor of that was the other lads being normal and down to earth, people that were put on pedestals by many but were just normal lads. We all had different backgrounds but just wanted to do our best. Stuart Pearson had come from Hull, I came from Millwall, but then you had someone like Lou who had signed for United from Celtic. From one dream to another. Even Lou on arriving from Celtic must have had a 'Wow' moment taking such a step up. He was a busy, industrious player who made you feel safe and secure in the middle of the pitch, but then the rest of the team were like that as well. The Doc made sure everyone was aware of their own responsibilities. Mine was to score goals, create and destroy the opposition.

Tommy Cavanagh would call Stevie and me the 'two little Dukies', wanting us to get the ball to do the damage. If we lost the ball we were told to tuck back in. Stevie was a natural hard worker but I was perhaps not renowned for that particular ability, as proved by an incident about a year into my United career when Martin Buchan gave me a clip around the ear during a game against Coventry. I missed a 1-2 and didn't pick up a player. When I got the clip I thought it was one of the Coventry players. When I realised it was Martin I chased him around the field, and the referee told us to calm down saying he'd never sent off two players from the same team. For me, Martin was the best central defender I've ever seen. Cool, calm, collected, very authoritative, very methodical. And that wasn't me. I can always remember going to a party at Martin's house just after I signed and most of the lads were there. Pancho told me to watch. We'd been there a couple of hours when Martin closed all the doors, went into another room and brought in a guitar. He played and sang for about half an hour. He's an absolute Elvis nut and would sing in the showers with a comb. He was always immaculately dressed and presented and it has to be said, a wonderful captain. He was honest and also told the truth when it needed to be told. It was hard to get to know him yet after all these years we're probably closer than we were when we played together. He really helped me through some difficulties which were to follow in my career. We were different and neither of us, in fact nobody on the team, were going to change our own character, we all had the collective goal of doing the best we could for Manchester United.

I was able to reap the benefits of the speed with which I'd settled at the club by putting it across in my performances on the pitch. The win against Newcastle was followed by a 0-0 draw at Middlesbrough that kept us fourth in the league with the top six separated by just one point. I loved playing against the teams in the North East as the supporters really loved their football, and that made for fantastic atmospheres in these great grounds. Ayresome Park wasn't the prettiest but had history, St. James' Park was great to play at, and against Sunderland at Roker Park you knew you would always be up against it. I said it a little bit earlier that after you've played so many times it's not always easy to remember everything, but I do have some vivid memories of playing up in the North East.

There was a game up at Middlesbrough where I raced for a loose ball that was rolling towards the byline after being cleared. I was being chased by a defender called Kenny Craggs who I knew only had one intention, and that was to plough right through me. I was able to think quickly enough to move my body and flick the ball a foot away from him as he went steaming through to tackle me in mid-air. I can still hear Kenny grunting as he landed in the mud, and still see the home fans move as one in the same shape as I did, because I'd thrown them the same shimmy as I did the defender. That was just typical of me. I'm not one to blow my own trumpet but I benefitted from great awareness and anticipation, so much so that I didn't always need to see a player coming in to tackle me, as was the case with Kenny. The defenders didn't know what I was going to do because most of the time, I didn't know either. I didn't normally make up my mind until the last minute, always acting on the spur of the moment to decide what I felt was the best action to take.

My first goal for Manchester United was typically something that was a little unpredictable. It was the decider in a 4-1 win at Bramall Lane against Sheffield United. I'd hit a shot but it was blocked by the keeper and came back out to me, and on the angle I struck the ball with my right foot and it went in the far corner. I must say I was delighted to have got that first goal. If you watched it without commentary then you might have wondered if it was me at all, a right footed goal in a white strip. I did like a white strip as I enjoyed playing in the Millwall one, and I really loved that white away United shirt. It was only in the last year or so that I managed to watch the highlights of that game against Sheffield United and as thrilled as I was to see me score that first goal for Man United, it brought me just as much pleasure to watch my old team-mates like Sammy McIlroy play with such class.

A week later, I scored the only goal in a win over Wolves at Old Trafford. It was a thunderbolt and I have to say that goal in particular gave me immense satisfaction. To score a great goal at Old Trafford, on the ground where so many greats had played and performed magic and miracles, was the moment more than any that made me feel I'd been accepted by the club. It was almost spiritual. We were top of the tree at Christmas though admittedly we'd played a game more than the other teams around us.

We closed out 1975 with a win over Burnley. My marker in that game just so happened to be the Gaffers' son, Michael. A ball came over and he came steaming in for a challenge near the half way line. I saw him coming so I knocked it over him and spun around but he floored me. He knew I'd done him and he took me out waist high. It was hilarious, the boss was going ballistic and yelled from the sidelines that he would have words with Michael later.

In January we kept pace at the top of the table, staying there when I scored in a 2-1 win over Queens Park Rangers. I scored from a corner at White Hart Lane against Tottenham, and then in the FA Cup a week later I scored a spectacular volley against Peterborough to take my tally to five goals in eight games. I couldn't have dreamed of a better start to my career at United.

It wasn't so much the goals but the way in which I'd settled into the side, and the way everything seemed to click. Don't get me wrong, I wasn't having love affairs with the players, I wasn't wooing them and taking them out for dinners, but we did have a chemistry on the pitch that was so natural that it was thrilling to be a part of that while playing my natural game. I was fortunate enough to have a good goal to game ratio that would compare with anybody in my position and even against forwards, but I couldn't have done it without the support of my wonderful team-mates. I was doing what came natural to me, and I certainly wouldn't ever hesitate when it came to striking a ball first time. I didn't want to let it drop. Ray Wilkins classed me as one of the best 'volleyers' of a ball in the world. That was my skill and that's what I brought to the table in a team that was full of special talents. The team played with a youthful fearlessness, it was one hundred miles an hour controlled football.

We progressed in the Cup by winning against Leicester at Filbert Street, and managed to maintain our fine league form through February. Home draws against Liverpool and Derby County were maybe games we might have looked back on in months to come as chances that got away but with those teams being around us, fighting to get to the top of the table, they seemed like good results at the time. And when we put four goals past West Ham without reply at Old Trafford, we closed February in third place, level on points with Liverpool and Queens Park Rangers but separated by the slightest of margins on goal average. Manchester United were back, challenging at the top of the table and in a good position in the FA Cup just months after returning to the First Division.

At the start of March we took on Wolverhampton Wanderers in what would prove to be an epic cup tie. Wolves were struggling at the bottom of the First Division and came to Old Trafford wanting a replay and try as we might, we couldn't break them down. As so often happens in cup ties, they broke away and got a lead, but thankfully Gerry Daly earned us a replay. In the return at Molineux we went two goals down early on, but managed to equalise and then win in extra time when Sammy scored.

That result took us through to the semi final against Derby County at Hillsborough. Good God, what a team they had. Charlie George, Franny Lee, Roger Davies and the best right back I've ever seen in Colin Todd. Derby were up there with us challenging for the league title, and everyone in the press labelled it as the 'real' Cup Final.

After having such a good season, there was always that thought in the back of our mind that this tie would be the one where we get our come-uppance. On the day of the game as we went into the ground, Derby's Leighton James and Charlie George were stood outside giving their tickets to their families. We went past them and Leighton turned around to tell us that it was not worth us turning up. Charlie told him he was an idiot for saying that. We thought it was great. Thanks Leighton, you just gave us our team talk. This was by far the biggest game of my career, facing a Derby County side who were chasing a number of trophies, in an FA Cup semi final, and for Manchester United. It was a very big game for us, just one match from Wembley. United hadn't been to a Cup Final since 1968 but now we were finally back challenging for honours. The club had won Division Two but the guys didn't acknowledge that as an achievement as they shouldn't have been there in the first place.

Regardless of the difficulties you could tell that with the size of the club the fans expected the win. It was choc-a-bloc at Hillsborough and when the whistle went we had to give it our all as Derby were expecting to go to Wembley just as much as we were. We just wanted to play as well as we could, because we knew that if we gave it everything and came up short, then the supporters would forgive us for trying to put on a good show. Thankfully everything went well and everyone was on song. I was the match-winner on the day with two goals but it was the team and the way they performed that won the game. It was surreal to score the goals in the fashion I did. I was able to use a little ingenuity to cut inside and bend the first one into the top corner but the goal was created by a fine pass from Brian Greenhoff and brilliant work by Gerry Daly. It was a special goal and I felt so great when it went in. In the second half we were awarded a free kick. I saw a gap in the wall and went to hit the ball there, it took a little deflection and went in like a rocket. I loved to take the free kicks, and I loved to try and put a bend on the ball, but the balls in those days were the hardest to try and bend. The Mitre Multiplex was a hard ball and if someone kicked it and it hit you, it left the Mitre impression on your leg for about a week. They really were hard balls. I can remember sometimes, Pancho would go up to head it and he'd complain about being dizzy afterwards. When you think about the level of seriousness that concussion is treated these days it's incredible.

Brian made a great run at the end of the game to nearly make it 3-0, and I couldn't see where he'd got the energy from because everyone was knackered. I see people complain about fitness in today's game and I'd ask them to watch a copy of that game. A full ninety minutes with only one substitute, on a pitch nowhere near the quality that you'd get today, and Brian was still charging up there in the final minute. Everyone in the team gave everything they had. The club was a top club, but the team weren't there yet. We were after Derby and Liverpool who were the top teams, and now we'd beaten one of them convincingly.

After the game we were due to go back over the top of the Woodhead Pass to Mottram Hall for a celebration. Being a neutral venue we didn't stay too long with the Derby lads but we did have a drink in the players lounge where Charlie George wasn't speaking to Leighton James. I always got on with Charlie, he was straightforward and I liked that, and such a good player too. Leaving Hillsborough was absolutely manic as we just about got in the coach and it was only parked about a foot away from the door. The supporters knew it was our coach because it was red and white and the crowds outside were absolutely incredible. We'd got back to Wembley, a cup final for the first time since 1968.

It was a brilliant and unique feeling. The club had really been in the doldrums for five or six years, and we were the players who had brought the glory days back. Loving the club as I do, I hope that they never have to go through that again, so maybe the feeling that we had as a squad in 1976 will forever be special to those of us who experienced it. All of the later sides that had success at United are great and I'm happy for them but it was a very special emotion to be part of the team that brought it all back. United supporters had longed for that since 1968, and had been with the team through the lows, so they really deserved it. It isn't the first time and won't be the last that I say how much credit the Doc deserves for his part in that. He upset a lot of people but that's football, and in order for the club to be reborn it was necessary.

The fans were delirious at Hillsborough and we were just as happy and ready to party ourselves. We managed to get on the coach and sit at the table. I think there was me, Sammy, Wee Dee and Greeno, absolutely elated and you couldn't wipe the smiles off our faces. The fans were hitting the bus, trying to get on it and knocking on the windows. At the side of the bus, there was a car, a BMW. It was trying to get out of the car park but it was in the worst possible position as it became a ramp and springboard all in one, as supporters climbed up on to it and were jumping all over it to get a view of us inside the coach. They jumped on the car until it almost literally sank. The suspension went and the guys in the car got out of it to find safety. It was crazy. They were trying to get a look at us, but we were doing the same to try and see what they were doing to the poor fella's car. Nobody wanted to disappear at that point. The more we were waving at them, the more they jumped. That car would never have been roadworthy after that.

As we were going back over the tops, we were all singing 'Tie a Yellow Ribbon Round the Ole Oak Tree'. When we got back to Mottram we had a room booked for our party, and it just so happened that a couple were also holding their wedding reception there. There was a disco, and on seeing us there we were invited to join in. The champagne was flowing and the Doc was enjoying plenty of it. He got up on stage and the song had changed from 'Tie a Yellow Ribbon Round the Ole Oak Tree' to 'Fuck off Derby, fuck off', It wasn't out of disrespect but I think it was more out of relief, the joy that the manager had from finally getting the club back. He'd had his criticism, so it was a vindication of everything he'd done at the club. The semi-final had been described as the final in the media because Derby were at the top of the tree and the other semi finalists were both from Division Two, but when that final whistle went we had no idea who we were playing against, we were simply elated to have made it to the final. In those days, both semi-finals were played at the same time and that is a tradition I'd like to see brought back into the game. As with everything else, that gets dictated by television these days, doesn't it?

TD may have been warming up his vocal chords but we were all doing that soon after. Another tradition that seems to have gone out of the game was the club Cup Final song, though I think singing might have been wide of the mark for us as we were more like a bunch of howling cats. The mixer and production team must have been geniuses. We went down to the studio in Stockport and it was hilarious as everyone was trying to be pop stars, dressing like Rod Stewart. Sammy came in saying he'd been listening to Al Green on the radio so I asked him if we were going to sing like him. It was a great day and we were all laughing at each other for being out of key. Tuning forks? We needed a whole set of cutlery!

Gerry Daly would sing the Simon and Garfunkel song, 'The Boxer', and of course it would not have been complete without Martin and his guitar. He wrote a song for the B side called 'Old Trafford Blues' with the lyric 'Then there's Brian Greenhoff, he's got lots of skill, and he really needs it to play with Gordon Hill!' At first I was scratching my head and thinking what the hell does he need a lot of skill for? Now I know it was just about the rhyme and it was only a joke. I had my own back though when I asked him if he could sing solo. He said he could so I replied that he should sing so low no one could hear him!

Everything came out okay with the song in the end and it was something that everyone did it at the time. It was a nice tradition and though we didn't all socialise together all of the time, it was really good for team spirit. You can only imagine what kind of production and seriousness would go into something like that today. I knew plenty of pop stars back in those days and they were all wannabe football players. I must say my own singing career was limited to that song and of course carol singing for a few shilling when I was a kid. I dread to think how many birds in the trees I killed with my singing.

With a Cup Final place secured against Division Two Southampton who'd defeated Aston Villa, and Manchester United in third place in Division One, three points from the top with two games in hand, some speculation about the possibility of us winning the double began to surface. The Doc tried to focus us and said that the Cup was a one-off game. I think he was trying to take the pressure off us in the league. That was our bread and butter, but we'd done far better than anyone had expected a newly promoted side to do. Frank Blunstone would say the same, keep it at one game at a time, and the boss looked at it very realistically.

Even for a club the size of Manchester United, anything above fifth place would have been far more than anyone would have hoped for at the start of the season. Unfortunately perhaps we must have had one eye on the final because our league form dipped. We were suffering a semi-final hangover when we were battered 3-0 at Ipswich, and though we beat Everton and Burnley in the next two games, we were defeated at home by Stoke City in late April in a game that really did for our title chances. We went into that game with two games in hand and four points behind, but the loss meant it was practically impossible for us to win the title. Defeat against Leicester on April 24th confirmed it.

Over the years I've been asked many times about what we could have achieved under the Doc. Indeed, I'll be talking about it as we go on. Of the many what ifs, that was as close as we got to winning the League and I dare say I'm not the only one who looks back at that Stoke game with disappointment.

Our league form wasn't the ideal preparation for the FA Cup Final on Saturday May 1st, 1976. It was the hottest summer on record as well, which hardly helped matters. Aside from Alex Stepney, none of us really knew what to expect as we hadn't been to a cup final. The FA Cup was the most coveted domestic cup competition in the world – and still is. Giants or minnows can get to the final.

We'd all played so well during the season and in the semi final, yet on the day the occasion got to me. It was the first time that they'd introduced cards with numbers on for substitutions. I was on the other side of the pitch after about seventy minutes of a game where we were really struggling to break through. Sammy Mac had hit the crossbar but other than that chances were few and far between. With around a quarter of the game to go, and the Cup Final still in the balance, I saw the number 11 held up by the physio Laurie Brown and realised I was being substituted. Nowadays it's common practice but there and then my response was 'Oh shit'. I was knackered and made the long walk across the pitch. As I got there I looked at the manager and said, 'What, me?' He replied that the whole fucking team could have come off. It broke me up and I had to laugh. Wee Dee went on in my place but soon we were 1-0 down to a goal from Bobby Stokes which I'm still sure to this day was offside, and unfortunately we lost the game.

It was upsetting for all concerned and we weren't happy because we hadn't played well. Everyone had their own reasons as to why we'd lost the game. Some put it down to superstition because we didn't stay at Selsdon Park where the winners normally stayed.

In the changing room after the game, the Doc and Alex Stepney, who must have had his own personal disappointment having never won the FA Cup by this point in his long career, tried to make everyone feel better by insisting we would be back next year to win it. And you know, that made a hell of a difference to our mood. We wished Southampton all the very best and then went back for what should have been a victory parade in Manchester. We got off the bus in Wilmslow and someone had made a mock-up FA Cup and it got on the double decker that was going to Manchester. There were big crowds there but we were still not really allowed to let our hair down and party afterwards, though there was a bit of a do on the night of the Cup Final. Sir Matt Busby and his wife were there, Gerry Daly got up and sang some Simon and Garfunkel and I did my Norman Wisdom impression.

We had one league game left to play after the Cup Final and that was the Manchester derby at Old Trafford. Funnily enough, United hadn't defeated City at home in the league for nearly ten years. I vowed to play well in that game, and I scored a dribbled goal in a 2-0 win. I wanted to let the supporters know that I could do better and that the cup final performance was a one-off. To be truthful, I think that was the whole feeling of the club. Sure, we were disappointed to have lost the Final, but it wasn't the result that mattered as getting there and finishing third in the league showed to everyone that Manchester United was back. You could feel it in training and you could feel it in the opposition when we played against them.

I've seen Laurie McMenemy, who was manager for Southampton that day, a few times over the years but the most recent was in August 2013 when we had dinner together in Florida. He told me that Peter Rodrigues played out of his arse that day and they knew the only person who would score or make a vital chance would be me, so once I had gone they knew they would win the cup. I told him that I thought I'd played shit, but he said he felt the whole team were below par and reminded me of that City goal a few days later.

It was nice to hear. In the immediate aftermath though, I couldn't be convinced that it was okay that I'd played poorly. All I knew was that I'd not performed, I'd been brought off and then we went behind and I was unable to do anything to help. It's okay to reflect, and of course I've had to do a lot of that in order to write my autobiography, but I don't like to dwell. Nonetheless, if I am reminded about Cup Final day in 1976, I am there in a second and can still feel the same frustration as I did then. The only thing you can do as a professional is look to the next game and try and improve and do better. I was lucky to get some short term relief with that game against City but the next step was to achieve something better the following season.

*****

Jackie and I were still living in Buxworth when our daughter Kerry came into the world. She was actually born in Chertsey, Surrey, but then my wife brought her back up to Buxworth. We are still very close and I absolutely love her to death. Your life obviously changes so much when you become a parent yet my life had changed a lot in such a short space of time that everything always felt like it was changing anyway. Still, your outlook alters when you have a baby. Everything has a new perspective and you have a different way of looking at what really matters. I wasn't to know it at the time when I was riding the crest of a wave, but a couple of years later that attitude was going to help me a lot. After living in Buxworth for a while, we moved house to Bollington, and my wife and I used to go down to a club called the Poco a Poco club in Stockport where the compere was Vince Miller. Even though he was a blue we struck up a good friendship, and we saw many good acts and shows at the cabaret club.

On the topic of change, my life had altered a lot in just a year. From Millwall to Manchester via Chicago, an FA Cup Final, a daughter, and now at the end of the season, an England call up. I'd actually been selected to play in an England under 23 game against Hungary at Old Trafford in April. It was a two-legged tie, the first had been lost 3-0, but I scored a great goal in the second leg in a 3-1 win. We ripped them to pieces in front of 30,000. Don Revie, who was England manager, came to me after the game and told me I'd be joining the full England squad from then on. I was delighted, because I knew that Millwall would be getting another payment for me getting an international cap. I was mixing with the elite, and when England travelled to the United States for the Bicentennial Cup in the post-season of 1976, all the top names in the country were there including Kevin Beattie, Kevin Keegan, Ray Wilkins, Mickey Channon. Again, it was daunting, but it helped that Stuart Pearson and Brian Greenhoff were getting their first taste of international football as well. Not only were we mixing with the elite, we felt like we were the elite and able to show that we could hold our own with all these great players, players for Manchester United and England. It was the greatest feeling in the world and you simply cannot go anywhere higher in football. So for me, and for us, it was about trying to stay at the level we had reached.

It was funny because United had travelled to the USA at the same time as the Bicentennial Cup. I actually missed out on a game with my old team Chicago Sting because I was making my England debut. We played Italy in the Yankee Stadium and I made my England debut alongside Ray Wilkins. We were 2-0 down in no time in front of 40,000 screaming Italian New Yorkers on a baseball field. Luckily we turned it around and won 3-2.

Afterwards, Ray and I could only muster up the strength to agree that it was a hard game. At the end of the 1975/76 season I have to say that my over-riding feeling was that I'm home. I was leading goalscorer for United and had been named runner-up to Peter Barnes as PFA Young Player of the Year.

I'd taken everything in my stride and part and parcel of what comes with being a Manchester United footballer is that you become something of a wanted commodity in media circles. I've always said that I felt the United team that I played in were equally great man for man. I would never pick one above another and I include myself in that, though it is a consequence of being an attacking player and scoring goals that you get noticed more. For better or worse, flair players tend to be attractive to the media and that's how it was in 1976 when the form that Stevie and myself had shown meant we were quite often asked to participate in various publicity events. We were flavour of the month when we were asked to appear in a commercial for Gillette razors, though this must have been the winter of the 1976/77 season. Just one problem, neither of us had any whiskers, we were still puppies. They also asked Tommy Docherty to be in it, and he has a bit of a dimpled face and is hardly renowned for shaving. None of us were exactly Ryan Giggs, who must shave every second.

Anyway, we had to go up into the gantry at Old Trafford where broadcasters used to commentate. It was freezing and the field had ice on it. They weren't exactly looking after us as we didn't have any gloves or anything like that and we had to climb up a ladder to get on the gantry. Once we were there it was a great view. I said that I would love to watch the game from up here. No prizes for guessing TD's response. He muttered that if I played like I did last Saturday I could be up there on the weekend. So we're about three feet from the roof and the cameramen got up on this rickety old gantry. The Doc had his script which read something like, 'Gillette Two – this will give you the closest shave and the old one-two'. As he said 'one-two', he was supposed to pretend to punch my chin and then glance on to Stevie's. Only the Doc didn't pretend and you can imagine how annoying it got after three dozen takes. I told the Doc to stop sodding whacking me as my skin was getting red as a beetroot. He said he was sorry but he was supposed to be coming off me and on to Stevie.

He was spinning my head as he was hitting me so hard. I asked Stevie to swap over and so he did. Then once we'd swapped he asked me why so I told him to look at the state of my chin. Then of course we had a bit of fun, it was taking double the time to get through it and the Doc decided that he'd warm up on Stevie's chin and whack me harder again. He must have been taking the piss. I asked him to take it easy on me, but he didn't though. The cameramen said afterwards that it was a great day, and that Gillette would love it. I told them that was because they still had all of their teeth.

We had planned to do more, a follow on, but then there was the shock news with the Doc but that's a story for another chapter, the next in fact. It was so funny though, I didn't even have bum-fluff and yet I was in an advert for shaving. Brilliant. I did grow a moustache but my mum would always ask me why my nose was so special that I had to underline it. If that was a little ridiculous, Stevie and I also experienced the bizarre. We were asked to open a Makro store in Swinton with the Typhoo chimps. There must have been close to a thousand people there and we thought they were there for the chimps, but apparently they were there for us. It was a bit of a circus when we turned up and we had to wade through the crowds because no one ushered us in and there was no security. We were pinned against the wall, someone ripped the chain off my neck, and someone else was grabbing my nuts. We tried to escape to the toilets but then we couldn't get out of there. It was bad for us but fantastic for Makro. The chimps were fantastic, but they'd have gone mad if they'd been with us. I'd have had some fun with them if I was given the chance.

Looking back I really can't believe there were no police or security. I had no problem at all talking with fans and I suppose my background with the Millwall supporters gave me good experience but the volume of it was something I really wasn't expecting. It was something I'd have to get used to, though. After that we were asked to open another store in Boston, Lincolnshire, so Stevie and I drove across there, and again there must have been about a thousand people. I'm left handed, Stevie is right handed, so we were signing things sat side by side. After a while my arm felt like it was going to fall off so we had a bit of mischievous fun when we decided to sign each others name. Some people out there have originals and some have original copies – sorry!

There were many responsibilities that came with being a footballer for Manchester United, and another was one that I took absolute pleasure in. We would have a kid come around from a charity to collect Christmas presents for poorly children in hospitals. I was asked to be Father Christmas and go and give some of the gifts and I was only too pleased, honoured even, to be asked to do it. It really played a tune on me, and it was very close to my heart. It was a privilege to be part of it.

I suppose you could say I was in demand a little bit as I was also asked to take part in some 'Focus on Soccer' tapes where I was in great company. Sir Matt Busby was the manager, Peter Shilton and Ray Clemence as goalkeepers, Colin Todd was the defender. For me, Colin was as good as any defender in the world at the time and I would have been happy for United to buy him in a heartbeat. I was the winger for it, we recorded what were essentially a series of instructional and educational tapes about how to play in our position, or in Sir Matt's case, how to build a winning team. That was recorded over a couple of weeks near Maine Road. Trevor Brooking and Kevin Keegan were also involved as well. It was incredibly flattering to be asked to do that as it suggested I was one of the best wingers in the country. When I look back on it, to have gone to that status from playing in the Third Division in less than a year was mind-blowing. There were suggestions I was one of the best in the world in the position but I wasn't about to take credit for that or even say I was the best in the country. I didn't think I was better than Stevie, no way. There were great wingers in Division One too, Dave Thomas for example. Maybe the reason I was selected is simply because I scored more goals.

I always say that the wheel always turns in football. Maybe someone, a greater force somewhere, had seen everything that had happened in 1975/76 and decided that with the Southampton game they had to give me a massive downer. Overall, I had to put it into perspective though. From being relegated to Division Three with Millwall, my disappointment now was not winning the FA Cup, and not winning the Football League. The club's disappointment had been similar and I take my hat off to the work done by Tommy Docherty in dragging the club out of the doldrums. People might have thought what he did was easy but he had an incredibly tough job and deserves so much credit for what he did for Manchester United. As a team we had proved that we were good enough to compete even if we weren't quite ready to win. The next challenge for us all was fairly obvious. For me personally, I just wanted to show I wasn't a one season wonder, and I was motivated by the disappointment of the Cup Final and the prospect of participating in a World Cup qualifying campaign to scale greater heights in the 1976/77 season.

5

King of All Cockneys

Everyone at Manchester United was looking forward to seeing how we could improve for the 1976/77 season. Perhaps it's true to say that our biggest asset proved to be our biggest downfall in 1976. The rest of the lads had a pre-season 'around the world' trip after their promotion in 1975, and with my spell in America maybe our higher fitness levels gave us an advantage as we started the season ever so well. However, it's a fair opinion that it caught up with us from April onwards. It was very difficult as we were playing so often and the team stayed unchanged. What was good for momentum earlier on was bad on the legs as the season progressed. We didn't get a breather. If players were injured we carried on, as we didn't want to miss a game.

Because the matches kept flowing, training would get less intensive, especially when we had midweek games. Nowadays, clubs have two squads for the competitions and it's no coincidence that the teams that do better have stronger squads as opposed to just a strong first eleven and nowhere is that truer than at Manchester United. But in 1976, Manchester United's squad was tiny by comparison. I admired the boss immensely as he remained true to the club's core principles regardless of the restrictions of the day. When travelling to away games, our bus could only carry eighteen, yet the Doc would always take some younger players, not necessarily to play but to give them the experience. That to me was the sign of a good manager. Today, clubs can afford to take everyone.

I'd been at Old Trafford for half a season and I was now an

England international yet I still wasn't feeling any pressure about having to win games. Maybe it's because winning came when we were playing our natural game and that gave us even more confidence to perform. I still had that eagerness to play. Every team in the division was a good outfit and you couldn't take anyone lightly, so I loved the challenge of competing. I can still hear the motivating words of Tommy Cavanagh as he asked me, 'Gordy, just get me one.'

Nobody enjoyed coming to Old Trafford – opponents were scared to play. We never suffered from nerves wherever we went because we'd always play in front of capacity audiences and our supporters were so great that we knew they could get us a point. We honestly felt that we could win every game, the spirit was that way and hadn't been dampened by the form at the end of the previous season, if anything that served as an extra motivator. Personally, I would always try and live up to Tommy Cav's words. Of course the most important thing was to help the team win, but I had personal goals, I always wanted to play well and score. If I couldn't score, I wanted to create as much as I could. It was the same way I'd played as long as I'd known and it was the same style that had thankfully fitted in so well with the United way. I wanted to entertain. Benny Fenton trusted in me to do it and now Tommy Docherty was putting his faith in me at the higher level and I was determined to justify it.

I have to say that there was a huge difference playing for England, though. Don Revie, who was managing the side, didn't always want to play with flamboyant players and sometimes played tighter for tactical reasons. He would pick the right time to use players to open up the game and that made me feel that I really had to earn my caps. I was being groomed, or primed, for the rigours of international football and the significant differences between that and playing for your club. I still feel cold when I think about pulling on an England shirt with the three lions and all that it means, after all I'm English through and through and would die for my country. When I put that shirt on I'd give everything. Having said that, it gave me considerable comfort to know that I had Manchester United behind me. I don't wish this to sound arrogant or rotten but I didn't arrive at England feeling out of place, wondering if I belonged because I played for an ordinary club. Did I have the right to play for England? I got my position in the England squad purely as a consequence of my form for Manchester United, and that meant the world. My first cap was my best one. As I've said, I made my England debut in June 1976 against Italy in New York but because the Bicentennial Cup wasn't recognised by FIFA, I didn't actually get a cap for it from the FA. But they certainly took all the praise for beating Italy.

After the long summer in Chicago in 1975 it was nice to have a little break in 1976. Arriving back at United for the new season, everyone had their own opinion about what we needed in order to win the title. In my opinion I felt we needed a goalkeeper. Alex Stepney had done a smashing job and had served the club ever so well but I just thought we needed new blood in that area. The boss obviously thought so as well as he'd dropped Alex the previous season just prior to my arrival. Paddy Roche came in for him and he was actually the goalkeeper in my first two games for United. But he'd made a couple of errors, one at Anfield before I came, one of them against Arsenal, and so Alex had been recalled. Anywhere else and Paddy might have got away with his errors but at United there was a higher standard.

Peter Shilton was the goalkeeper for Stoke City and had become England's number one goalkeeper after the World Cup winning stopper, Gordon Banks, had to sadly retire due to an eye injury he'd suffered in a car accident. I spoke with Peter when I was with England and the Doc made no bones about it, in fact he urged me to speak to Peter to convince him to sign for United.

It wasn't about getting rid of Alex, it was about bringing in the England goalkeeper who wanted to come to United. I know that because Peter told me personally and I can remember him coming to Old Trafford to meet the Doc and speak about it. He made no secret of his desire to move to United and I'm sure he'd be pretty open about that today. He'd have been up there in a heartbeat. He'd ask me at England training if I had spoken to the Doc about him. I said I didn't need to which was true. Everyone knew Peter's ability and TD was no different. The board said no as they wouldn't sanction the fee of around £275,000, and that was that. Alex was a good, steady goalkeeper, but Peter would have made a big difference to our team.

The pre-season trip to Western Europe might have seemed like a fairly comfortable tour but it was frickin' hard. We played against Hamburg in Germany and Nuremburg where the difference between training fitness and match sharpness was apparent but we won both games with me scoring in the win over Nuremburg. A 0-0 draw with Alkmaar of the Netherlands followed before we played Red Star Belgrade. That match sticks out for me because on the Red Star side was a player called Joe Raduka, who's still a very good friend of mine today. Joe and I often speak of that game because there were some fabulous players on view.

The trip was memorable for more than the game because the boys locked Paddy Roche and Gerry Daly in their room all night. We were staying in rooms where the doors opened outwards and they'd left their key in the door, so Lou Macari and some others sneaked into their room on the top floor and disconnected the telephone before we went out for dinner. When we were due to leave the boss was asking where they were, little did he know that they couldn't get out of the room, and he told us that he would deal with them later. It was hilarious, you could hear them bickering in the room in their Southern Irish accents wondering how were they going to get out. They didn't for three or four hours. They could get out on the balcony but because they were so far up nobody could hear them, even if they'd been able to understand. Gerry had bought loads of duty free cigarettes and Paddy had cigars. They were put together because they smoked and when the lads opened the door a rush of smoke came out. The boss had a go at them because of it as well, but they took it all in good spirits.

When we went to actually play the game against Red Star it was bizarre, because when we went out for the warm up before the game nobody was in the ground. As we went back out to play the match there were about 40,000 army boys sitting in the stadium. They'd been waiting outside with their battalion in their military coats and hats and had been marched inside all at once. It was a good game which we lost 2-1 and we were able to visit the commemorative plaque that the club had in honour of the Munich disaster.

I was too young to know about the tragedy growing up but not too young to read and learn about it afterwards. It's something that's very difficult to comprehend and takes on another meaning when you become a United player. Listening to the stories of the survivors and their memories of great team-mates, you know from their achievements that these aren't memories that are over generous, they are accurate. Hearing Wilf McGuinness tell you about Duncan Edwards for instance ... even the conversations I'd had with Bill. He never spoke of Munich much, but he would say small bits and pieces, like when he told me about Duncan. Now there was a player. Everybody said he was as strong as a carthorse, a lad who looked like a fully grown man.

The club is steeped in tradition that went before Munich. The rivalry with Liverpool that was a city rivalry due to the canals, the changing of the name from Newton Heath, Old Trafford being bombed in the war. So Munich, on the playing side of everything, is a significant part of the history. Stories of success are often tinged with sadness and so it is with United and Munich. Think of that team going out as pioneers, competing in the European Cup against the wishes of the League secretary Alan Hardaker. The young men whose lives were taken much too soon, the heroes that were born in such tragic and terrible circumstances, and the resilience of the club under Jimmy Murphy to begin to rebuild in the immediate aftermath. See, when people talk to you and question you about the pressures of playing for Manchester United, and succeeding the likes of George and Bobby, there's a deeper meaning to everything. Sure, you're doing that, by the process of evolution, but you're also playing in the shadows of those who perished on February 6th, 1958.

Maybe that's something specific to United and their connection with European football as they were the English pioneers and there is something special about those nights. You are playing with the memories and the shadows of all that has been and passed. I loved playing at Old Trafford more than anything because of every single emotion that was involved with it. It felt like it was my pitch when I was playing on it and it did feel like

I belonged, but as soon as I stepped off the turf it belonged to those shadows once more. Maybe it would be better not to be conscious of that, not to be aware of it, but it made me appreciate everything that much more. Did it add extra pressure? Possibly, but I just knew I had to go out and do my best, the same way that had been done before me in years gone by, and the way that had been done before them too.

And now I'm a shadow, Bobby Charlton is a shadow, Denis Law is a shadow. That's what we all are, those players who were lucky enough to wear that shirt. There's never any pressure from the club or the supporters to replicate the 1958 side, to try and match that potential, or that of any successful United side. But every player is aware of it, every player is striving to meet that potential to be the best they can possibly be in the hope that one day they can be mentioned in the same breath. I don't know if anyone can live up to it, it may be impossible, but it's a very unique feeling at the club and that is why, for me, supporters have a very special relationship with those who bust a gut. There are countless players over the years who the supporters have adored because of that connection. Every player has their own specific feeling and today there are so many of those who are remembered fondly. I hold an immense respect for those that paved the way.

I'm jumping ahead of time here, but I was to enjoy a moment against Juventus in 1976, one of the standout memories of my career that was made possible by the club who made those brave first steps into Europe. Because of them, all kinds of ideas of greatness had been made achievable. Whenever I return to Manchester and Old Trafford I make a point of spending some time to observe the Munich plaque and pay my respects there. To have a few moments to myself to walk slowly down the tunnel and remember the stories of some of the players who lost their lives on duty with the club that I have taken to my heart so much. To remember the few, poignant words that Bill Foulkes would share with me. Then when I get the opportunity to go back into the stadium, particularly when it's empty, to just have a seat and allow the memories to come flooding back into my mind. Going to Belgrade to play for Manchester United was never going to be simply a 'friendly' when remembering their history. After playing in such a game, especially less than a year after playing against the 1968 side in the testimonial for Pat Crerand, I was in a place where I was under no illusions about what representing the club was all about.

Stories came out around the time of that trip to Belgrade that Lou Macari was set to leave after falling out with the Doc, but he stayed after sorting it out. That was good as not only was he a great player but Lou was fantastic to have around and a real joker. If there was a scheme being hatched, he would be the one pulling it off.

Talking of jokers, Ashley Grimes had come over for a trial and was going to sign for us, but came along with us on a trip to Leeds early in the season. The boss said he had to have an initiation on the way home on the coach, and that was to sing the song 'Danny Boy'. Ashley refused, so the boss said that if he wasn't going to sing then they were going to stop the bus and he'd have to get out. Now, anyone who's done the Leeds to Manchester journey on the M62 on a cold night knows how freezing it can get. And bloody hell, if he didn't kick him out. Ashley could have got pneumonia. The bus set off and Ashley chased after it and was allowed back on the bus after agreeing to sing. There was some fun had on that coach. We had a fruit fight going to the Cup Final, though I'm not sure our driver Bob appreciated it when an orange hit his windscreen. That was the team, and we had such a great combined spirit.

Sadly, one of my good friends left at the start of that season. Jim Holton was a good player who had represented Scotland in the 1974 World Cup, but he suffered such terrible luck with injuries and was transferred to Coventry City. I was saddened greatly to hear that he had died in 1993 at the young age of forty two. A fit Jim could have made a huge difference to our fortunes in the early stages of the 1976/77 Division One season. We had signed Colin Waldron as cover and he was a nice guy but not a player at the level capable of deputising for Martin Buchan or Brian Greenhoff. We couldn't do with either of them getting injured but unfortunately Martin did. Colin came in and so did Steve Paterson who was an apprentice, but that showed just how thin the squad really was. United didn't pay the best wages so couldn't fill the squad and players who became available tended to go to clubs like Derby, who at the time were able to attract players of a similar talent.

Martin's absence was a blow as he was the natural leader and thinker of our team, while Brian's cavalier defending as a foil for Martin was important to the way we played, but being completely honest, every single player in that team brought something special that meant their absence would be felt. As good as that first eleven was, the fragility of fitness and the reminder of the damage just one injury could do, showed that we weren't in the best shape. And that was a shame as we had taken the First Division by storm, got to the FA Cup Final, and were now preparing to try and repeat that as well as perform in the UEFA Cup. Entry to that competition was the reward for finishing third in the league and saw United in European competition for the first time since their ultimately unsuccessful attempt to retain the European Cup in 1969. A trip to Ajax awaited us on September 15th, by which time we'd already had a little stumble in the league.

We began the season playing against teams from the Midlands, drawing two and winning the other at Coventry in a game in which I scored. We found our form in a 5-0 League Cup win at home to Tranmere where I netted again, but suffered the hiccup of a home defeat to Tottenham in the league. A draw at Newcastle continued our indifferent start and we went into the Ajax tie in eighth place in the league. Ajax were a fantastic side, proved by their hat-trick of European Cups from 1971 to 1973. Johan Cruyff had just left but they had many great players and they had a fabulous footballing philosophy. We knew we'd be up against it and the thought crossed our minds that we'd be eliminated at the first hurdle. At that point we had to remind ourselves that our own style had brought many admirers and gave the opposition something to fear. We were still playing good football, fast and controlled, and the boss trusted us to take that same approach into European competition.

Ever the pragmatist, Tommy told us not to worry if they scored one, just make sure we scored two. We looked at their style of play and had to admire their technical ability but at the same time we were also blessed with players who were very technical. Lou was one, as was Stuart Pearson and myself. I felt I could match anybody at Ajax and relished the chance to come up against the experienced Wim Suurbier. We had a belief in ourselves that again stemmed from the fact that we were not only being utilised to our strengths, but also playing our natural way.

The boss has to take the credit for putting us in the shape we were and the instructions we were given were hardly rocket science. For me, I just had to tuck in when we didn't have the ball. And as much as we knew our own strengths, we were more than aware of our opponents strengths too but we were just confident in the ability of our team-mates to handle it. We knew Martin and Brian, international defenders, could cope with anything thrown at them.

Despite all of the best preparation, sometimes results just don't go your way, and that was the case in the first leg at the Olympisch Stadium where we lost 1-0. It was my first game in Holland and my first exposure of seeing a style and a way of playing that I admired so much. I love World Cup tournaments and I was mesmerised by the Dutch team of 1974 with Cruyff, Neeskens, Rep and others. I wouldn't say I was inspired by any particular style, as I was very much my own player, but watching such a great team with so many talents certainly reinforced the belief that being an individual could be a huge blessing. I was eager to show them what I could do on my own patch.

Our league form picked up between the European legs with wins at home to Middlesbrough and away at Manchester City. Perhaps proving how tight the league could be when it was two points for a win, those results took us into third place, just one point behind Liverpool who were top.

All the while we were looking forward to Ajax coming to Old Trafford. Having seen what they were capable of, we wanted to take them on and were looking forward to having our supporters behind us. I'm not sure they knew what hit them. I've already said about how the stadium has a unique atmosphere on European nights due to the history of the club and this was my first experience of it and the first time United fans had seen a European game at Old Trafford since they were knocked out of the European Cup in 1969. With Ajax being such formidable opponents, all the ingredients were there to make it a memorable occasion. The roar that went up when Lou Macari put in the rebound after the goalkeeper spilled my fierce shot inspired us and we were able to add to that with a goal in the second half when Sammy McIlroy put us ahead and ultimately decided the tie. We were thrilled to beat them and afterwards it was a case of 'who's next?'

The answer to that question was Juventus, so it wasn't going to get any easier for us but at least, Europe knew that Manchester United were back. We opened up a lot of eyes around the continent with that result but before we took on the Italians there was some work to be done on the domestic front.

We won at Leeds before overcoming Sunderland in a tough League Cup tie that went to two replays. Then there was an international break in October where I played my first competitive match for England, coming on as a substitute against Finland at Wembley with a quarter of an hour left. I'd played at Wembley for England in a friendly the previous month when I came on for Charlie George who was making his debut against Ireland. England won the Finland game 2-1 to keep up their hopes of qualifying for the World Cup in 1978.

Our warm-up game for Juventus was a trip to the Hawthorns to face West Bromwich Albion. Unfortunately this was the first game that Martin missed and it hit us hard as we were well beaten 4-0. It wasn't the ideal preparation for a game against a team full of Italian international players and we were well aware of the strength and ability of everyone on that team, considering that Italy were in England's World Cup qualifying group. In fact, with England struggling to qualify, the game almost took on extra significance as far as pride for the country was concerned. Nobody could take them for granted that's for sure, but following the Ajax game we were already used to the toughest opposition that the competition could throw at us. When some English clubs' achievements are evaluated from the seventies and eighties the lack of strength of the opposition is something that is often used to downplay how well they did, but we certainly could have had nobody telling us our baby steps into life on the continent were not as difficult as they could possibly be.

There are many things said and written about that United team of 1976/77 and one of our great attributes was that we all had that hunger to prove ourselves as the best and re-establish the club. We relished the bigger games and enjoyed testing ourselves against the best around.

When looking back at the first leg with Juventus at Old Trafford, I have to say that it was one of the best nights of my career. Juventus had plenty of world class footballers and they double-marked me with two men, but fortunately I got half a yard during the game and was able to score on the volley. It was the kind of goal I could hit a dozen times. As big as the night was, and it was the biggest of the year, it was yet another of those games where the entire team were up for it and we knew we could turn them over. The game finished 1-0 although we might have nicked a second.

That was the first meeting between United and Juventus and obviously since then there has been a lot of history between the clubs. There were epic battles in the mid-nineties as Sir Alex Ferguson saw Juventus as the pinnacle, and everyone remembers that game in 1999 where Roy Keane led a great fightback on the way to United winning the European Cup. Back on that evening in 1976 we were just happy to have got such a great result against a team who were undoubtedly the top dogs in Italy. After all they had won Serie A in 1972, 1973, 1975 and would also win it in 1977 and 1978. We were under no illusion about how tough the return leg would be. I went out for a drink with my friend Mario after the game and he was a big Juventus supporter. He told me it would be harder in Turin. Not much!

We weren't mugs but we were a young side who came up against a brick wall over there in the return. It was brutal. Sammy got a whack under his right eye from Marco Tardelli in the match while I got a boot to the head. I nodded a free kick against the post which rebounded into Dino Zoff's hands. Even luck was against us as we went down 3-0 on the night and were eliminated 3-1 on aggregate. The fans didn't like us so thank God there was a track and that they pulled out the canopy to the edge of the field. Coming off the pitch there was fighting in the tunnel and we gave as good as we got.

We may have been out but our performances had been good enough to let Europe know that Manchester United were a force again, and it was just tough on us that we faced two very strong teams in the early rounds of the competition. I sometimes can't believe that game finished 3-0 as it was very harsh on us, it was a scoreline we didn't deserve and just as the first game stood out as one of the very best moments in my entire career, the game in Turin was definitely one of the low points.

The home leg had been the start of a good run of form for me personally, and buoyed by the winner against Juventus I just wanted to take on all-comers. The team were playing well too, with Sammy McIlroy and Lou Macari working wonders in the engine room.

I scored in a home draw against Norwich before we faced Newcastle United in the League Cup. Record books say I scored a hat-trick but I contest that to this day. I scored four that night as we won 7-2 and I was delighted as Newcastle had some good players. It was the performance that pleased me more than the goals and once more I was glad to help the team show that the season before hadn't been a one-off.

I loved to score goals and entertain yet I knew I was selfish at times. But then I needed to be. Others would be too, development was about choosing the right times to be selfish and knowing when not to be. The boss was pleased for me to get the hat-trick and I can remember taking the Mitre Multiplex ball home with me as is customary to do. I would give it to the kids outside so they could play with it on the street. People would ask me if I was going to treasure it, and I did, but I had a lot of fun with it and the kids had a lot of fun with it too.

A run of eight goals in seven games was fine but there were two games during that run where the team didn't score at all, a 1-0 home defeat to Ipswich and that loss in Turin. Ipswich were a top team, though, and had a wonderful defender in Kevin Beattie who could head the ball as far as I could kick it.

After scoring in a defeat at Aston Villa and then in a home draw with Sunderland, the international break came around again. As ever, the headlines stayed with Manchester United despite there being no games as the Doc made a signing from Stoke City. Not Peter Shilton, but Jimmy Greenhoff. In my eyes, Jimmy was the best uncapped player around. He gave us the experience we needed to help Stuart Pearson up front and he took some of the pressure away from Lou who would occasionally play further up so he gave us an extra option.

Jimmy's signing was great for the team but I didn't see it as taking any pressure from me, in fact it was quite the opposite. We were looking for the double whammy now, so instead of just targetting Pancho in the box, we could look for either of them and they both made really intelligent runs. It added an extra dimension to the way we played and really solidified the Doc's game plan of a 4-2-4 formation. If we wanted to tighten it up, Stevie could move inside to make it a 4-3-3 as well. It was a fabulous signing from the boss and at just the right time .

Our form was really sticky and going into the international break we were in fifteenth position, nine points behind the leaders Liverpool. We were determined to catch Liverpool and do better than we had the previous season but even with Jimmy, our fortunes couldn't instantly improve due to Martin still being out. By Christmas, following defeats to West Ham and Arsenal, we were well and truly out of the race in seventeenth place and thirteen points behind top spot. I suppose you could draw a comparison with the signing of Robin van Persie for United in 2012 and Jimmy signing for us in 1976. He was a wonderful signing, and just like Robin, Jimmy would go on to make such a great contribution. He was billed as the player who made the difference, and while that is not a false statement, it's just as right to say that if TD had been allowed to address more pressing needs we might have gone on to achieve more than we did.

It was no coincidence that Martin's first game back at Old Trafford saw an instant up-turn in our form. From that game on December 27th, a 4-0 win against Everton where I scored, until the end of March we were beaten only once, on January 3rd at Ipswich. Our form improved so much that by the end of March we had put ourselves in fifth position with three games in hand and now we were only seven points behind leaders Ipswich. Despite that we knew deep down we'd given ourselves too much to do to win the league, but we had resolved to ensure we were not going to suffer cup heartache again.

Our cup form was good and possibly helped our league form as a consequence. The third and fourth round games were decided by a single goal at Old Trafford. I scored in our win over Walsall, and Lou decided the fourth round tie against QPR. That set us up for a revenge clash against Southampton in the fifth round at the Dell.

Having lost to them in the final in 1976, we were delighted to knock them out although they took us to a replay. I scored in the first game. We never underestimated our opponents because we knew first hand what they were capable of and were determined to prove the final was a one-off. That was a stumble for us and we were going to carry on doing well. Jimmy Greenhoff scored both goals to get us through to the quarter-finals where we were to face Aston Villa. Despite all our problems, once we got past them and had a semi final place and also a good position in the league, we were similarly placed to where we had been the previous year.

The week before Easter we faced problems of a different nature. A defeat to Norwich City at Carrow Road was marred with problems in the stands. The Red Army was what it was, but with the numbers that came to watch us on the road and the way the fencing was put up at grounds just added to the tension. Supporters shouldn't be put behind fences, and I felt that the Manchester United followers got a lot of unfair criticism. It was described as a hooligan problem but to me, they were just the Red Army. I'm not going to sit here and dismiss it and paint everyone as angels, they weren't, but there were problems from both sides and it was going to remain that way for a long time until it reached a head in the most tragic of circumstances in the 1980s at Heysel and then Hillsborough.

What I didn't agree with was the fencing. Not only did it look bad, but it also sent out a provocative message that one side was at fault. If more open and less confrontational dialogue had been attempted then maybe a lot of heartache could have been avoided. I can only say from my view as a player that it didn't look right from the pitch. And years later, when disaster did inevitably strike, I was right there in the stands to see it unfold.

My relationship with the United supporters was very special to me. Was it a sign of how good we were or just what they did for everyone? I don't know. But walking out of the tunnel in front of 50,000 United fanatics who had a song for each of the players was very special for me.

The nickname Merlin had stayed with me from my Millwall days, it was a press thing, I certainly didn't encourage it, and I would never have dreamed of asking any of my team-mates to refer to me as Merlin. There were nicknames around the squad, obviously 'Bucko' or 'Greeno' for Martin Buchan or Brian Greenhoff, though we'd also call Martin 'Elvis' because of his love for the guitar. Brian, we'd sometimes call 'Roy Orbison', because he'd got tinted sunglasses. Alex Forsyth was 'Bruce', for obvious reasons, while Gerry Daly was 'Catweasel' because he was spindly like him. I liked Gerry and would play with him again later in my career, but he smoked a bit too much, liked a drink and liked to put some money on the dogs – three things that I wasn't really into. Steve Coppell was 'Stevie', or 'Poppy', and Stewart Houston was the 'Six Million Dollar Man' because he ran like him!

I was 'Hilly' or 'Gordon' to my team-mates, and to the Stretford End, I was 'Gordon Hill, King of all Cockneys' To hear one of the most famous ends in world football sing such a song for me made the hairs on my arms and neck stand right up. I loved it when they went around the team chanting 'Greenhoff, Greenhoff', or 'Skip, skip to my Lou Macari', and when they'd get to my song, I'd pretend not to acknowledge it. In fact, I'd turn my back on them just to get a reaction. They'd perhaps sing it again, then boo me, and as soon as they booed, I'd turn around and clap the fans. I loved it!

These things may be considered small but it's part of the football culture that I absolutely love. You can win awards and they're great but for me, maybe the true measure of how good you are for a club is how much the supporters take to you. Certainly I treasure the memories of my name being chanted as much as I do winning the Cup in 1977. I cannot begin to tell you the pride I feel, and the pride I felt, at being referred to as 'the King' in any fashion. The previous 'King' at Old Trafford had been the one

An early photo of me with Mum at my
Nan's house at Hampton Hill

Mum and Dad at my brother
Tony's wedding

Young pup. My first picture
at Millwall in July 1973. It all
started here
© *Popperfoto/Getty Images*

My first club
photo with
Millwall. I loved
that all white
strip

In the thick of the action for Millwall. I felt the full brunt of that one

Performing tricks in the warm up

I think I was double marked!

With the legendary Bill Foulkes in my loan period with Chicago Sting

Now in a Manchester United shirt with the ball at my feet – there was no better feeling

The first goal against Derby County in the 1976 FA Cup semi final catapulted me into the public eye

Publicity photo at Old Trafford. That's some haircut! Why did I have that moustache?
© *Howard Talbot Photography*

One of my proudest moments. With team-mates Stuart Pearson, Alex Stepney and Sammy McIlroy celebrating our 2-1 victory in the 1977 FA Cup Final
© *Popperfoto/Getty Images*

My daughter Kerry – she didn't
fit in the Cup!

In the air at Derby County – did
I really know what I was doing?
© Bob Thomas/Getty Images

Evading two defenders on international duty against Luxembourg
© Bob Thomas/Getty Images

Happy family – with Claire, Sam and our first dog named Cleo

Collecting one of many awards in North America

In 1981 my love of the North American game was reborn

Relaxing at home in Kansas City with Sam and Cleo

These make me very proud. Caps from representing all the different levels of England

With Tommy Docherty, Vince Miller and my wife Claire

Coaching youngsters. A team talk against Home Farm

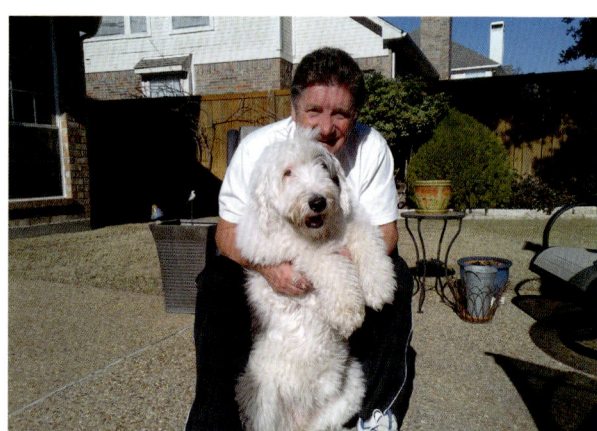

Our special dog ... Cleo is a real beauty

Showing the girls how to score having just netted with my head. No wonder I'm so happy!
© *Stacey Barton*

The girls get a team-talk as well
© *Stacey Barton*

One of my summer tours, talking to a group of young American players at Old Trafford
© *Stacey Barton*

Wow! I made the wall. Some great players on there
© *Stacey Barton*

Returning to Old Trafford in March 2014. Looking out at the pitch I can't help but feel nostalgic
© *Stacey Barton*

With my grandchildren Grace and Cameron, on the left, and Gabriella, on the right

and only Denis Law, a striker who I had so much admiration for, a tremendous figure in United's history. For most of the squad to have songs for them in the stands showed me what a loved team we were and I hope that we managed to justify that with our performances.

*****

Going into the 1976/77 season, even though we were optimistic, we were also realistic in feeling that we might have it tougher in our second season back in the top flight. That had proved to be the case but from the turn of the year, with the Cup in our sights, we had really picked up and were looking forward to the big games. Our League form meant we didn't have a serious chance of winning the First Division but that didn't mean that we let some things lie.

In April we came up against Stoke City who had got a result against us in the previous season's run-in that cost us a shot at the League. We were determined to make sure that wouldn't happen again and I said as much. It was on our minds but we had Jimmy who was keen to make a mark against his former team. He didn't score yet we still won 3-0, but to be honest that was one of the few highlights from the final run-in to the League that season.

In the FA Cup semi-final we faced a very good Leeds United side but a great Stevie Coppell goal decided it for us. We were going back to Wembley and that was great. The celebrations after the game were not quite as flamboyant as they had been the previous year but I was just as delighted as I had been twelve months earlier. I was so happy for Stevie that he had enjoyed a moment like I had done against Derby. He was such a fantastic player and deserved it so much, so it wasn't that the victory didn't mean as much as the previous year that we didn't let our hair down this time around. You could put that down to a determination within the group to make sure we remained focussed and concentrated, particularly as our opponents this time were going to be all the more resolute.

This time we stayed at Selsden Park, the hotel Southampton had used the previous year. I don't know if these things are fate but we certainly weren't reading anything in to it. Liverpool were going for the treble of League, FA Cup and European Cup and they were not a team that we thought we could beat just because of the hotel we were staying in.

Having been favourites the previous year, we were now billed as underdogs against Liverpool yet I felt we were just as capable as they were. Liverpool were the better team, but United were the better club and the better club won the final which sprung to life early in the second half after a cagey opening. Stuart Pearson gave us the lead, Liverpool equalised, and then Jimmy Greenhoff became the cup hero when his chest deflected Lou Macari's shot into the net. I was disgusted with my own performance as yet again, I didn't perform in the Final and was substituted. The Doc brought on Dave McCreery, our super sub, to shore up the defence and make sure we kept our discipline. David could buzz around when Liverpool were tired and make it difficult for them.

Looking at it now it was a clever tactical move from the boss and it was great because it worked as we won the game 2-1. Afterwards, people even said that we won it with a jammy goal. A goal is a goal. I don't care what anyone says, the currency of one ball going into the net is the same no matter how it goes in.

As I've explained, I try not to let my emotions show but that certainly doesn't mean that I don't feel them. When I was in a losing team it would hurt and even if I didn't play well or feel like I made a good contribution to a win I could still be in a foul mood. I was impulsive on the pitch and I could be just the same off it. In the aftermath of the final I was asked by a Daily Mirror reporter about being substituted, and if I felt that a second successive Cup Final substitution meant my time at Old Trafford might soon be up. In the heat of the moment I said that although TD hadn't made his decision with any bad intention, sometimes you have to face the facts, and that was enough to fuel a report that I was considering my future. At the end of the match the thought had fleetingly crossed my mind, not because I was throwing my toys out of the pram just because I was brought off but because of a moment of self doubt, the same moment I'd had the previous year. Was I not good enough when it mattered? Couldn't I be trusted? Yes, we'd won, and I was happy for that, but in a way that was part of the problem as it added to a cocktail of emotions

I was feeling, and I was still so upset with how I'd played that it clouded the bigger picture and made everything appear worse than it was. It was no longer than a moment when I had that feeling, and it so happened that a reporter caught me at that very time.

I knew in my heart I never wanted to leave. My response from the disappointment of the previous year's final was to strive to do better, after all I'd had a good first season, a very good first season. If you don't have the attitude to be better though, you ain't gonna last long at Manchester United. I'd scored ten goals in thirty three games in 1975/76 and I had a great second season, was top scorer for the club with twenty two goals, scoring in every competition for United. That brief moment of self doubt had been replaced by the motivation to do even better the next year.

To top it all off, my family were there to witness the triumph, my finest achievement as a player even if it wasn't my most glorious performance. I say my family but there was one notable absentee. In 1976 all of them had been there, my mum, my dad, my brothers and sisters and many more besides. There were United supporters recognising my mum and bowing down to her to say thank you to her. She was terribly embarrassed and humble and hated the fuss and, as it turned out, Dad thought he was a bad omen and told me he wouldn't ever come again if we ever got that far. Mum told him not to be so stupid and looked at me saying don't worry, he will. To be fair, it's not like they would come and see me play anyway as it just wasn't something that they did. They had so many kids that they couldn't be going up and down the country every week. I knew that and I appreciated it, but obviously the FA Cup was a big deal, a different story, that's why they all came in 1976.

And I thought Dad was joking, that if we ever got back there he wouldn't come. Turns out he wasn't, and he actually didn't go, instead he sat at home and watched it on the telly. That was a shame, more of a shame that he thought he was a bad omen because he wasn't, and that was just thinking silly. From his point of view I could see why he might have thought he was, but once he'd made up his mind there was nothing I could do. It was a shame that he didn't but then it was just as much of a shame that they never got to see me play at Old Trafford either. I guess that's life. Sometimes you don't worry because you think everything will last forever. I must confess at this point that looking back at this incident, I do have my own sense of guilt which I hold to this day. As much as I think of it as a shame now when I'm looking back, at the time I didn't because life was such a whirlwind and I was almost in another world.

I was kept grounded by those I was around but I was in a whole different society. In Buxworth, we lived close to a family called the Whiteheads, Eric and Dorothy. Eric was fantastic, a Bolton Wanderers fanatic, but kept an interest in me and what I was doing. We'd play snooker up at the Chinley snooker hall and we'd have many a night up there talking football. He was much older but it wasn't as if I saw him as a surrogate or substitute parent while I was so far from where I grew up, we just got on really well. I think they still live in the area and both them and their children were really great. They had a son and two daughters, one of the daughters Hilary used to babysit Kerry for us. We also enjoyed the company of Chris and Edna Broadbent who were two doors down. They were City through and through along with their sons Jamie and Adam. Sadly they suffered a tragedy which I will speak about a little later. I should also mention Simon and Li-Lin Fenton, also Man City supporters who I enjoyed mixing with in the local area.

I mentioned that I felt guilty because as much as these people helped me feel down to earth and I know them to this day, at the time I was so caught up in the bubble of being a United player that I sort of lost touch with my own family for a couple of years and that should never have happened. Moving to Manchester, getting married, having a baby, at times it seemed like I was almost a different person. It was only a couple of years but that was one regret I do have. I got carried away with my life and I suppose when you do move away the natural consequence is that you spend less time with those you leave behind. I love them all dearly and I should have spent more time with them. I love all my brothers and sisters even if they think I'm a pain in the arse. If only I knew then what I know now, eh.

Over time I understood that the substitution in the 1977 final wasn't simply because I'd played poorly, we weren't on the rack, but it was the last ten minutes of a Cup Final. Maybe I could've held my discipline, I'm sure I could have, but I could have also done something unpredictable, for better or for worse. TD knew with Wee Dee he was getting a guarantee. It was probably the only time he could be accused of being conservative in his managerial career and who could blame him. Unsurprisingly, as soon as he'd heard about the Mirror report, the boss asked me about it and I told him it was nonsense and I didn't want to leave.

Looking back, I was more disappointed with my performance against Southampton in 1976 than I was against Liverpool. Against Southampton I came off, we conceded and lost, and all we were left with were 'what ifs'. We all should have played better and I was no different, but I'll forever have the question in my head about whether I might have been able to make that difference if I'd have stayed on. Against Liverpool, there were no 'what ifs.' We won the game and won the Cup, and with the benefit of hindsight, even though I'm still bitterly disappointed I didn't play better, I contributed to my team winning the FA Cup and that is something that I can at least be proud of.

I wasn't the only one overcome by emotion. There were tears again, but tears of joy this time around, and everyone was delighted. We were able to know finally that we could take a trophy home to our supporters in Manchester. We knew plenty of the Liverpool players as not only did they live fairly close, but we played with so many of them when away with England. I said to some of them afterwards that we've won today boys and it was a tough game, but I really hope you go and turn the Germans over so we wish you the very best of luck. They went and beat Borussia Moenchengladbach in the European Cup Final to complete a double for themselves, but we had denied them the treble. Bill Shankly had said to his side that there's a team up the East Lancs that are gonna take the trophy from you. We were truly delirious as it was the first silverware the club had won since the European Cup in 1968. It was a statement to prove that we were as good as we had threatened to be, and it was something that we could use to prove that we could be good enough to win the league, which was our ultimate goal. It was also vindication for those players who had gone down with the club to Division Two and helped them back up. They didn't belong there, United were synonymous with being the top club in England, heading the division and competing for trophies. In a season of us attempting to make landmark statements such as going back into Europe beating Juventus and winning the Cup, possibly the biggest was that from Shankly. That really stuck in my mind because as we parted after the game he told me that one day I would be a good player. I thanked him but said that I already am. He laughed and told the boss that he liked me.

Bill was right to be concerned. We were a team, a club in great shape. Even with thirty-five year old Alex Stepney in goal, our average age throughout the team on Cup Final day was just twenty five. To put that into perspective, the average age of the United side that beat Liverpool in 1996, with all those kids that Alan Hansen said would win nothing was twenty five! You cannot underestimate the value of experience that older heads like Alex brought to the team, but there was also the experience that you get from playing together more and more and what you take from the opposition. We were fearless, and that provoked concern into anyone we played against.

The FA Cup Final win of 1977 should have been the start of a golden era for Manchester United because we had the potential to achieve anything we wanted. I know I spoke earlier about TD wanting to add Peter Shilton to the side and Peter himself wanting to come, but Alex was still one of the best goalkeepers around. And we were all so happy for him to finally win the FA Cup, it was the one trophy missing for him and he dearly wanted to win it. He played his part on the day too with a couple of good saves. We felt safe with him in goal, and I think the potential signing of Peter was more of a move for the future. The manager was already thinking like that anyway with the experimentation of playing Paddy Roche, but fair play to Alex for sticking at it and getting that special day.

There were good players throughout the team, class players such as Jimmy Nic who was a good full back, though obviously with him playing at right back I only played with him directly in short spells when I would switch sides with Stevie. Nic was industrious, had a smashing engine, and wasn't afraid to play a bit. He was very similar to Arthur in that he would encourage me to take players on. Arthur had only played around thirty times for the first team himself so was the baby of the team, but he played so well on the day and showed that he was ready to make such a big step up. Arthur's place in the team was guaranteed the second that Stewart Houston broke his ankle at Bristol, otherwise perhaps Stewart would have played and Arthur would have been on the bench.

There were players missing from that defence who were fantastic. Alex Forsyth was a smashing defender, but we had some good young players coming through. Jim Holton was another one who missed out. It was good at the time that the club rewarded Stewart Houston with a medal as they had so many extra to distribute amongst the non-playing members of the squad that day. With the large squads nowadays there are so many players named on the bench with little chance of getting on that you can feel a bit sorry for those who just missed out back in our day, but that's football. I felt sorry for Stewart when he suffered his injury because the pitch was shit, and you just knew as soon as he did it that he would be out of the final.

No talk of our defence would be complete without once again mentioning Martin and Brian. I really don't need to keep singing their praises and repeating how brilliant they were, you only have to look at highlights of any game from that era to see how important they were, and on Cup Final day both of them gave shining examples of that once again. They were outstanding, but not just on that day because the way they demonstrated their seniority was a sign of things to come from the rest of the team. Their partnership had blossomed to a level that they could dominate a strong Liverpool front line and we were all close to clicking to that kind of standard.

Our midfield was the perfect example of that. Martin and Brian had played together for a while and built that understanding and after we signed Jimmy Greenhoff, Lou Macari moved back into midfield and we began to build a similar chemistry. All four of the midfielders, myself included, worked hard to win but in myself, Louie, Stevie and Sammy you have to say that our primary goal was to attack. Maybe I am biased but I'd put that midfield up there with the best in United's history. Sammy and Louie were so hard working but always forward thinking. Before Jimmy arrived, Lou would act as a link man between midfield and attack and not much had changed with how he played afterwards.

We all had quality, skill on the ball, and although I played in that team I am being completely honest and truthful when I say that Sammy Mac or Lou Macari would have fitted very nicely into the Manchester United midfield in recent years. They really would have been perfect for what supporters have been crying out for and what the team needs. Even Gerry Daly would have fitted in well, and what's the thing they all have in common? They were all from the British Isles.

United have always had a strong British and Irish core in their central midfield and when you look at their entire history it's difficult to find that many examples of a successful foreign import in the heart of midfield. From our team to Bryan Robson, Ray Wilkins, Gordon Strachan, Roy Keane, Nicky Butt, Paul Scholes, and you can even see in the modern team that United haven't played better than with Darren Fletcher at the heart of things.

Moving back to our team, it's not with sentiment that I say my midfield team-mates could have walked into any United team. Up front we had a fantastic strike force and I've got so much time for Pancho. He was a hard working, clever finisher. We had a good partnership, not perfect, but promising enough to be one of those combinations that would only have improved with time. Jimmy was signed to be the difference and I guess you would say it was symbolic that he was the one who actually made the difference in the final. He was a great addition to the team and brought the experience that we needed as a young side to lead the line.

As a player you only get stronger with experience and we had all the attributes to have gone on and reached the pinnacle. We were all gelling together and, in a footballing sense, we were feared. It doesn't matter if it's Manchester United or any other club, but to go from getting promoted to being arguably a top class goalkeeper or a top class defensive replacement away from winning the league. that was some achievement and I'm not sure the Doc gets enough credit for what he did. We had proven we could beat the League Champions and, as it would turn out, European Champions and our problem wasn't in beating teams, putting teams away, or inconsistency, it was simply that the squad we had wasn't big enough to sustain a full season. That was the next step.

As for my own role in the way it all went together, well it's not for me to say, other people can have their thoughts and opinions on it. I wanted to score, provide and attack. I wanted to be like all the legends that had done so well for the club in the past. From day one I had dreams of scoring at Old Trafford, playing in cup finals for the club, winning trophies. Now I had accomplished all of that and knew I was doing well enough to continue to play and contribute, but I didn't let it go to my head. It's a different world being a Manchester United footballer, like I said, everyone wants to know you, you get kids telling you they want to be like you and it's the most incredible feeling in the world. That was what made me tick, that and the motivation to win football matches. As I say, I was not happy with the way I played for the second year in a row in the final. I was gutted, but I was absolutely over the moon that we picked up the trophy and gave something back to the supporters who had been there through thick and thin.

I'd not been in the team that had played in Division Two but I'd played against them and in front of those supporters as a Millwall player. After games at five or six o'clock we'd watch the results and every week United would win. To be part of a new generation of players winning trophies at United for the first time in nine years was great, but actually being there I understood that this was the way it was meant to be, these were the days this club was supposed to have. And these were the days I was enjoying with this magnificent club that had brought success back. Any mixed feelings I had on my own performance were soon outweighed by the relief of winning the Cup, though I would always strive to do better and prove myself to the fans. This was the club's destiny, but it might not have been mine. I didn't have a divine right to be there, I felt that I still had to perform to a higher standard to prove myself.

It's hard to put into words but that might be what separates

United from other clubs. Even on a day when there is so much to be happy for, there is a moment when you consider that you have to improve to carry on being a part of it. I'd enjoyed a special moment, a career defining moment while playing for Millwall when we walked out at Old Trafford. The feeling I had as I walked into the arena and heard the fans was unlike anything I would ever experience again. Playing for United you don't feel that awe, but other teams feel it against you, as I well knew. The only feeling that came close at club level was playing in European stadiums, grand and famous stadiums that you knew you had to earn the right to play in by being one of the best teams in England. It was the ultimate satisfaction as a professional footballer to represent Manchester United because you knew it would always be the ultimate test, and you knew that in order to prolong that feeling of satisfaction, you had to give your all in the ninety minutes you were wearing the United jersey.

There was no better feeling as United were top of the tree. Teams hated to come to Old Trafford, and teams hated us to go to their ground because they knew we'd play exactly the same way anywhere. Our crowds were always as good as a goal for us with the atmosphere they provided. People say that crowds don't make a difference but I've played in front of Manchester United supporters and let me tell those people now, when those supporters are roaring for you, and you find that extra bit of adrenaline, it makes you feel as though you can conquer the world. That's part of the beauty of the sport which had given us the tough times and now the good. You can be shattered and feel like you will never score, you can play in a game and feel like it's going nowhere, but then you score a goal and you get a new lease of life, and the momentum is all changed. You can be dead on your feet and the next minute jumping over rainbows, and we were certainly jumping over rainbows after the Liverpool result.

Beating the Champions in the Cup Final had proved that we could compete with them on any given day though I'm not sure I could say that we thought we were the better team. I thought they were a great side who were enjoying a rich period of success and we wanted to follow it and restore United to that level. That was the ambition of the club coming out of the Second Division as mere consolidation was not an option, the club wanted to compete for the best prizes, the First Division, the European Cup, and take them too. That was the motivation of the manager and he'd built a squad that was young enough and had enough potential to share the ambition. It felt like the only thing that could stop us fulfilling that potential was something completely unexpected.

And, lo and behold, that's exactly what happened.

I was absolutely devastated to discover that Tommy Docherty had been sacked as manager of Manchester United. The board had taken that decision because he had an affair with Mary Brown, the wife of our physio Laurie. I first learned of the news of the affair when I bumped into Sammy, completely by chance, on a holiday in Ibiza. He had gone on holiday after an international trip in the post-season with Northern Ireland and it just so happened we had gone to the same place. I was walking along the beach and he was there sunbathing and he spotted me.

'Hi Hilly, have you heard about the Boss? Its been found out that he has been seeing Mary Brown. I know the club and they won't stand for this,' Sam said. I didn't know what to think. I didn't know how the club would handle it, or how they should, it just appeared to be a mess. I just remember telling Sammy that I hoped they wouldn't get rid of him. I couldn't argue because the club did what they did and what they thought was right, but it takes two to tango and the whole story hadn't been told.

I feel that maybe a reprimand might have been sufficient and I certainly didn't want the Doc to be sacked. People say that he was in the wrong and that he had an affair. I think it's incredible that it's described as such when they have been together ever since and remain married to this day. Shortly after I met Agnes, who was Tommy's wife, and she was a tremendous lady. I just didn't know what to say. Regardless, I couldn't judge the boss, I just couldn't.

As for the future of Manchester United I hoped that the new manager, whoever it might be, would realise that he had a winning side that barely needed changing. As the saying goes, if it ain't broke, don't fix it. That squad was ready for a manager to continue the great work that Tommy had done and on reflection, perhaps it might have been better if Ron Atkinson had got the job at that time. Ron was on a similar wavelength to the Doc and could have been a natural successor. Looking around at who else was available, well there was Brian Clough. I'm not sure Brian would have had the best relationship with the board considering what happened for him at Leeds United, but with the success he had at Nottingham Forest you wonder what he could have achieved at Old Trafford.

Personally, I feel there might have been too much of a personality clash there, and after the controversy of the Doc and then Brian's infamously disastrous time at Leeds, he was probably not someone the board would have touched with a barge pole. For me, Bobby Robson was the best man to take the job, and he could have brought some players with him from Ipswich. But you never know. It's always, 'if, if, if', and the reality is that none of the above got the job.

The best man for the job was the man who had been removed from it. It was later reported that TD had verbally agreed a new four-year deal before the Cup Final but hadn't signed it, and then the news broke. It's another 'if', of course, but had Tommy remained in charge of Manchester United I am convinced we would have gone on to win the First Division within that spell and gone on to challenge in the European Cup. This was the world that Manchester United belonged in and the one that they were in for most of the time under Sir Alex Ferguson but I strongly believe that they'd have been there under Tommy. We were so close. I'm certain that the board did what they thought was right for the club, but what is right and what is best are not always one and the same and I don't feel that the decision to sack Tommy was the best thing for United, as was proven by the difficulties over the next few years.

I did feel sorry for Tommy as he was just cast aside, but he wasn't exactly popular with a few figures that were dubbed 'the silent voices'. Because he wasn't popular with those people the success he brought wasn't either, but they couldn't fault his style or knowledge. Tommy was and is an excellent reader of the game and was a flamboyant manager who would go to win games. They wanted rid of him in other ways and in that respect maybe it wasn't as straightforward as to say that the board themselves wanted rid of him. After all, Tommy had delivered at Chelsea, Scotland, and at the biggest club in the world. He seemed to get on well with Sir Matt Busby and Louis Edwards but I have to say as a player there must have been many things in the management side of the game that players were simply unaware of, as I was to learn later on in my life.

There were many 'what ifs' hanging over the future of Manchester United but the only thing that was certain was that Tommy Docherty was no longer manager.

6

Reality Bites

It wasn't Bobby Robson or Brian Clough but Dave Sexton who was chosen as the manager of Manchester United following Tommy Docherty's departure. I felt I would get on with Dave. I didn't know him beforehand, but he came from Chelsea and had done really well with Queens Park Rangers so he must have done something right. People accused him of having no personality but in my opinion he was just someone that you had to get to know. He was a very dry individual and he did smile although I can only remember that happening a few times! He wasn't a man to show his emotions. If the Doc was upset with you, then you knew that for sure, whereas Dave wouldn't be so forthcoming.

It is known that Dave and I did not exactly enjoy the best of times together in terms of our relationship but sadly he died in 2012 and the last thing I want to do is speak ill of those who have passed away. To be honest, I didn't really know him personally and our differences were purely on a professional basis.

Nonetheless, I will be honest with my account. I got on OK with him and actually lived not too far away from him. I knew after he had been at the club for a few months that he wanted to change things. I was aware that he was more focussed on defending and stopping rather than scoring after playing against his teams, and that wasn't the way that Manchester United had played under Tommy Docherty. QPR were good in defence, but then most teams were in Division One and we had been too, even though we were cavalier and flamboyant. And to be honest, when we were playing against teams we were concentrating on the players rather than the managers. This isn't a criticism of Dave but an observation of what I felt we needed at the time. I thought the Manchester United manager needed to be a charismatic person and I felt that after TD, Dave represented a safe option going forward. Don't get me wrong, Dave's teams did attack, and there wasn't anyone coming in who would have had a philosophy like Tommy's anyway, so we knew whoever took over would be perceived as being more cautious than the Doc. It was a symbolic change by the club in more ways than one and maybe after the controversy they went too far the other way.

Changes occurred on the training pitch almost immediately. Tommy had trusted the squad so implicitly that we didn't always have to train intensely and he knew the right time to step in and give us instructions or make a change. This was demonstrated by changing the shape in the Cup Final even though it was to my cost as I was substituted. Training under the boss was straightforward, he knew what we were good at doing so we could go and enjoy ourselves. Dave was much more intensive and he would have us go over the same thing again and again and again, drilling routines into us where, for example, Jimmy Greenhoff would step over the ball, Stuart Pearson would knock it and Jimmy would turn into space. I can remember going through a training routine later in the season for a corner and we were trying it for ages but never seemed to be going anywhere. After about an hour, Gordon McQueen, who had signed from Leeds, suggested we try this corner where someone kicks it into the box, he gets his head on it and scores a goal!

We would spend up to an hour and a half sometimes perfecting routines. Dave wouldn't stop us practicing on our crossing by ourselves for example, and we were all motivated to improve ourselves anyway. But where there had been a more relaxed approach under the Doc, everything was more methodical. One day after training Dave called me up to his office and we sat and watched a film of Hungary defeating England. He wanted me to observe how hard the wingers worked and followed the managers instructions. It must have been difficult for the staff who had remained at the club after the Doc left.

Tommy Cavanagh had been with the boss and saw us develop

and improve the way we had been and I'm not sure he was into watching all the videos. I don't think he knew which way to turn. Ultimately he had no choice but to coach us using Dave's methods. It was get on the bandwagon or find yourself another club. That was certainly true for me. As a TD man who loved the flair, Cav would still encourage us where possible to express ourselves as he knew that was when we would play our best, but training was a world apart from how it had been under the boss. And like I said it must have been tough for them, not only Cav, but Jack Crompton, Jimmy Curran, all those guys who had worked with TD to create a great team and had been through that journey with us and now found themselves on a different path.

For whatever reason the Manchester United FA Cup winning team was never to fulfil its true potential, but that wasn't to say that Dave Sexton wanted the club to fail. Of course he wanted the team to succeed but he wanted to do so having put his own footprint on the team and club, and you would expect that of any manager. If that meant change then so be it. The main issue though, was that the boss hadn't been sacked for footballing reasons, which in itself made it an exceptional situation, and the team that he had left to be taken over was a successful one. Though we accepted we needed some improvements in order to make that next step, they were small changes that could have been made, but instead, being the new manager, Dave attempted to change the character of the side.

Training had changed, but because Dave was not going to alter things overnight, we still went out to play the way we had done under the Doc and that sometimes meant it was confusing to the players. That in turn made it difficult for us, for example me going in to watch a video of what he wanted a winger to do when I was doing so well anyway. It was much more defensive than I was used to yet I had the ability to do well for the team. The Doc never told me how to take on a defender but said when we didn't have the ball to tuck in and make it difficult for the opposition, and to be fair that's what I did. It's not as if I had great big holes behind me to exploit and I had Stewart Houston or Arthur Albiston behind me who were wonderful defenders.

One of those two would tell me to tuck back in and that was

fine, I'd do as they said. More often than not they'd encourage me and Arthur would tell me to go and smack the ball in the net. I cannot say strongly enough just how great Stewart and Arthur were. Arthur had a great left foot, one of the best I've ever seen and neither of them would ever get embarrassed by an opponent. I felt confident in their ability to defend and keep the team secure behind me and I knew that Stewart and Arthur had confidence in my ability and what I brought to the team. We felt comfortable playing alongside each other because we believed in our strengths. Some players are good at tackling. I could take the ball but I wasn't pronounced as a tackler. You could say the same of any of our midfielders at the time as none were hard tacklers, but we were all very good at nicking or pinching the ball. I felt it was a fantastic way of playing, it was just like the Brazilians did.

United weren't exactly mugs and knew what they were getting when they signed me, so I didn't understand why I was being asked to change my game so much as I'd done well. I'd been encouraged so much to play my natural game under the Doc and Tommy Cav. Even wingers in today's game lose the ball and don't run back to retrieve the it. I've lost count of the number of times I watch a winger lose the ball and walk. It's been going on for generations and will continue to do so but that doesn't mean it's a bad thing. It's not as if we were without surprise or our own revolutionary approaches. Nowadays it's commonplace for teams to switch wingers during a game but Stevie and I were doing that under the Doc before it'd even been thought about elsewhere.

Dave Sexton was methodical and concentrated heavily on tactics, and by comparison Tommy Docherty seemed a carefree relaxed manager. But I absolutely believe that the Doc does not get the credit he deserves for a tactical masterplan ahead of its time. The difference was the Doc didn't put it on a clipboard, he just told us on the training field and we put it into practice. Tommy Docherty's team talks were simple but they were that way for a very specific reason, and that was because the opposition was scared of playing Manchester United, and the Doc was building us up to live up to that and to prove them right to be scared. Concentrating too much on the opposition automatically gives them a reason to be confident because they know you have concerns, and that kind of attitude can also creep into the players.

It will always take a while for the mentality and atmosphere from one manager to fade under the guidance of his successor so we weren't feeling negative. The management structure had been perfect. Tommy Docherty would give the instructions, Tommy Cavanagh would act as the go-between for the players and the Doc if he needed to calm down, and Frank Blunstone was a real thinker. It was a great unit. That was the past, though, and for better or worse, we had to trust in the board's decision to move forward.

We spent most of our pre-season in Scandinavia scoring loads of goals against teams like Rosenborg and Stromsgodset. Our final 'friendly' was against Liverpool at Wembley in the Charity Shield. Wembley was becoming our second home. It was 0-0 and a really hot day when with about three minutes to go, me and Phil Thompson shouted to the referee to end the game because we were knackered. Lo and behold, he called it up. We played hard but there was nothing like the intensity of the FA Cup Final in May and we knew there was a long season ahead of us. We shared the Shield with Liverpool. I know it is classed as a warm up game but against such strong opposition, when we both had a point to prove to one another from the last campaign, it was always going to be more competitive than a normal Charity Shield and it was a good work out for us all. We certainly took it seriously enough.

With all the difficulties behind the scenes we were delighted to carry on where we had left off and start the season well. We had a special win in our season opener at St. Andrews with a thumping 4-1 result over Birmingham. Lou Macari scored a hat-trick but my goal was arguably the pick of the bunch. The ball came over my shoulder into the area and I connected so sweetly on the volley that the goalkeeper had no chance. I've scored many goals of that nature and that was one that actually was recorded so watching it back gives me a nice sense of satisfaction. Four days later I scored in another win against a Midlands team, this time Coventry at Old Trafford. It was very much one game at a time and Dave was never going to come in and wave a magic wand to change it all around instantly. He didn't tinker with it too much and our form benefitted from that stability in the early weeks of the season, and we went unbeaten in our first four league games before falling to defeat in the Manchester derby. That wasn't the ideal preparation for our return to Europe.

Winning the FA Cup meant we were to play in the European Cup Winners Cup and we were drawn to face St. Etienne in the first round. We went over to France for the first leg and I put the ball in the net three times but only one counted with two ruled out for offside. I'm not sure what the referee or linesmen were looking at but when I did finally score a goal that was permitted, we all looked at the referee half expecting him to disallow it again. It was a peach of a goal not too different to the one I'd hit against Juventus a year earlier, on the volley from a right-sided cross. We absolutely tore them apart but it finished 1-1 and the offside decisions provoked chaos in the stands with the United supporters wrecking the fences which were penning them in. UEFA ruled that we were not allowed to play the return game within two hundred miles of Old Trafford. Going north, we couldn't play in Scotland because it would have been on a field. Going west, we'd have been in Ireland, and going east, we'd have been in Holland.

The only place we could play was down in Plymouth so we took on St. Etienne at Home Park and won 2-0. The Green and Whites were no mugs as they'd won the French League four times in the Seventies. It was odd playing at Plymouth as the home team and it would have been easier to go back to St. Etienne but we still did the job. As it turned out, we had to go back to St. Etienne anyway to play a game and give the proceeds to the club to repair the fences. I thought it was a bit of a joke as we'd already been punished, and I don't think you can say it was the crowd's fault either because they were all there to support us. As it always is, the minority ruined it for the majority, and the result was us traipsing all the way to France to play a meaningless game in December. The problem we had with United was that so many people went away to follow the club and there had been a recent history of trouble, so it did follow us around the country and then into Europe. France isn't hard to get to. You can have a thousand good supporters but between one and ten who give the others a bad name. It was the same as with Millwall, but due to the size of Manchester United it was always going to be on a much larger scale. I still don't think that damage was caused to the extent that we had to go and play in the Parc des Princes for them. But that's what they ruled and that's what we did.

We had mixed form in the league. A home defeat to Chelsea was followed by a couple of personal milestones. In my ninety-ninth appearance for United I scored to earn us a 1-1 draw at Elland Road against Leeds. For my one-hundredth we played against Liverpool at Old Trafford and I played my part in an impressive 2-0 home victory which put us in fifth place, three points off the top. It was a statement of intent that said even with the changes, we were still good enough to beat the Champions.

We had been drawn to play Porto in the next round of the Cup Winners' Cup with the first leg away again. We knew what Porto were all about and we knew we could turn them over. We would have done too, if not for one of the most ridiculously timed friendly games ever to be arranged. A game had been scheduled for the week after the Porto game in Iran as the Government wanted us to help with a British Trade Week in the country. We had to have injections for various illnesses and it had a negative effect on lots of the players who were ill as a result. Arthur was struggling, so was Jimmy, as well as others. We had the injections on the Friday before a game against Newcastle who we beat 3-2, but some of the lads were already starting to feel it and on Sunday and Monday it really took it out of them. We went out to Porto and were beaten 4-0 which would never have happened. We were sluggish and lethargic, it was like someone had taken all of our energy. The players still weren't right for the weekend game and we were also beaten 4-0 at West Brom. We flew out and played in Tehran against the Iranian national team on the Monday after the West Brom game and won 2-0. So it's not all bad.

When Porto came to Old Trafford we knew what we had to do. We were all set and determined to overhaul that deficit and in no uncertain terms we were going to go gung-ho. We walked on to the pitch with the home supporters singing 'Five nil', believing in us despite the fact we lined up without both Greenhoffs and

Lou Macari. We took an early lead but Porto equalised meaning that we had to score another five. But by God, we went for it. A Porto defender put my cross into his own net and Jimmy Nicholl made it 3-1 at half time. We just couldn't quite get level with them but they were shell-shocked by the fight we put up. If anything, it was only down to the fact we had taken the game to them so much that cost us because we were committing too many men forward but it was the price we had to pay. The atmosphere was electric. I'm not quite sure there are too many places in the game of football that a team can be losing a tie 4-0 and the supporters want and almost expect their team to qualify. Yet at Old Trafford the fans can make you think that anything is possible and it almost came off for us against Porto. We were comfortable that we could have won that competition and without a shadow of a doubt the injections cost us the first leg. It just wasn't to be.

The Porto return leg was something different from the norm in more ways than one. The game came right bang in the middle of four league defeats in a row that had begun with the West Brom game and left us in sixteenth position in the table, a full twelve points behind the leaders Nottingham Forest, who rounded off our run of defeats. We tried to improve with wins over Norwich and Wolves at Old Trafford but when Forest came to Manchester for the return game and won by a convincing scoreline of 4-0 sending us into Christmas in fourteenth place we knew things weren't right. Paddy Roche was in goal but apart from that it was just about the same team that had done so well the previous season.

Something wasn't quite right and the supporters sensed it too and they began to get bored of the football that Dave wanted us to play. We were a side that responded to encouragement but we were feeling dejected because we didn't feel we were allowed to express ourselves. Furthermore, we could feel that having taken his time looking at the team, Dave was now going to make his own mark and bring his own players in. He did, by going to Leeds and signing the big centre forward Joe Jordan, and the tough Scottish centre half, Gordon McQueen. Both were great players but very, very different to the style that we had been playing.

Before they arrived we welcomed Tommy Docherty back to

Old Trafford. He had not been without a job for long, and in Derby County had found himself with a top club too. There was an hilarious subplot to the fixture. After the Cup Final the previous season, Tommy called Martin Buchan into his office and showed him a suitcase with either £5,000 in it. He told Martin to share it among the players and Martin said, 'Fine, but I don't want to take it yet, can I take it at the start of the pre-season instead?' And of course we never saw the suitcase again. We all talked about it and had a laugh. We ribbed Martin and asked why he didn't take the money in the first place but perhaps, by never following through with the money, the boss burned some bridges with other players because of it. I didn't get involved with it although I heard about it so I was a little bit disappointed. A few of the others were peeved about it and Martin is nothing if not honest, so they wanted to have a few words with the Doc when he came back.

There was no point crying over spilt milk. It was something that was offered to us after winning the cup and the boss wasn't obligated to have made the offer. Martin scored against Derby and I scored twice, but it wasn't personal against the boss. I was there to do damage and even though the team wasn't having the best of times, I was still doing well and scoring goals. Though I held the boss in the utmost of respect I was not going to stand on ceremony, he knew what I was capable of. It was lovely to see him and it was nice to see him back in the game and at the top, though it must have been strange for him to see all of his boys but then have to go and tell his Derby team they're playing against his team.

After that 4-0 loss, he must still have felt a lot of pride deep down about the way we performed. It wasn't going to be too long until I was seeing the boss again. It's a bit ironic that after such a performance where we showed what we were capable of, Dave decided the time was right to inject some of the new character he wanted into the team. Jordan and McQueen were great players but they were very much Leeds style players, tough and uncompromising. We weren't sure if Joe was going to partner Jimmy or Stuart, if one was going to be dropped or sold.

All of a sudden, after having a settled side for so long, we were accommodating new faces. Gordon McQueen was to take Brian Greenhoff's place in the centre of our defence and that indicated there was going to be a significant change in style from then on. Even when United have had strong players in their team, the club was never renowned for playing a physical game, yet this seemed to be the road we were going down. Brian, being an attacking defender, was one of the players who characterised the Doc's style, and my unpredictable wing play also fitted that description. I had concerns that something was going to happen and that I was going to be replaced by someone who replicated one of those Hungarian wingers that Dave seemed to be so fond of.

We didn't need to be reined in as it wasn't our performances that were holding United back. Do you rein in Lionel Messi, Andres Iniesta, Cristiano Ronaldo? Do you rein in Gerard Pique, who reminds me so much of Brian? Or do you trust in them to provide something unique to the team? I have, and always have had, so much admiration for the work rate and engine that Stevie Coppell had. He gave so much in every game and in training, but he would be equally forthcoming with praise for my natural ability. I would score more goals and stop fewer attacks than Stevie, but then the obvious point to make after is that he did stop more attacks. It was that way through the side and that's what had given us such a great chemistry. All of the players had their strengths and weaknesses, but the strengths of one compensated for the weakness of another. Jimmy Nicholl would support Stevie and likewise, I would try and do the same with Stewart or Arthur. But more often than not they would tell me to get up the pitch as I'd be doing more harm than good coming back. That was the team, it was hardly anything ground-breaking. But then the most successful styles rarely are, and the most remembered and celebrated are those where a team naturally expresses itself.

The Doc had taken four years to assemble that team, one that complemented every component so well, and that was proved by the success we had. We weren't perfect, I've said about the areas that I felt we needed to strengthen, but Dave had different ideas and in my opinion that was damaging the team and its chances of success.

The win against Derby had only moved us into eleventh and we were still fifteen points behind Forest. Any chance of building from the Cup success and mounting a challenge for the League was well and truly over and by the end of January it was even worse as we were knocked out of the FA Cup in just the fourth round by West Brom. We had drawn at Old Trafford and they took us to a replay where I scored with a twenty-five yard strike that I was very pleased with, but Cyrille Regis netted to knock us out in extra time.

After getting to Wembley twice in a row we were now out at the second hurdle and it was tough. Having got so used to winning in the Cup it was difficult to take. Playing for Manchester United and having nothing to challenge for but pride at the end of January was very, very disappointing. We were dejected but still wanted to do as well as we could until the end of the season to generate some good momentum. We weren't playing poorly but just not as well as we had the previous two seasons and now, with the arrival of two new players and a new manager as well as our change in philosophy, it felt like another man's team to the one we'd enjoyed much success with.

After our Cup exit we didn't win in eight league games and I was told by Dave that he needed me to concentrate on helping the team stop goals going in rather than going forward. I asked him if he still wanted me to score goals as restricting my movement on the pitch would also have an impact on our creativity. I was aware of what he wanted and I was conscious of that in games, but then I was playing within myself. The Doc has said I was a player that couldn't be coached and though I wouldn't go that far, he had a point in what he was saying in as much that if you tried to coach me and direct me away from my natural game, you were taking away some of what was good about what I did.

I wasn't stupid and I knew that not following the manager's instructions was likely to mean one thing for my place in the team. I went into every game with the best of intentions, but then you are influenced by the individual circumstances of every game and being the kind of player I was, I just couldn't play within myself. I was top scorer after all, justifying my place in the team, and I was happy with my own form. I wouldn't go as far as saying the team would have struggled without me as we were struggling anyway, and maybe the goals I scored could have been scored by someone else.

As much as everyone likes to speculate, the only thing you can ever really go on is what actually happens, and I had scored the goals. It's not that I didn't try, I did, and I know it sounds strange, but maybe scoring goals at the rate I was gave proof to Dave that I wasn't going along with what he wanted. He was trying to make his team more functional, compact, or defensive, and it was clear to everyone that I wasn't exactly what he was looking for. It was no secret what he wanted, but in order to show his authority and control at the club he had two options and they were to drop me or sell me.

I've since been a manager so you wonder what goes through someone's mind in that situation. Dropping me would send a message that it was 'my way or the highway' but it would also be cutting his nose off to spite his face to drop the top scorer from the team, especially one in form. Perhaps dropping me would provoke questions from inside the club which Dave didn't want to answer. It was clear that something along those lines was on his mind but with the run we were on, he couldn't afford to take that chance. We were in the middle of March and we hadn't won since that comprehensive result against Derby. Ten games for Manchester United without a win is just not acceptable, but I'd played my part to make sure it wasn't even worse, scoring six goals in that run. Without my goals, four of the seven draws would have been defeats. It's not for me to speculate whether seven defeats in ten games would have made Dave's position untenable, and to be honest, I haven't really thought about it since. Looking at the cold hard facts, it might have been one of those cruel ironies that football can throw up when my goals helped preserve the position of a man who was about to bring my whole world crashing down.

I also scored at Leicester in the win that ended our bad run, in fact I was in a good run of form scoring five goals in my last six games. But after that our form dropped again and in the run up to our game with Queens Park Rangers in April, Dave told me he intended to rest me and play me in the reserves at Preston. Later,

I got a call saying he'd changed his mind and I was going to play. Even later, I had another call saying he'd changed his mind yet again and I wasn't. When Dave called once more indicating another change of mind, I made the decision for him by saying it would probably be best if I played for the reserves at Preston. I was all over the place and informed Dave that I was concerned that if I had a bad game he'd be on my back again. So I went to Preston, but at half time Jimmy Curran said to me that he'd had a call from the boss and they were bringing me off. He told me that the club had accepted a bid from Derby County.

I felt straight away as if Dave had planned the entire thing. I went to meet Tommy at Mottram Hall with the Derby secretary Stuart Webb, where they told me they'd made an offer of £275,000. Tommy said he intended to have Derby fighting for the title and I believed it with the players they had in the side such as Colin Todd, Charlie George and Roy McFarland. We agreed terms with no need for agents and that was it, I was to join Derby County.

It was strange how, just like the move to United, I'd been pulled away from playing to be told a bid had been accepted. I hadn't needed an agent when I signed for United, didn't need one for the advertising ventures, and I wouldn't have needed one to have signed a new contract if I'd have been offered one. I would have treated a new contract the same way I treated signing for the club in the first place.

It broke my heart to leave Manchester United. To have one man show me I was no longer wanted at the club that I felt such a part of was devastating. I could have said no and stayed, trying to fight my way through the reserves, but I just wanted to play. In fact, if I'd have been dropped, I could have handled that, I would have buckled down and played so well it would have been impossible to leave me out. But I doubt if that would have achieved anything. I had still been playing well, scoring as many goals as ever and was top scorer for United. But that brought a reality check to me, where I thought that though I might be scoring, some coaches may not want that. Obviously, managers do want goalscorers, so maybe there was something in my style that wasn't pleasing to Dave and it wasn't going to earn me a place in his first eleven so what could I do.

When I say it broke my heart to leave, it really did, and it's something that upsets me to this day if I think about it for too long for a number of reasons. I didn't have much of a choice in the matter, the club had only recently hired Dave and had shown great faith in him so were going to stick by him. As a professional I loved the club but I had my pride, I didn't feel I deserved to play in the reserves and obviously I'd done well enough at United for other top clubs to want me. I'd been at a club where there had been so many great entertainers and great players in history, and I was hoping that my involvement with this great team would see me mentioned in the same breath as them, but then all of a sudden it was over. I knew that under the Doc I could have stayed for all my career, yet as soon as Dave came in with his videos of Hungarian wingers, the writing was on the wall and I could feel that something was happening and it alarmed me. I don't think I warranted being dropped, and for Derby to pay a fee that was around five times what United had paid for me in the first place showed that I was a good enough player.

I say I saw the writing on the wall, and that was quite literal as when I went to Old Trafford to collect my things to leave I saw graffiti on the wall that said 'Hill in, Sexton out'. It was the first step of breaking up a team that had dragged United out of the doldrums and back to glory, I can't imagine there was anyone more delighted than all connected to Liverpool Football Club with what was happening to our team. The supporters were quite rightly upset. It's a fair argument that in letting go of Tommy Docherty, in the twelve months that followed his departure, the club were put back more than they had been after suffering relegation. Hurried, rash decisions and a desire for change when there needn't be any at all took its toll. Tommy had overseen such a dramatic change at the club where he basically had to end the United careers of Bobby Charlton, Denis Law, George Best, and then rebuild a side that could challenge. After doing all of that in such a short space of time all the hard work was now being undone. I might have been known for my sense of humour but there was nothing funny about my last game for Manchester United at Arsenal, falling on my twenty fourth birthday.

In the midst of a poor run, I'd done as much as anyone to help

United, working incredibly hard and scoring goals to get some vital points on the board. I don't know if I can say I'm relieved but it's a source of comfort to me that my departure from Manchester United wasn't wanted by the supporters and that the attempt to use me as a scapegoat for our poor form wasn't accepted by the fans. I'm sure anyone reading this knows that perception can be everything in football and sometimes the truth gets ignored but the United fans were great to me and they have been ever since.

When a manager makes such a bold decision as Dave made he has to be vindicated by the long term results of that decision. And, as someone who had given his all and absolutely hated losing, I cannot begin to tell you my frustration with only winning one of my last thirteen Manchester United matches. At the time it felt very much like I had unfinished business with the rest of my team-mates. From what I knew we were all capable of, I knew that the form we were in was not a true reflection of our quality. Instead of dwelling on the way it ended you have to look at the positives. It's a small crumb of comfort that I scored in my last appearance at Old Trafford against Everton and it's better from a personal perspective to think I scored five goals in my last six United games, certainly better than thinking we won only one of the last thirteen, but at the time it was no consolation whatsoever. There should have been League Championships and European Cups to be won with my team-mates and there should have been plenty of opportunities in the future for me to overcome those Cup Final personal disappointments, but no more. I was bewildered by the dramatic turn my life had taken.

Arriving at Derby County was quite a culture shock compared to life with Manchester United. The Baseball Ground was much smaller than Old Trafford and I was still a little concerned that some of the supporters hadn't completely forgiven me for the two goals against them in the 1976 semi final. My new stadium might not have held half the supporters that Old Trafford was capable of but Derby County supporters could still generate a great atmosphere. The clubs may have been poles apart in size but Derby as a team were just as competitive as United. They had been chasing trophies throughout the Seventies and I had joined a team with a manager who I knew believed in me and a chairman and board who had great ambitions for the club.

Football supporters can be fickle, hating you one minute and loving you the next if you sign for their club, and thankfully I scored on my Derby debut in the last game of the season against Arsenal to win over a few. Saying that, Manchester United supporters never did that. They never turned against me after I left and gave me a great reception whenever I returned to Old Trafford. That might have been because I was still scoring goals for them as on one trip back I was stood in the wall and deflected a free kick into my own net. The headlines read 'He scores for United again!' It was a sad experience to leave United, but I was determined to do my best for my new club. Did I want to prove Dave Sexton wrong for letting me go? There was an element of that, sure. But being back with Tommy and Frank Blunstone who had also joined up with the Doc, I had hopes of winning more trophies and going on to have a long and successful career with Derby and England.

It was a significant move. Derby were top class in terms of your average football club and I don't mean any disrespect when I say this, but United is a completely different kettle of fish. TD said after he left United that he spent his time trying to build a club like that but it was impossible and I agree completely with him. I'd been brought up at Millwall, and before that I'd played local football, so I wasn't spoiled by any means. I'd been used to seeing clubs get by on what they could scrape together and Derby was well above that. You might have thought it was a culture shock heading from Millwall to United but honestly, I think having got used to being at Old Trafford, the change from United to Derby was a lot harder to get used to.

Although things had changed, one thing that remained the same was the will to win in the dressing room. It was just as intense as it was at United and that suited me. To be honest, maybe I wouldn't have noticed if it was any different, because that was my attitude right back to when I was a kid. I wanted to win. Oh god, did I want to win and score goals. I said I would cry when I was a kid, I would take myself away and cry where no one could see me if we lost a game because it upset me so much, and things hadn't changed now I was a professional. I could take defeat on the chin a bit better but you have to believe that losing put me in a foul mood.

I wasn't in the best of moods having left Manchester United, but I must stress I wasn't unhappy to be joining Derby. They were a top class team filled with great players and with the Doc at the helm, I had every confidence they could challenge and I had no reason to believe that I couldn't go on to fulfill my potential with them. That extended to my ambitions of playing for my country, too. At the end of the season, I was called up by Bobby Robson to join the England 'B' tour. The 'A' team had played the Home Internationals and won them, with my old team-mate (I was still getting used to saying that) Stevie Coppell getting the winner in Scotland. The team I travelled with was named the 'B' team but went with a view to sounding out which of the players could break into the squad for the European Championship qualifiers which were due to begin the following season.

Of course, England had failed to qualify for the 1978 World Cup and so there were plenty of us feeling we could break in if we performed. I hadn't played since a match against Luxembourg though I honestly couldn't tell you the reason I hadn't been selected after that. Peter Barnes was being picked in the left wing position yet I was still scoring plenty of goals for United at the time. Maybe the public message that Dave Sexton had sent out by saying he didn't think I should be playing for Manchester United had affected my chances on the international stage, though it should be said that competition for places was a lot fiercer than it is now. Squads were smaller and there were barely any foreign players in Division One so all the top players in the Liverpool, United, Derby, and Arsenal sides were mostly British.

In the February of 1978, I'd played for the B team in a friendly in West Germany where we had won 2-1. There were plenty of players vying for a place in the England squad, let alone the team. My thoughts were not 'why haven't I been selected' but more, 'I'm going to make sure I will get selected' and that was the aim for me on the tour. It didn't matter what level it was to me, when I pulled on that white England shirt and the blue shorts and white socks, I felt an incredible pride.

The tour was a great experience. I'd always separated my

feelings about club and country anyway, they were two different things to me, so it wasn't as if I was relieved to get away from a tough time, I was just excited to be going away with my country. None of the other players spoke to me about my move, I think all of our collective focus was on proving ourselves and playing the best we possibly could. Regarding the destination, you're never quite sure when you have so many 'suits' travelling with you if it's one that is meaningful or one for them – they go to their director's boxes and smoke cigars, drinking champagne mingling with other directors. They're representing the FA and loving it, but whatever the motivation for them, for me it was all about pulling on the Three Lions on my chest.

I only needed one look around the changing room to know just how fierce competition for places was – Joe Corrigan, Viv Anderson, Steve Daley, Mel Eves, Brian Talbot, Paul Mariner, Alan Kennedy – some great players. It was Alan who scored in our first game of the tour, a 1-1 draw against Malaysia in Kuala Lumpur. It was boiling, in fact it was so hot you couldn't move ten yards without sucking air through your arse! From Malaysia, we flew to Sydney in Australia and spent a couple of days looking around the harbour and exploring before we flew to New Zealand. New Zealand was a beautiful place and the people gave us such a great reception. The local FA had arranged for us to play games in four or five different locations so that the local supporters could see the England players. Their teams were made up of ex-patriots, a bit like an amateur team, but it was still a tough test as they were going to give it their all against an England squad who were all out to make their own point too. That was no difference to me, I was used to players wanting to kick me when I played for Millwall and wanting to beat us when I played for United.

We played three times against the New Zealand select side, in Christchurch, Wellington and Auckland, and we won all three, and I scored in two of the games. I felt like I'd made my mark and continued my good form when I scored twice in our final tour game which was an 8-0 win in Singapore.

New Zealand really was a beautiful place but it was so far away, that's why I never went back! Having said that, years later my son got an opportunity to play in New Zealand and I advised him to take it and he really enjoyed it when he went down there. The tour was great, and after I got back I had a call from Bobby Robson congratulating me on my performances and saying he was looking forward to working with me again. I appreciated that, and I have to say that my experience of working with Bobby only reinforced my belief that he would have been an ideal candidate to succeed Tommy Docherty as United manager. I looked forward to working with Tommy again, though we were both to learn how cruel football could be.

7

Dark Days at Derby

With no disrespect to Derby County Football Club, the transfer there from Manchester United seemed to be the trigger for the low point of my career and my life. Not just because I'd been devastated to leave Old Trafford, but because I suffered a lot of bad fortune. I didn't move away from Bollington to begin with. I would commute from there daily for training. The funny thing was that Colin Todd, who I'd loved playing against and wanted to play with, actually ended up signing for Everton in the close season of 1978/79 and so we would end up crossing each other as we went to our new clubs. Sometimes we'd stop and have a chat on the way, it really was like ships passing in the night.

We kicked off the season with a 1-1 draw against Manchester City in front of 26,000, then lost at Everton, before getting a draw at Birmingham when Gerry Daly, my old team-mate from United, scored for us. My career was to change forever more on August 30th, 1978, when we played Leicester City at Filbert Street in the League Cup. I'd scored the winner as it turned out, but as the game entered the final minute I went for a tackle against the late George Armstrong that I didn't really need to make and got injured. Incidentally, George was playing his last match for Leicester.

I was initially told it might have been strained ligaments but it was a mis-diagnosis that was going to have a significant effect on my rehabilitation. I was put in a cast for a month, but when that was taken off, it was even worse. I had to build up my left leg again so I was training hard, not realising that I was doing more and more damage to myself. I should have had it operated on straight away but didn't. I was running up and down the stands with David Webb on my shoulders. I played a game against Blackpool reserves and a guy lent into me, nothing too serious, and I felt like my knee had opened up again. I had some more time out and came back training hard once again, but my knee always felt heavy and although the doctor kept insisting everything was alright, I knew something wasn't.

At least I had an inkling, unlike in my personal life when I was rocked by a bolt out of the blue. My wife didn't want to move to Derby. I think she just wanted to go back to London. I was away a lot and her family were all based down south. She came from a wealthy family that had everything she would need. One day I came home and there was just nothing there in the house. She'd left and taken everything, lock stock and barrel. We'd sold the house because I thought we were moving closer to Derby. I was in the midst of buying Charlie George's house. Everything had been agreed but when I arrived home that day I discovered that the furniture was being moved, but it was being taken down south and my wife wasn't coming back. I had to pull out of the deal with Charlie which I'm sure upset him but I could do nothing about it as my wife took literally everything, including all of my money. The house proceeds had been put in the bank and she had moved everything into her account. I later discovered that it had been premeditated and that her father had encouraged her to do it as he wanted her back. She was his only daughter, and we didn't really see eye to eye.

I went down South to try and sort it out and was surprised to find that she already had a house for herself. I couldn't even go in my Mercedes as she'd also taken that. I had a Mercedes because I wrote an article for Shoot! magazine which paid for it, but the number plates had been taken off so I couldn't drive it. I had to get my clothes from there but she'd put them all outside in boxes.

I moved to the Midland Hotel in Derby and still had to pay maintenance when she had everything. I've not seen my FA Cup winners medal since the day I picked it up from the Queen, and I don't have my losers medal from the year before either. I'd never seen a lawyer or solicitor but now I was having to concentrate on that while trying to get myself fit again.

I was back in the team for the visit of United on December 9th, 1978 and we took the lead when my volley was saved by Gary Bailey but Gerry put in the rebound to score. Later on I hit another long range shot which was saved, all the while not realising that it was doing me more harm than good. United turned it around to win 3-1.

I was also in the side for Derby's next three league games, losing at Arsenal and then drawing with Aston Villa and Nottingham Forest. We were drawn against Preston North End in the Third round of the FA Cup. During the game I was taking on a defender and sending him the wrong way, but as I changed direction my knee completely opened up and I was brought off immediately. I saw a surgeon in Derby and he twisted my knee and you could hear it grind. He then told me that he couldn't guarantee that I would ever play top class football again.

I almost fell off the bed and broke down in tears. Just four months previously I'd been flying about all over the place and now all of a sudden I was a damaged product. It was so serious that he said he was going to operate on the Monday morning, and advised me that if I woke up with plaster on, then he had inserted a ligament ... but if I woke up with a bandage, then he had worked on my cartilage. Everything was going through my mind as I'd heard about cartilage operations and injuries and how they could finish you. My nightmare continued further as I learned my wife's family had tried to have Kerry's name changed and that really upset me. Let's put it this way, I wasn't having a good time and yet I still had to try and recover to salvage my career. At one point, my wife made an utterly confusing attempt to get back with me which I'm sure wasn't genuine.

I was receiving the support I needed at the club and in that respect I was happy to have familiar faces around. Frank Blunstone supported me by saying I'd be okay with the operation, and Tommy had seen many players get injured and recover too. I was so disappointed that the injury had struck when it did. I had fallen out of the England reckoning with the last of my six caps coming against Luxembourg in October 1977. England needed to score goals by the bucketful in that game to have a chance of qualifying for the World Cup in 1978 but could only win 2-0.

At the tender age of twenty four I had ambitions of playing in the World Cup of 1982 four years later, knowing that should be my peak time. Instead of being at the top of the game I was now at the very bottom. People tend to say, 'He went off the scene quick', but there was just nothing I could do about it. I hadn't gone off the scene because I wasn't good enough. I wanted to prove to the Derby people that I could play as well for them as I had done for United, but most of all I just wanted my natural game back and I was deeply worried that it had gone.

It was a tough time because as well as the injury, the newspapers were often featuring me because of the breakdown of my marriage and I would get followed about by reporters. The only thing I could say to anyone was that I wanted to get my first team place back, and then my England place. But at that time I had nothing, no house, no money, in fact the only thing I could say was mine was the Saab sponsored car I got from Derby. And even that wasn't really mine! I eventually got some bits and pieces back, memorabilia, some shirts that I'd swapped with players, but it was barely half of what I had. I got back the miniature Charity Shield replica we had for taking part but all of these things I literally had to collect from my wife's doorstep as they had been left there in the street where anyone could have taken them.

I had to turn things around and it was perhaps at this time the words of a man who I had encountered while with England had some resonance with me. Ken Burton had been a coach under Don Revie, and with the differences in playing for your country compared to with your club, I would pay attention to the things he would say. He taught me the importance of dedication and determination and for the first time in my career, in my life even, I found myself in a position where I would really need to call on a fighting spirit. Ken Burton was very good at putting things over to you and making you understand the importance of your attitude and effort and it was advice that helped me tremendously. It was good to have people to talk to yet I wouldn't discuss my injury or my marriage problems with any of my fellow players. I would still go to training every day and while the others would train in a morning and then go home, I'd be there morning and afternoon, putting weights on the bottom of my foot to make my leg nice and strong again.

In the absence of a face to talk to, I would go into a local wine bar and have a drink there. The only option other than that was to go to the hotel where I was living out of a suitcase. Most of the clothes and possessions that I did have were now with my mum at her house.

I had a low point when I went to my Mum and Dad to take my stuff there and I broke down, saying, 'Why me?' Dad consoled me while Mum reassured me that I would always have a place with them. But my lowest point was probably back at the wine bar. As I've said previously, I didn't drink very much so I was completely out of my comfort zone and felt as if I was in trouble. I had my knee in a plaster pot as it had only recently been operated on. All thoughts of playing for England again were out of my head, I was just hoping I would be able to play again. My marriage and personal life had really taken its toll on me and I was distraught thinking everything was collapsing. I sat there at the bar with a bottle of Green Label wine, I looked it and had a sip. I put the cork back in and said to the waiter, 'You won't see me again. That's it.'

After that I focussed myself and concentrated on my fitness. I had it in the back of my mind that I wanted to repay the Doc's faith in me and also justify some of the price tag they had paid out so I worked my arse off. I wanted to play so badly and it was so frustrating that I couldn't. The Doc knew that I hadn't become a bad player overnight and, as always, showed he would stand by me and give me the support. He would tell me not to worry and so, after a lot of hard work and dedication, I was able to report back for a full and intensive pre-season in the summer of 1979. Unfortunately, Tommy had resigned in the May of 1979 and was replaced by Colin Addison. In a fashion, Derby's struggles in the 1978/79 season mirrored my own. The club finished in nineteenth position, one above the relegation places, although the gap of six points between us and Queens Park Rangers in the highest relegation position illustrated a small degree of comfort. It was one of those strange sporting coincidences that QPR was where

Tommy would end up next and both club and manager had been a part of the history of my career and would provide some part of my future too, though I wasn't to know it at the time.

Off the pitch I had help from the good people at Derbyshire Building Society who offered to help me get a mortgage. I told them I needed to get some cash together and I got around £3,000 back from my wife. However, it wasn't in the shape of money, it was in my Mercedes! The manager, Mr Mitchell, helped me and I got a house out in Mayfield in Ashbourne which is a beautiful place. I didn't have a pot to piss in but I got a £19,000 mortgage for a lovely detached house. There was a director at Derby County called Freddy Fern who had a carpet company that came and carpeted my house for nothing and it was fantastic kindness, I was so grateful to him for his help. I'd got my affairs just about back in order with Mr Mitchell who also looked after my accounts.

Freddy also helped me out with a loan to furnish the house. Again, I was so grateful and I became close friends with Freddy and his family and I never forgot what he did for me. I was shown warmth, generosity and love that I didn't expect and it meant so much.

Back in training, I could tell I had lost a yard of pace. What had started as a physical problem had now also become a mental problem. I was wondering if I could play my natural game like I had done before, and all the while thinking if my knee would go again. With that awful thought, I always felt as if I was playing or training within myself.

While preparing myself for a return, I went to take part in an episode of the TV show *Superstars* in Southampton with Mickey Lyons amongst others where footballers were taking on athletes such as Geoff Capes. I'd arranged to stay with my Mum as I'd planned to see my daughter while I was there, but it turned out she'd been taken to Ireland without my knowledge. My knee was feeling better and we had an absolute blast doing the challenges.

While doing the show I met a young lady named Claire but we didn't say much as she was there to watch one of the athletes. I was doing the obstacle course against Daley Thompson and banged my knee so I had to stop. I went to the medical room to get some ice put on it and Claire walked past to see if I was alright. She said that I had taken a bit of a tumble but I was way out in front at the time!'

It turned out she lived in Windlesham which was just up the road from where I grew up in Sunbury. She gave me her number and I said that if I was ever down that way she could come to a game to watch me. I left, said goodbye to mum, and thought nothing of it. About three months later I was going through some fan mail when I opened a letter from Claire who was an air stewardess for British Airways. She had sent me a letter from where she was staying in Inverness saying how nice it was to meet me and that she'd love to see me if I was ever free. She left her telephone number so as I was driving home from training I decided to stop at the top of Ashbourne Hill in Derby where there was a telephone box. I thought she might have been working, but to my surprise she answered the phone. I told her that I was sorry to phone out of the blue but wondered if she was free. When she said she had three days off I asked her if she would like to spend the weekend with me and I was delighted when she said that she would.

She boarded a plane, I picked her up at the airport, we spent the weekend together, and we've been together ever since. There was a little bit of trouble from Jackie when she thought there had been something going on, but that was ridiculous as not only had I met Claire long after Jackie had left me, but Jackie herself was also seeing other people. I was still hopeful of meeting up with my daughter but she would always be taken away from me. My brothers and sisters supported me saying that once Kerry was old enough she'd want to see me and thank God, that came true, but it took about six or seven years for me to get to see her. Jackie sent her to school in Ireland and I never interfered with it as I wanted Kerry to have a settled life, I didn't want her to see me arguing with her mother and grandparents. Claire came into my life much later on, when I was on my way back to fitness at Derby. She is of Armenian descent but was born in Larnaca and had British citizenship.

After that first weekend together, Claire came up as often as she could, always bringing home Lladro porcelain figures. The house looked a little bit better. She had an Old English Sheepdog called Cleo, and one time I insisted that she brought her up too as there were fields nearby which were great for dogs. She brought Cleo up a couple of times and then the dog just stayed with me. I would take her all over the place but she was still Claire's little baby, her first dog. As a dog lover I fell in love with Cleo just as I did with Claire and both were cemented in my heart forever more from that point onwards.

*****

The 1979/80 season started quite badly for Derby. I was back in the team for the first game of the season, a draw at West Brom, but four consecutive defeats saw us near the foot of the table. A defeat at Middlesbrough also saw us eliminated from the League Cup at the first hurdle. In the next game I was to suffer one of the lowest points of my career when I received my first senior red card. We were playing at Crystal Palace and I was up against Kenny Sansom. I got the ball and hit it against Kenny's leg and it went out of play. The linesman was five yards away and the referee about fifteen yards. The linesman then gave Palace the throw! I told him he had to be joking and at that point the referee came over. It was then in a moment of madness I called him a 'fucking cheat'. I can't even remember the referee's name, but I can remember as clear as day the moment he instantly pulled out a red card. Five minutes into the game, as well.

Claire and my brother Adrian had come to watch and they'd not even sat down. Of course, when they did get in they asked someone where I was, and learned the ugly truth. Adrian came down to the changing room and asked me what happened. It was difficult to explain because I could barely believe it myself.

Colin fined me two weeks wages for it and rightfully so, I'd let the team down and we lost heavily in a 4-0 scoreline. The only thing that annoyed me was that Roy McFarland was sent off a couple of weeks later and nothing happened to him. I was up in arms about that. Overall, it was a very disappointing start to the season. There was a spell in the Autumn when I did well, scoring twice at Stoke and then in a home win against West Brom, before I made my final appearance for Derby, at home to Ipswich on

November 17th, 1979. A 1-0 defeat in front of 16,000 fans was not the way I expected that my top flight career would end, but at the time I had no reason to believe that it would be so as I was only twenty five ...

I had thought for a while that Tommy would leave Derby at the end of the previous season. It sometimes felt as if the club wasn't big enough for him, that he too was struggling with the aftermath of leaving United. He had gone to Queens Park Rangers and they were at least at the right end of Division Two. QPR had, of course, been challenging with United for honours throughout 1976 and 1977 so the boss had a similar task on his hands as he had when he first took over at Old Trafford, trying to rebuild a once great club. He got in touch with Derby to make an offer for me. At the time, Derby were out of the relegation zone only on goal difference while QPR were in second place in the Second Division. There was no reason to believe that Tommy wouldn't bring QPR back up. The plight of both clubs at the time, considering the success they'd had less than five years before, was proof of how competitive the divisions were and how quickly things could change in football.

I saw a move to QPR as a chance to finally sort out all the issues from my marriage and I was able to do that. Claire and I sold our houses and bought one in Sunninghill, Berkshire. As a motivator, the boss was without comparison, and he felt that by paying another big transfer fee of around £150,000 getting me into the Second Division and back in London around comfortable surroundings, he would be able to get the best out of me. Unfortunately neither of us had reckoned with the psychological damage that was lingering from my injury and the self doubt that was plaguing me about whether I could actually perform to the standard I'd set myself in the past.

Ipswich had shown an interest in me and they were to finish third in Division One, but I was that restricted by what I had gone through that maybe I felt the same as Tommy. I tried my hardest at QPR, the club I had left as a schoolboy all those years ago, but it just wasn't right. QPR had Don Shanks, Tony Currie, Gerry Francis, a lot of top seasoned professionals and had been tough opposition when I'd been up against them.

I was only to play only around a dozen games in total for QPR, but my time back in London was marked by the most wonderful memory as my son Sammy was born in 1980. We were playing a game, I think it was a reserve match in midweek, and afterwards Dave McCreery, my former United team-mate who had also been signed by Tommy for QPR, and I went to the hospital to see him. The best thing for me about the entire move was the fact that my son was born locally, in Ascot. I was over the moon. I'll talk about Sam in more detail later on but it was an absolute dream to be blessed with him.

Surrounded by my family I was convinced that I could get back to my best, and I was positive and trying to get there, yet I just couldn't shake off the feeling my knee might go again. It was my left knee that was injured and, to be honest, I'm glad it was that one out of the two. You might ask why, as that was my natural kicking foot so I'll tell you. Obviously my right leg gave me all my support, the one I stand on, turn on, the one that held me upright and gave me balance when I was shooting. I was able to use my right leg to protect my left, so I was still able to volley or connect with the ball as naturally as I had done before. However, if I'd been in a position where I had to use my left leg to turn on the ground, then I think I'd have had a major problem, and it was that which was the very basis of my psychological struggle with the injury. I knew that would damage me and I would not be able to play at all.

So much is said about today's game and the game when we played. Which player would be better, which era was better, for example. One thing that is for certain is that the injury I suffered would have done in any player in any era without the right treatment. The difference is that in today's game, what was actually wrong with me would have been identified a lot sooner and I wouldn't have had to suffer such a long time without knowing what was really wrong. I've gone into detail about the injury but being completely honest with you, it was the mis-diagnosis or the time it took to make a correct diagnosis that annoys me rather than the injury itself. It did then and it does now. Injuries happen, but I should have been sent to see a specialist right away. You deal with it the best you can at the time and you can only trust what the doctors are telling you as after all, your fate is in their hands. I trusted the doctors and they got it wrong. In the years that have passed, when it comes to the operations I've had on my knee, I'm always wary of what the doctors tell me because I feel I know my knee better than they do. I won't say that I don't trust them because some have really helped, and today they use all the proper equipment to make a full analysis but not then, and it had such a huge impact on my career.

Looking back, it could be said I was fortunate to have got away as I did. Kevin Beattie had done his cartilage, had an operation on it and was having problems with it immediately, and it ended up having such an effect that he could barely walk. I wouldn't say I was lucky, but in comparison it wasn't as bad as it could have been. Still, I just wasn't completely certain about the move to Loftus Road. And believe it or not, I just didn't feel comfortable playing in hoops! Top club as QPR were, and they were no slouches, the drain of feeling the way I had for two years since the injury was beginning to take its toll on me. It was a shame that it was such a tough time mentally. I'd recovered in my personal life thanks to Claire coming along and then giving me my beautiful son, and I could not have had a better set up to try and really push on professionally. My family were around me and my mentor was there too, I was close to where I was brought up as a kid, and yet something wasn't quite right. Was it that I was only in my mid twenties, and that I'd gone from being top scorer for Manchester United to taking a gamble of a move to a Second Division club in little more than a year? I don't know, but something seemed to be holding me back.

Hindsight is great. Looking back, maybe I shouldn't have taken that step down to QPR, maybe I shouldn't have left Derby, or maybe I should have joined Ipswich. But I had to be honest with myself. As well as the psychological hurdle which I was struggling with, I'd also suffered the natural consequences of a serious injury and lost a yard of pace. Like I say, with hindsight I perhaps should not have gone there, but at the time I was still battling against those self doubts I had and trying to get back. But then TD went and got sacked again!

QPR had finished in fifth place in the 1979/80 season, just a couple of years after they had been one of the best teams in the First Division, and the Doc started the 1980/81 season under pressure to get the club back into the top flight. Things didn't go well from the off with a win against Bristol Rovers in the second game of the season the only bright spot from a miserable start, and when we lost three games in a row against Notts County, Newcastle and Sheffield Wednesday, time was ticking for Tommy. It was clear that all wasn't well and so it wasn't really a surprise when he was sacked and replaced by Terry Venables. Venables had done a great job at Crystal Palace, getting them promoted from the Third Division to the Second in 1977, and then to the top flight in 1979. In the 1979/80 season, he led them to their best ever position of thirteenth in the First Division, and it was that kind of success which the board obviously wanted at QPR.

After leaving QPR, Tommy had a short spell at Preston, and then at Wolves, but I wasn't about to join him again. He had been great for me in my earlier career and nothing could ever change that. My most enjoyable playing days were with him at United but I think we were both looking at the situation and thinking neither of us were likely to reach that high again, and that was a shame for both of us.

I won't say that the Doc did me a favour by signing me for Derby and QPR. I felt I'd showed what I could do, and the Doc felt he was the man to get the best out of me. I was grateful for his faith in me yet I think there came a point in those final few months at Loftus Road where we both realised it wasn't right. As a manager, maybe he looked at me and felt that as much as he wanted me to be, as much as we both wanted me to be, I was never going to be the same. And maybe there's some truth in the theory that he didn't quite have the same passion for the job after what had happened at United. I felt Derby wasn't the 'big' club he needed to get that buzz back, and QPR certainly hadn't done that for him either. As for not playing me often for QPR, well, that was fair enough, he had seen me first hand for a number of years so he was probably very aware of the damage that had been done to me. If I wasn't fit and confident I just wasn't the same player and maybe that's why I didn't play as much.

Terry came in and made changes and I was one of those who immediately bore the brunt of it. He called me and a couple of players into his office shortly after his arrival and said we were surplus to requirements as he would be putting younger players into the team. George Graham, who would later manage Arsenal to great success, was looking after the youth team and they had some promising young players. As Terry had done exactly the same thing at Palace, I certainly wasn't surprised that he made that choice. Fair enough, he'd done well, but I wasn't that bothered as I wasn't a big fan of him personally. I'd known him and been around him when I was just a young player, and I knew people who had known him and told me about him. Events involved in my eventual transfer confirmed that to me.

Though I can't say I wanted to work with Terry, it certainly wasn't the greatest thing for my self confidence to be deemed surplus, or even have it suggested that I was too old or past my peak when I was only twenty six years old, especially with the way that I'd been feeling for nearly a year. I was still supposed to be approaching my peak and here I was no longer wanted by a Second Division club. Even when I had played, I accepted my form wasn't quite what it was, and maybe that was because I simply felt that I couldn't do what I could do before the injury. I was inhibited by the psychological repercussions of it all. The time at QPR put a lot of things in perspective and instead of sitting and feeling sorry for myself again, I had to handle what I had been dealt and, unlike when I first suffered the injury, I now had a stable relationship, a strong partner and a baby boy to look after. I could accept that I might not be able to overcome those obstacles and get back the top flight career and the England place I wanted so badly. I could have had a transfer back to a Division One club if I'd recovered my form, but at what level? If I was to be a reserve player for a mid-table team, I would not have been enjoying my game or have felt comfortable, so what I wanted first and foremost was a platform where I could enjoy my game again.

At the end of the 1980/81 season I'd not really featured much again, and with the knowledge I was soon to be moving, I was hopeful of a place where I could just get back to loving the game.

A transfer was imminent but it was still a bolt out of the blue when I received a phone call that a Canadian team had just been taken over by Molson Coors, a big brewery in the country, and they wanted to buy me for £175,000. The manager over there was Eddie Firmani, who had played for Charlton and I'd known him at Millwall.

I met Eddie in London and discussed the move. He sold it to me and I felt excited about it, yet at the same time I just couldn't understand it. I was damaged and not the player I'd been before. Something didn't quite feel right. I went to have a medical at Harley Street where it was confirmed that my knee wasn't very clever. QPR hired a another doctor to provide a second medical, and I passed that one. I don't want to use this time to point the finger at anyone but £175,000 was more than I'd moved to QPR for in the first place. I'd like to sit here and say my ability justified the fee, and when fit maybe it could well have done, but I can't help feeling there was some skullduggery involved.

Whatever the reasoning, I was looking forward to enjoying a new lease of life somewhere afresh, and that helped me come to terms with the fact that my top flight career in England was over. I won't lie, it wasn't easy and took some time to get used to, especially seeing my friends playing in the World Cup in 1982. That the injury had followed almost soon after my transfer to Derby seemed to signal that everything stopped as soon as I left United and to some I'd dropped off the radar as soon as I left Old Trafford, but it just wasn't the case. I look at what could have been if not for the injury and even playing for Derby, or another team, I felt that I would have been there in 1982. The injury had obviously had an impact on my England career. I was still hopeful at Derby and even at QPR that I could get fit, that my knee would sort itself out and that I would make the 1982 World Cup. I saw playing for England at a World Cup as the pinnacle. How can it not be? If they had qualified for the 1978 tournament then maybe I'd have made that squad as my last game had been in the qualifier against Luxembourg in October 1977, but even after leaving United I finished the season as their top scorer.

Peter Barnes was the current first choice on the left for England, but I felt I would have made the squad in 1978 if they had qualified. I was confident enough in my ability to feel that if I was fit and had a proper run of games, I could show I was still worthy of consideration. I absolutely loved playing for my country, but unfortunately the FA weren't quite so keen on me. It's like I've said, everyone loves you when everything is going well but when you hit misfortune then the phone stops ringing and people don't want to know. I would have appreciated it if Ron Greenwood had picked up the phone after the injury to talk to me, not to give me re-assurances but just to wish me well or be honest with me about my long term chances. What would that have cost? Nothing, or very little.

I love England, but the FA and the board, I'm not sure I could say the same about. Aside from the knee, I never had another injury, and I still kept myself in good condition by avoiding the bad habits. But I was just one of a list of players to feel that way. Kevin Beattie was an unbelievable defender, someone I roomed with for England, and he suffered injuries that stopped him reaching his potential too. Maybe there was something in the water? I'd learned that fortune, or the lack of it, played as much a part in the career of a player as talent or application. You can have all the skill in the world or try harder than anyone but if the luck ain't with you then you ain't going anywhere. And when you've been at the top and suffer bad luck, you learn that the world of football can be a very lonely one.

Regardless of all the 'ifs and buts,' what happened had happened, and what was real was that I was close to moving to Montreal. I sat down with Claire and we discussed everything as I wasn't going to make the decision without consulting her. She had seen so much of the world in her job and we both knew how beautiful Canada was. We came to the conclusion that maybe it would be best to move on, move away from a bad situation in England and start a new page in our lives.

8

Back West

Montreal, Chicago, San Jose, New York, Kansas, Tacoma. I'm told that my life in the early 1980s sounds like a Johnny Cash song, though the only 'Johnny Cash' I was really familiar with has a completely different meaning ...

Coming back to North America was like a fresh start, a new life, and it was completely exciting. It wasn't just my career, football as a game and a sport seemed to be struggling in England, it didn't seem to be progressing and the prospect of everything starting afresh was very appealing. That was one factor. Another was moving away from the personal troubles that had dogged me, so the move across the Atlantic Ocean was a chance for everything in my life to feel like it was brand new. Don't get me wrong, there are people and players that have had it worse than I did, but any individual who goes through a rough patch wants to come out of it and would like to start with a blank page, and so I was no different to anybody else in that respect. Even though English football might have seemed like it was in a bad place, it wasn't as if the Canadian or North American game was a bed of roses, or 'the promised land' by mere virtue of the location. A lot of good players had gone out there, not set the world alight, and gone back home.

As far as I was concerned, I had received a boost in morale by the fact that someone still wanted to buy me, and a vote of confidence that I was still seen as a player talented enough to build a franchise around. There were details to be sorted out before I made the move. I learned I wouldn't be allowed into

Canada unless my divorce was finalised, so I sorted that out and Sam, Claire and myself went to Montreal looking to start a brand new life.

This wasn't like my visit to Chicago. I wasn't going there knowing I was going back to the United Kingdom in six months, this was a move that had every intention of being permanent and so everything had to be right. Claire spoke French which was a benefit considering we were in Montreal. With the thought that the move would be permanent, we took the appropriate steps with our ties and responsibilities in England. We sold our houses, and I pulled out of a pub called the Slug and Lettuce that I had been a partner in. To be honest, too many tunes seemed to be played on the till in that pub.

Montreal was beautiful and we arrived when the snow was down, it really was fantastic imagery that we were welcomed with to begin our new life.

At Manchester United I'd been part of a great team, yet at Derby and QPR I'd perhaps been 'damaged goods.' At Montreal Manic, I felt like a big fish in a small pond. The transfer fees paid for me had all been big in their day. With Montreal the latest club to pay a sizeable amount for me, and the good feeling that surrounded the move, I was really positive about finally getting over the demons of my injury and re-starting my career. I had a sense of belonging and with Eddie Firmani I felt comfortable. Eddie wasn't blind, he had been over to watch me play for QPR, so he saw that I was still capable, and that went a long way to reassuring me.

The NASL still had a lot of people who I knew from my time there six years prior. A lot of people from England had come over and settled down too. Tony Towers, the great former Manchester City and Sunderland player, had signed for Montreal at the same time as me. We became very good friends and the sense of belonging that I spoke about really helped me get off to a flyer. Ever since the injury at Derby I had felt haunted. Not just by the injury and the constant attempts to repay the faith that TD had put in me, but haunted by the entirety of my time at Loftus Road. I don't even think that Claire knew how unhappy I'd become. I was desperately sad at having to come to terms with knowing I'd never reached the upper limits of my potential. I shouldn't have had to leave England to restart my career at the age of twenty seven. When Eddie made the offer and explained the franchise to me, selling the Manic as a team that I would spearhead alongside great players like Tony as well as Fran O'Brien, a great Irish player, and Bobby Vosmaer who was a fantastic Dutch forward, it helped me rediscover my confidence. Perhaps subconsciously I had accepted my fate and that had triggered the return of my careless, 'sod it' approach to my knee.

There were no bad memories of my time at Chicago and the game hadn't changed so much in the time that had passed, and perhaps it helped that the club itself were on a blank page too. The Montreal fans really took to us and the support was phenomenal. We had a great fan club with a European connection. In our team we had Scottish, French, Yugoslavian and Egyptian players. Thinking about it, although it wasn't necessarily the same calibre of player, the demographic and cosmopolitan flavour of the squad was very much a blueprint for what is in the English game today. They were very much ahead of their time in the way they approached some aspects of the game even though other areas would leave much to be desired.

Our club were being taken seriously. The Manic was named after the Quebec Dam at the mouth of the Manicougan River, and we were to play our games in the Olympic Stadium. Years later, the next soccer team to play in Montreal, the 'Impact', would use the same stadium for some of their games too. They now play in Major League Soccer and are owned by the wealthy Saputo family who were supporters of the Manic when we were playing. The stadium was fantastic even though it was normally used for baseball, and we would attract around 23,000 there regularly.

Molson Breweries had bought the Philadelphia Fury, a struggling club with a small attendance, and as often happens in North America, the entire franchise was relocated to Canada. Though they had made significant changes, they kept Eddie on as coach, and that was a wise move as Eddie was the most successful coach in the history of the NASL. Eddie had won titles in Tampa and New York. In fact, in my first stint with Chicago I'd played a blinder against his Tampa side and scored two goals.

I think Eddie never forgot that. He'd seen me at Millwall, and after that first game he said that if he had known I was coming he would have signed me. Upon eventually signing me, he said that he knew I was lacking in confidence but he just wanted me to play with freedom. Eddie had managed Pele at New York so he knew good players. He was trying to bring in the calibre of player that he'd had there so to be considered the big name was very pleasing. Eddie had chased me for ages, even when he was at New York, so I knew he was keen. I've been very good friends with him ever since.

With such positivity it was hardly a surprise that we began the season really well with three wins out of our four games. My own form was strong and I would go on to score sixteen goals and create a dozen more in just thirty one games in 1981. As the season went on we began to attract more and more supporters to the games, in fact only New York Cosmos, the most famous side in the league, had a higher gate than us. When the Cosmos came to the Olympic Stadium in early June, there were more than 38,000 present.

The schedule of the league was much like the format of the way the Scottish leagues used to run, with teams playing each other home and away twice, so when the Cosmos returned in July, over 40,000 were in attendance for our biggest gate of the season so far. New York won on both visits with the same score of 2-1 but other than that our home form had been really strong. So strong that the fans turned up regardless of the strength of the opposition. A shoot-out win over Washington Diplomats in the last game of the regular season was watched by over 50,000 supporters who had come to celebrate our achievement at qualifying for the play-offs.

As if to underline the point about the strength of the league, Washington had the great Johan Cruyff on their roster in that season. It was fantastic to be playing in front of crowds that were as big as most that I'd encountered during my time at United but the atmosphere was also incredible. And the fans were a credit to the game. We had a large Italian following and they were fanatical. The president of the fan club was a fella called Tony Incollingo, who is a lovely guy. During the Washington game all the supporters wanted to get their players shirts. The supporters would gather around the area of the stadium where the players would run on to the field so we knew that we wouldn't be able to get out of the game that way without being mobbed. Perhaps the supporters knew that we wouldn't be going back there as halfway through the game, they sent some pigs and pigeons on the field to send everything into a frenzy! It was a sight, seeing people chasing pigs around a football pitch. After the game, the supporters converged on to the field and we couldn't get off the pitch. In the Olympic Stadium, there was a complete underground system where people could get around more easily, so as the fans were grabbing at me, I took off my shirt and threw it in the air, and did the same with my shorts, and then I legged it to the nearest exit! I walked back to the changing rooms in only my slip, socks and my boots. Normally we wouldn't be allowed underneath but I got away with it. What a way to celebrate, but what a great set of supporters. Canadian people are very passionate about the game. Perhaps ice hockey is their number one sport but they are passionate about football too.

Our play-off opponents were Los Angeles Aztecs, who played in the Coliseum in LA. One of the great things about the league is that all of the soccer clubs played in superb NFL or baseball stadiums, wonderful arenas that had histories all their own. The Aztecs had great players. Cruyff had once played for them as well as George Best, though their roster at the team when we played them was not too shabby. Gilson, Dragan Simic, Marcelino, Chris Turner in goal.

Our home win over the Aztecs in front of 46,000 set us up nicely for the second leg. The Aztecs won in the Coliseum, but in the third and final playoff leg we won in the Coliseum to earn a tie in the next round, the quarter final, against my old club Chicago Sting. In that first leg we attracted a club record of more than 58,000 as we won 3-2. That was to be our final home game of a season where we had played in front of well over a quarter of a million spectators at the Olympic Stadium.

Unfortunately, Chicago went on to win the next tie and then the play-off at Wrigley Field to eliminate us. Nonetheless, it had been a good season and a strong first year for both me and the new franchise. I'd said to myself that I didn't need to worry about my knee but in fact I'd underestimated it as it held up really well and I was able to play freely without any concern. I worked hard, the knee was strong and I had all my strength back. It was unfortunate that I'd left the English scene by this point but I have to be honest and say that I was enjoying myself so much that I wouldn't have relinquished it anyway. I did, at least, get the opportunity to show some of my re-born self confidence back at the Theatre of Dreams.

*****

In November 1981 I was delighted to take part in Sammy McIlroy's testimonial back at Old Trafford. Sammy had richly deserved that recognition and invited the 1977 FA Cup winning team to play against the current United side. Like most of us in that side, that FA Cup was sadly the only major trophy Sammy won with United as Dave Sexton had failed to add to it while he was there. The club reached the 1979 final, where Sammy scored, but lost to Arsenal and never quite looked like reaching the potential we all had together in 1977.

Dave had been sacked and replaced by Ron Atkinson, and Ron quickly set about stamping his mark on the team. He'd bought Bryan Robson and Frank Stapleton and his side were labelled the 'seven million dollar men'. Both Frank and Bryan scored in the game, which was a 4-4 draw, but Jimmy Greenhoff netted a hat-trick for us and Gerry Daly, who hadn't played in the Cup Final but was a guest due to being Sammy's friend, got the other. The Doc was managing the 1977 side and knew Ron was looking for another wide player and actually told him to buy me as I would score him goals. Eventually, funnily enough, Ron signed Peter Barnes, the player who had hit the scene at the same time as me. Jesper Olsen had been signed by that time too.

It was nice of the Doc to have said that, and showed once again just how much he thought of me, and I felt that I'd given a good account of myself in that return to Old Trafford.

*****

After being named in the NASL All-star team of 1975, I was again named in the team in 1981 after my return and both made me proud in equal measure. Getting to know Pele and playing against him was a professional accolade in itself, a huge honour, as were the comments he made about me being a Brazilian-style player. The inclusion in the 1981 team after all the troubles I had been through, and proving that I still had the ability to play at a high level, gave me a different kind of pride.

After the outdoor season back in Canada, the Manic played an indoor season and that was quite funny as we'd be playing in the Ice Hockey arenas. It was odd, because after we'd finished playing, we'd have to roll up the pitch and prepare the ice so the likes of Wayne Gretzky could come on and play. We had a strong winter in the Indoor League, being named the 1981/82 Champions of the Eastern Division. I really found form, blitzing the competition with twenty nine goals and nineteen assists in just sixteen games. We were still filling the arena there too. I could have stayed at Montreal as they offered me a deal, but the tax was absolutely killing us as it was so high. I was losing sixty percent of my wage to tax and I could kiss my bonus goodbye to it too.

When the opportunity came up to move back to Chicago and play for the Sting again just into the 1982 season, it made financial sense to do so. I'd started well, with two goals and three assists in the first five games, when Chicago made the offer. I'd recaptured the kind of form I'd showed at United and had people saying I was the franchise. I didn't see it like that, it was the team, but there is no denying that I had done well there. It wasn't just me that was haemorrhaging money as the club were too, spending well beyond their means in order to try and establish themselves. On the other hand, Chicago had been named North American Soccer League Champions in 1981.

The Chicago owner Lee Stern made the offer and there I was, back at the club where I'd done so well seven years earlier. The German coach Willy Roy was there and had filled the squad with his fellow countrymen. There must have been more than half a dozen German players there. Duncan McKenzie, my compatriot, was also there but the German style of playing and the English style were not really compatible and this lead to a fair few problems.

Willy was pissed off with me right from the off as the deal had been done direct with Lee. I was close with Lee and his family but the way it had been handled obviously didn't sit right with Willy, and that got us off on the wrong foot. I still enjoyed being back in Chicago as a lot of the same people were still at the club and a lot of friends that I had made on my first stay were still in the city too. There was Doctor Rosenzweig who I'd known since that spell in 1975, along with his wife Lois, and Claire and I became very close friends with them. Many faces were the same but things had changed with the franchise. Since I'd been there they had moved from Soldier Field to Wrigley Field which I knew having played there the previous season. The difference was that Wrigley Field, and Comiskey Park, where the Sting would also occasionally play their home games, were both baseball stadiums. It wasn't the same atmosphere due to the layout.

The rules of the game changed in 1982, with the offside rule now applying from the halfway line to come in line with FIFA demands. This was great, as it meant the game in North America was now adapting to change. Previously they'd made the rules up to suit themselves but it was obvious that conforming to the way that the game was meant to be played was only going to be of benefit to everyone connected. For one reason or another, Chicago failed to rediscover the form they'd shown the previous year. In twenty six games I still managed a healthy return of nine goals and ten assists, but the Sting achieved the stigma of being the first defending champions not to qualify for the play-offs.

One brief moment of glory came during the season when we played in the Trans-Atlantic Challenge Cup. We drew with Uruguayan side Nacional and then defeated Napoli of Italy 3-1 before facing New York Cosmos in the decider. I scored in a 4-3 win to help us lift the trophy. The final was played at the Giants Stadium and I met Mick Jagger and the Rolling Stones there. To me, it was just football as usual. It was great to play Napoli as my old friend Rudi Krol was there. I'd played against Rudi in the United and Ajax tie of 1976 and he came into a restaurant to see me in Chicago.

To be honest, the tournament was little more than a pre-season friendly for the European teams. The NASL were trying to promote their own game by inviting top teams over and it was commendable as there was a lot of interest due to the relative lack of the television coverage for the Italian supporters in America to see anything of their compatriots. There was never any thought that the tournament would develop into something more serious than a friendly, but it still served as a judging point to see the difference in quality. As well as we did, it still felt as if the European sides would have wiped the floor with us if they treated it as a competitive game. The NASL had gone about what they wanted to do in the right way but it was always going to take time to reach the level of the European game. You can't put the game in a microwave and instantly reach the level of 150 years of history, it just doesn't happen like that. Make no mistake though, the Cosmos wanted to win that final and treated it very seriously, as did we at the Sting. It was competitive for us, and that's what made it a good workout for the European players.

The outdoor game began to fall apart quite quickly when it was announced that Mexico had won the right to host the 1986 World Cup and fewer teams were participating in the NASL due to either going bust or lack of interest. As a result, there was an increased focus on the indoor game which was gaining in popularity.

I don't think that the failure to get the World Cup directly led to the NASL ending, I just think that the financial pressure had become too great for many individuals. I was looking for a contract to play indoors as I'd enjoyed the winter season with Montreal because it was like playing five-a-side to me. Five-a-side is like pinball compared to a full-sided game but if you're good at the five-a-side's in training in the professional world then you can adapt to the indoor game quite comfortably. I took to it like a duck to water, but there had been a change in the transfer system. A club could now transfer you to another and you wouldn't have a say in it, and that meant that you could be forced to move to another city with about three days notice.

Most of the contracts I had included a 'No cut, no trade' clause, meaning I couldn't be dropped so the club couldn't get away without paying me, and that my club couldn't trade me without my agreement. After scoring ten times in eleven games indoor for Chicago I went to San Jose Earthquakes where I played just four times before I was on my way to New York in a player exchange deal. It was never going to work with Willy at Chicago but everything happened so quickly and before I knew it I was in New York playing for the Arrows. There were lots of games with a very fast turnaround. The matches were an hour long and demanded a lot from you physically. Though it was still technically the same game, to me it wasn't football. Football had collapsed, and the indoor game wasn't the replacement for it, no matter how much they wanted to say it was. I made the best of it by scoring ten in twenty two games for New York before the opportunity to play the outdoor game came up with another project in Montreal in 1983.

A supporter started a club called Inter-Montreal FC to play in what was called the Canadian Professional Soccer League which consisted of six clubs. The name was misleading as the teams were essentially semi-professional teams with a few professionals added in. Technically speaking the league lasted a season but it was much less than that, it felt like a month of just going out and doing something to get paid and then coming back. During my time there Inter-Montreal played friendlies against European opposition where I excelled. Against Marseilles I scored twice in a 2-0 win, and I netted our only goal in a 1-1 draw against Udinese. Inter-Montreal's spell in the CASL lasted just over a handful of games. They had good intentions with the league but as seems to be the story more often than not, they just couldn't fund it.

Moving back to the indoor game after that failed venture, I moved to Kansas City to play for the Comets. Once again I performed well as in my first season I scored forty six and created twenty four goals. I began the 1984/85 indoor season with them but only played nine games before a move to Tacoma Stars in Washington. While there, I played with Roy Wegerle, who would go on to play for Coventry City in the Premier League in England as well as clubs like Blackburn and Chelsea.

Everything about the indoor game felt like a winding down of the NASL game in general, and for me, I felt as if my contribution towards it was to see it through and not just run away from it. I was there for about three months but it was always going to be a temporary stay. but it was nice to be in Washington as the weather was fairly similar to how it was in England.

Afterwards we drove from Seattle back to our house in Kansas and then down to Florida as we were moving there. I love driving in America and I was able to share moments with my family that were just incredible, like going across the Rocky Mountains, through Nashville, and going over the continental divide. Motorways where we couldn't see the end and tumbleweed like in the movies.

Throughout that time, we tried our best to maintain stability even though I was moving around so much. Claire was absolutely fantastic and kept everything ticking over nicely on that side of things and made sure we would always have a base somewhere. Claire and Sam would come and stay with me wherever I went and we bought a house in Florida as a base because Montreal was so cold!

We'd have a base wherever I was playing. When we moved from Montreal to Chicago I bought the owner's son's house in Northbrook, Illinois. We thought we would be staying there so we sold the house in Florida and would only go there for a week on holiday instead of moving back there permanently. When we moved to Kansas, I had a house built and we stayed there all year round. I was happy there and could have stayed but the life of a footballer means that you are always moving. I didn't buy in New York as I knew that move was temporary. After we eventually sold the house in Kansas we rented in Florida for a short time.

Though we moved around, we did make a number of close friends. America is so transient, particularly in soccer and despite being so used to staying in the same place when I was younger, I got used to the change and seeing the different places. Being able to see America and everything about it, and doing it for work, was of course an absolute dream.

From growing up in Sunbury to being able to drive five miles down the road and see deer was something special. Americans don't have to leave their country to see some of the most spectacular sights in the world. Lake Shore Drive, Chicago. Lake Michigan. Lake Erie. The desert in Phoenix. Florida and the Gulf. Through what I did for a living, I was so fortunate to see some incredible things. We played a game in San Antonio and while we were there I went to see the Alamo. These are things that you only see in movies. With all due respect to Brighton, it just doesn't sound the same!

That's not being detrimental to my country as I love it but I have been lucky enough to have seen all the different corners of the world. The Far East, Australia, Europe, but the only place I wanted to settle down was in America and the four years I spent there in the early 1980s changed my life forever. I played in every major city in the country, played in most of their major stadiums both indoor and outdoor. However, moving around so often, all the inner cities would feel the same, and playing in the indoor leagues was never going to be right for me long term and it never felt like the proper game anyway. We played tons of games, one after the other, so I knew I was fit enough to play, but playing on the surfaces was terrible. The astro turf over ice was one way of saying goodbye to my knees. I wore Nike Tiempos that would grip the carpet very well, but although I wasn't worried about my knees anymore, the point remained that I wasn't going to be doing it long term. Like I've said, it was a five-a-side that was played in front of eight thousand people, although I do have some fond memories of my time playing it.

A few years later, I was invited to an NFL dinner and they showed footage of a bicycle kick I'd once scored for Chicago at Phoenix. The ball came to my chest, and I turned and hit it and it went like a rocket into the top corner. We lost 9-2 but I got a standing ovation for what felt like five minutes! John Gorman, who went on to be the assistant manager of England under Glenn Hoddle, was playing for Phoenix in that game and he couldn't believe it, just as those in attendance at the dinner couldn't.

The NASL played an integral part in establishing football interest in North America. After the outdoor game folded the national team was filled with players who weren't contracted to clubs for a number of years. It took a long time, almost ten years, until a structure was put in place for the MLS to be created. I scored forty three goals in the outdoor game in North America. I'd score goals wherever I'd played, it was one of my strengths, but the record proved that I was still capable after my injuries.

The indoor league had also seen me score goals by the hatful though I still wouldn't class that as the game that I knew and loved. I was confident in my ability to play and score but I knew in 1985, at the age of thirty one, that I would never get back to the way I played in my prime. I'd come to terms with that. If I hadn't got injured, I wouldn't have left England when I did, I would have continued to fight for a top level career.

When I left QPR to go to Montreal I had a new found freedom that allowed me to express myself and I was able to rediscover my game. The collapse of the outdoor game in North America and the failed attempt to re-ignite it in Canada meant that I still had an unfinished chapter in my on-pitch career. I had done it all and seen it all in the American game and felt a sense of completion which made me feel that despite all the problems, I had a great career, and that gave me a wonderful sense of optimism when reaching my next decision. I wanted to finish my career playing outdoors and I knew I would have to go back to Europe in order to do it. The big question was, having played indoors, would I be able to adapt to playing the outside game once again?

9

Back to Europe

After deciding to move back to Europe to finish my career in the outdoor game, I now had to find a club. Harry Redknapp's Bournemouth were in the Third Division but had been in the headlines when they knocked out the FA Cup holders, my old club Manchester United, in the 1984 competition. I went down there for a couple of days and took my family as Harry said he would cover the expenses, but when it came to a deal he said they couldn't afford to sign me. We moved back north to try and get settled and bought a house in Box Tree Mews, Macclesfield. While I was looking for a club Ron Atkinson, who was still at United, would run Friday afternoon games for a bit of relaxation and he'd ask a few of the old boys to go down to the Cliff and play. I could still play and every now and then I'd do something that would make him turn and exclaim that he knew he should have signed me.

It was good fun, but I never thought of it as anything more than a nice compliment. I was a lot more confident than I had been when I left England to go over to Canada and I was on the lookout for a club, but I was never going to beg Ron to give me a chance. I was looking to settle in Macclesfield having just bought that house there but I certainly didn't look at those sessions at the Cliff as any serious way back to playing at United. I was only thirty one, so who knows what might have happened if I'd played those years in between injury free, but when a serious offer came up I had to think about it.

I got a call from FC Twente in Holland, and though they

knew I wasn't in the best of condition I went over for a trial anyway. At the end of the trial they offered me a deal but I had a clause inserted into it saying that if my knee went again we could terminate the contract, shake hands and walk away. I was confident that I could do well and was determined to do so but I didn't want them to feel like they were taking a risk on me.

The coach at FC Twente was Fritz Korbach, God rest his soul, and he had assembled a good squad of Dutch players. It was nice to see Dutch football. The club had a community system where they were part of the town. It was a nice club with a great following and upon seeing that I was instantly attracted to the idea of playing there. For such a long time I'd admired Dutch football and now, seeing it up close and how much the clubs were associated with their communities, it really made me think it would be the right place for me.

Because I had played indoor football for so long I was absolutely awful in those early weeks. The indoor game is short and sharp but because of how quick it is, it takes it out of you, and it took me some while to adjust. One of my first games was against Heracles and I just couldn't get going and that was just symptomatic of my first six months there. They beat us 3-1 and I couldn't get past a defender to save my life. It hurt me a lot to have played so poorly and there were a couple of things I could do as a result. I could call it a day, or I could go back home and put it down to a bad experience. But I was damned if I was going to have my final memory as a professional be such a let down, and the only thing for it was to get myself in a position where I was happy with the way I was playing.

When I say there were options, there was only one thing I was going to do. I wasn't comfortable with the lingering perception that I'd 'disappeared' from the English game and I was not happy with how my return to the game had been viewed in Holland. It wasn't in me to give up and I wasn't going to do that. More than having to justify it to the Twente supporters or the footballing people in Holland, I had an obligation to myself, a professional pride that there was no way I was going to allow my return to be consigned to such disappointment. I was thirty one, but any professional who is in love with the game will tell you, especially if they've suffered an injury that robbed them of their true potential, there's no way you can allow yourself to just fade out of everything. Some may say that was the case anyway but I was not about to accept that. I was going to fight with everything in me to make sure I did myself justice.

So, with that in mind, it was back on the training pitch to improve and get used to the game once again. At Christmas time I was training three times a day and I honestly didn't mind. In the morning there were five or six professionals there, and in the afternoon all the semi-professionals that made up the rest of the squad came in after they had finished their other jobs. Freddy Rutten had been there for some time as part of his very long association with the club as both player and later manager. He also went on to coach a very good Schalke side in Germany.

I found everyone in Holland very pleasant. Fritz saw in training that I was still capable and felt I was worth persisting with so he encouraged me. I was trying my best but it just felt difficult and something wasn't quite working. It must have been the indoor game that was still in my system as physically I felt okay. The astro turf surfaces are notoriously bad for knees and I'd come through that okay, but now I was just struggling to come to terms with the outdoor game which, I suppose, wasn't a surprise considering I'd been away from Europe for so long.

FC Twente were also struggling. We played against Ajax at home and were thumped about 9-2. Fritz asked me afterwards what I would have done. The Ajax team was brilliant, but it wasn't the team of 1976 even though it had Ronald Koeman, Frank Rijkaard, Marco van Basten and was managed by Johan Cruyff. I just told Fritz that we should have closed them down and paid them less respect, but in 1986 perhaps that was easier said than done. Ajax, PSV Eindhoven and Feyenoord all had full-time professional teams and as such were very much the top three. It was a scenario like Scottish football has been for most of its history. That made it difficult for other teams who simply didn't have the resources to compete.

Away from those three though, the league was fairly competitive with evenly matched teams and it was great when a good player came through and they'd get signed by one of the top clubs. The boys knew how good Ajax were but after our heavy defeat they looked like they didn't know what had hit them. I was not surprised as I knew what they could do with the difference in class. They had admired Ajax instead of pressing them.

Fritz thanked me for my opinion. We had another discussion about my future and although I'd tried my best, I had decided that I wasn't going to play the second half of the season. I said I'd had enough and I just couldn't click into the outdoor game. In training sessions I could still light up the sky but it wasn't happening on the pitch. Fritz persuaded me to play against Heracles in the return fixture against them amid talk in the press that I was finished and it was clear I didn't have it anymore. Perhaps I was given extra motivation by that, or maybe I felt free as I had almost certainly decided I was leaving, but I had a blinder scoring twice and burning the defender who had laughed at me in the first game. After the match Fritz told me that I had got my form back. I said I didn't know but Fritz had seen enough to convince me to stay and play the following weekend. Once again I played well and scored a marvellous goal. Now I'd finally found my feet again I agreed to stay.

I had a really great time there for the rest of the season, and towards the end of the campaign as I was faced with the choice of staying another year or going home, I had support from many of my team-mates who were sure I could play for another year or two. Twente had finished above the relegation places so would play in the Eredivisie. After Fritz had taken on board what I'd said, we got a 1-1 draw in Ajax in a game where I hit the bar from about forty yards. There were good players in the team, too, not least the goalkeeper Theo Snelders. He was so good that I recommended him to Man United. They ignored my advice and signed Jim Leighton from Aberdeen while funnily enough, the Scottish side signed Snelders who went on to have a great career at Pittodrie.

While at Twente, I was also made aware of another talented individual, a young boy who had travelled over with the Newcastle youth team to play some friendly games in Holland. Because of my background and the set up with semi-professional players in the league, I was known as Twente's 'star' and so was often introduced to teams and players. Anyway, as we played our games on Sundays, Newcastle were at Twente in a small tournament on the Saturday, and I walked down to the ground to watch them play. It was a nice afternoon and as it went on one of the Newcastle coaches recognised me and came over for a chat. He told me that they had a player with them who deserved a look as he was flamboyant, and played with his instincts just like me. He told me his name was Paul Gascoigne and that he was already some player.

He was brought over and introduced to me saying that it was a great, great honour to meet me. I knew straight away he was a player who would make his mark, very much a controller of the game, and he was all over the place. I could see he would be the future for England as he played with such a childlike enthusiasm and that never left him. Even when I watched him play years later, he would do things that reminded me of watching him that afternoon in Holland. It was lovely to see.

Sadly we all know what happened to Gazza later in his life and I, like so many others, wish I could do something to help. I have suffered from personal issues and I was on the brink but I was able to put everything into perspective when I saw people who suffered from real afflictions and handicaps and then compared it to my own minor problems. Paul had everything but was also surrounded by so many of the wrong people who used him. Sometimes maybe it's better to have no-one. I had nobody when I was in that bar in Derbyshire, I was injured and my daughter had been taken away from me. Well, I thought I had no-one, but it still humbles me to think of the compassion and generosity of others and that attitude rubs off on you. I often wanted to reach out to Gazza and offer my help as what happened to him really saddens me. When thinking of him, I prefer to see that enthusiastic kid with the world at his feet who gave pleasure to those who watched him play.

As for my own future, I had to be honest and say I missed my family who hadn't come to live in Holland with me. Sam was going to school in Macclesfield so we couldn't take him out and I wanted to go home and be with them. I planned to do just that when I got a surprise call offering me a short term move to Finnish Champions HJK Helsinki for a couple of games. I went over and scored a couple of goals for them in a brief stay. Their season was short and I was only there for a month. I had a smashing time staying in the centre of Helsinki, though I had to get big heavy curtains to keep out the daylight in the land of the never-setting sun. It really was beautiful there, but I knew that I had to go home to be with my family.

I wasn't back long before Stuart Pearson, my old pal at Man United, found out I was home and asked me if I fancied going to play semi-professionally at Northwich Victoria where he was managing. No-one had come in for me for a full-time contract even though I'd had a strong second half of the season in Holland's top division.

I decided I wasn't going to play any more I was going to retire, but Stuart convinced me to turn out for a few games. Northwich are a very traditional club and were in the Conference. They played at the Drill Field close to where I lived so I could train on Tuesdays and Thursdays just down the road. I did very well there, contributing to help keep them up.

It was good enough for me but not for Stuart, who left his post as manager. Afterwards, I was given the keys by the board and asked to become player/manager. I didn't want to do that as I wasn't ready to play with others and then stand and criticize them from the sidelines. I was enjoying my time there, but then Ron Reid asked me if I would go and play for Stafford Rangers.

After a year at Northwich, I took Ron up on his offer and played for a short while in Stafford. The problem there was that it was quite a bit of travel, so when Northwich called me and asked me to go back and help them as they were down the bottom again, I took them up on their offer – and I was able to help them stay up. Moving down the levels, with all due respect, I was able to show the kind of form I'd shown at higher levels, and furthermore I was confident in expressing my natural game too.

My second spell at Northwich was notable for my second career red card, the third if you count the one I got as a child. I'd accepted the red card at Derby as I was in the wrong and it was out of character for me to react in the way I had. However, the red card given to me while playing for Northwich was a completely different kettle of fish. The referee accused me of spitting in a game, ironically enough against Stafford, and I would never stoop so low in a million years as to do something as disgusting as that. A decision went against me so I asked him politely, what the decision was for and he just turned around and held up the red card. I asked him what for and he never even answered, so off I went as one of the directors went bonkers at the referee as well.

Later on it transpired that he manufactured the tale that I had spat at him. I didn't even realise until I turned up for training on the Tuesday and there was a letter inviting me to an FA hearing. I couldn't believe it but I was determined to have that hearing and clear my name, and I had been lucky that it was right in front of the Director's box so they could vouch for the fact I'd never spat at anybody. I went to Nottingham Forest for a hearing and the Northwich chairman Derek Nuttall came with me, the referee was there too. The panel was made up of a few people I recognised, including the Liverpool chairman, and I just asked them if they thought I was capable of something like that, bearing in mind that I was in a position where I was setting an example to kids. I was let off and I never saw that referee again. Maybe he just wasn't a United fan!

It was nice to be revered by the supporters who had really taken to me and I had a high point in a local derby game against Altrincham. Jeff Wealands, who had played about eight games for Man United, was in their goal and they had a good side with a strong history of giant killing in the FA Cup. Their manager had kept blasting Jeff, telling him not to kick the ball down the middle but he ignored the advice and did just that. When it came to me just behind the halfway line, I chested it and volleyed it back into the net. Everyone was full of praise with the chairman saying I was the best player to play the non-professional game. I would put the ball in the net from anywhere though, that's just what I'd done my entire career.

The best run in football is the one back to the halfway line after you've scored and I didn't have far to walk at all after my goal. I'd still got some of the magic and it wasn't as if it was easy playing at that level. After all I was now thirty four, I'd had my injuries, and I came with a reputation which meant everyone liked to have a kick when they could. They wanted a name, but even then

I wasn't going to give it to them.

I have such fondness for my time at Northwich and the club itself. I also loved going back and watching games there after I had finished playing for them. I had started the game at semi-professional level and gone on to play for the very top team. I had gone around the world before the game that I love brought me home and back to my roots in the sport. Yes, it would have been nice to have had a longer career at the top and finished my career there, but this was the path I had been given and it wasn't due to lack of ability that I'd not done so.

In finishing up playing the semi-pro game at a local level and still managing to impress, my career had come full circle and had a nice sense of closure. It gave me some fantastic memories and a sense of returning home to where I came from. To watch kids make their way in the manner I did, working at very well respected semi-professional clubs, was very much a joy of mine. I loved going back to Northwich and watching the game at its purest, at grass roots level. When Sammy McIlroy was at Macclesfield I would go and watch there as well.

My attraction to football and my passion and love for the game is for the sport itself. It's in my blood, it's in the blood of thousands of others like me, and I was happy to have had the chance to finish my career playing outdoors in a way that had seen me return to my roots.

While I was playing as a semi-professional I owned a sports shop which Bryan Robson came and opened for me. I would teach tennis and re-string racquets, as well as teach a class in Macclesfield about football. I was delighted when players I coached managed to get professional contracts but I have to say that being behind a counter in a shop wasn't me. I enjoyed it, and it's nice to this day that some people say pleasant things about their memories of it, but I've always been someone who wants to be actively involved in football and maybe taking that short time out strengthened that feeling.

*****

April 15th, 1989, some months after hanging up my boots, I went to watch the FA Cup semi-final between Nottingham Forest and

Liverpool. The venue was Hillsborough and I went there with a close friend called David Brown. I thought nothing of it, as would normally be the case at any other football match. From what I saw, the police and the FA made a ricket when they put the Liverpool fans in the wrong end. We were sat down about half an hour before kick off in the main stand. We knew there was going to be a big crowd there, after all there always was at Hillsborough as that was the traditional home for the semi-finals.

It started to fill up with people coming through the tunnels and it all seemed quite jovial as where we were sat there were a mixture of supporters, Liverpool fans, Forest fans, all with plenty of conversation. Some people were asking for autographs, others asking me who I thought would win, so no different to any other game. Hillsborough was of course, a special place for me. David said that he could still picture my goals, one at the Kop end and one the other end. Now THAT was a semi final.

I reminded him that Stevie had scored a great goal at the ground against Leeds too. The stadium owned so many memories. It was so special. As kick-off got closer I said to Dave that I was worried about what was happening in the Liverpool end, 'They're going to be squashed to death in there, Dave.' I didn't know what the hell was happening nor how prophetic my words would be.

You could see people's faces being squashed up against the bars and then we heard that the doors had been locked. What were they playing at? Who gave a toss about the game at that point? It's only a game. Everyone in the stand was screaming for them to open the gates as everything bottlenecked, people were suffocating, and it happened in no time at all. It was chaotic, nobody was interested in the football!

Observing Bruce Grobbelaar realise that something tragic was happening was a sobering moment. The police reacted but by that time it was too late. The game stopped, the players were stunned. Seeing the fans on the pitch and watching them move bodies on advertising boards was absolutely horrific. I couldn't stand anymore, I couldn't watch it, I was too shaken and I didn't want to see anymore. I'll never forget it, seeing all those ambulances. Walking away was one of the most harrowing and sickening experiences.

I didn't find out until later that my sister-in-law Bridget's sister had sadly died in the disaster with her boyfriend. I was floored. I said that I was so sad and sorry, but they were just words. She was watching her football team with the person she loved in a city where she was attending university. Her whole life gone for nothing. Such a tragic loss.

Unsurprisingly it changed how I remember Hillsborough. It had gone from giving me so much pleasure to a place that was bone-chilling in a matter of minutes. I had seen hooliganism and I had seen supporters behaving badly on the terraces but to me, the Liverpool supporters were wrongly given the blame for a long time. It was an accident that had been waiting to happen for some time due to the almost barbaric way supporters were treated and caged, and it disgusted me as time went on that those responsible dodged accountability. Lives were lost. Nobody should go to a football match and not go home afterwards.

*****

The spell at Northwich Victoria had been my last as a footballer, professional or not, though I made no official announcement about retiring. As far as I'm concerned I never retired, I just gave up playing. Even so, you have to come to a stage where you say enough is enough. I would play in charity matches but I wasn't ready to commit myself to another team.

I had done my coaching badges and was looking at what I was going to do in terms of management, but because I'd been a professional for so long I still had to adapt to being out of the game. Even when I wasn't playing, every Saturday at 5pm was when I would have a bath. Instead of reflecting on what had been, I was faced with the struggle of every day life wondering what would I do for a living now I'd finished playing.

I had saved some money for my pension but it was never going to make my life comfortable forevermore. Your run-of-the-mill squad player in today's Premier League earns more in a year than most players did in their entire career. I earned £25 a week at Millwall which went up to £60 when I signed for United and eventually to £275. I earned £400 a week at Derby and £425 at QPR. Even so, I wouldn't have given it up or swapped my time for anyone.

I had some great advice from Ken Merritt who looked after the payroll when I was at United. He told me to think of the future, and put me in touch with an accountant friend, Phil Gabby, who sorted me out with a private pension. I put my signing on fee in that and topped it up. When I couldn't put any more into it, I took out a second pension with Abbey Life which turned out to be a waste of money. I was even more grateful to Ken for his help in getting me a secure pension.

I have no regrets about the way my playing career went. Of course there are 'what ifs' and of course there are moments when I'd still love to be playing – tell me an ex-professional who wouldn't. I had ambitions of winning trophies that I didn't get the chance to and also playing in the World Cup which I never managed. It was sometimes difficult to deal with, especially when I was going through the worst part of my injury hell at Derby. I've never been one to take anything for granted though, and I've always been grateful for what I did have. I look at my record of scoring great goals and my good goal to game ratio and I scratch my head wondering what might have been if the Doc hadn't been sacked or I hadn't got injured.

The one thing that upset me at the time was talk that I was 'here today, gone tomorrow' but that wasn't my talent it was my injury. I think I would have preferred a broken leg rather than the knee injury I had given the respective problems in healing, but I am not bitter about it. How can I be bitter after learning the ropes at Millwall and playing for the biggest club in the game? How can I be bitter about the path that was laid out for me, even with my injury, when that path led me to my wife?

When going back I can look at a period from 1975 to 1978 when I was an attacking player and top goalscorer for the most exciting team in the world. It warms me greatly to hear the nice things that people say about what they saw me do, or how good they thought I was. I could never surpass George, Denis or Bobby but I hope for the time that I was at Old Trafford that I gave those supporters as much excitement as anyone did. At the end of the day they were great, incomparable players but they were people just as we were. I got just as much pleasure and thrills from playing with Sammy McIlroy, Lou Macari and Stuart Pearson as I'm sure Bobby did with Denis and George. The era that we played in was United once again at their best and most exciting and to be a part of that was something incredible.

I knew that I had to get involved with the game again but for the first time I felt perhaps held back by the stigma that had been attached to me. I was a joker and somebody not to be taken seriously. At least, that was the memory associated with me in England. I had been carefree at Millwall and Manchester United, but that was just my personality, my character. But because I liked to be the one who would try and lift spirits, people wrongly assumed I wasn't serious, yet as I've already explained, losing a game hurt me deeply and I would often think about it and dwell on it afterwards.

To this day, people ask me about the Cup Finals in 1976 and 1977 and I wish I could go back and play them again. Not because it was a great day and a brilliant feeling to win the Cup in 1977, but because I was so unhappy with my own contribution that I would have loved the opportunity to do it again and do it properly so I could show the 'REAL' Gordon Hill. And that was serious to me.

I had what couldn't and can't be taught, and that was a winner's mentality, and more than that, a professional desire to be the best I could personally be. I hoped to be able to at least pass on some of that experience and put forward my own ideas but without a situation I couldn't really propose hypothetical ideas. I can't say that I was turned down for any opportunities as the 1990s beckoned but then I wasn't put forward for any either. Football can be an environment that is very much 'jobs for the boys' and I had been out of the English game, or the spotlight in England at least, for quite a while. I'll tell you what is funny though, years later, when I did get looked over for positions, it would be said that I'd been out of the English game for too long. And who gets the jobs? Foreign managers!

There was a meeting with the FA to talk about flair players with a bunch of people who hadn't even played the game. Sometimes you can't make it up. I've been all around the world and seen players from all continents and cultures and yet get overlooked for positions in my own country. Back in 1991, when something did come up, it was no surprise that it was from a place where they knew I meant business.

10

North West, Nova Scotia, North West

They say football is a funny old game. Even Tommy Docherty, who said so many nice things about me, said I couldn't be coached, and as I've documented earlier in my story, Dave Sexton tried his best to get me to watch videos and that didn't make me change my game. So I guess you might ask, why did Gordon Hill decide to become a manager? The first thing I thought was, 'tactics? What the hell are they?' I chuckle to myself thinking about it, but that's not to say that I wasn't going to approach being a football manager with the seriousness and the dedication I'd shown as a player.

Having put all I had into the playing side, I now wanted to put that experience to good use by trying to bring through players. My style as a player had always been to try and express myself and entertain and my number one philosophy was to instil that into my teams and players too. You would hear, 'Football is a simple game complicated by coaches,' and to an extent that's true. I would try and keep it simple, though not ignoring the essential basics of the game. The best form of defence is attack and I was very much of the same mindset as the Doc had when he managed Manchester United when he would say that he didn't mind them scoring one as long as we scored two. That's the objective of the game after all. I'm not a fan of playing with one striker and fewer forwards. There's a natural consequence to that in having fewer opportunities to score and to me, that is

170

against the natural principle of the game. I sought advice from others and took courses in management with the likes of Sammy Lee, and I also looked for guidance from certain individuals.

Being the kind of player that I became, I was never going to be able to physically teach people what I did, but what I planned to share were the fundamentals that I grew up with and then hopefully develop similar players that way. The way I see it, football management is just like every other aspect of the game. There are periods of evolution but the success of a certain tactic has as much to do with your opponent as it does with your own team, and the game has never changed. Management, as far as I can see, is much the same as it had been when I played, and I honestly feel that since the time I was managing until the present day it hasn't changed.

Picking a management team today I'd have alongside me a top class goalkeeper, defender, midfielder and forward. There can be nothing better than a team that you can rely on and a team you can expect to cover the various aspects of the game. It's no coincidence that you see managers of whatever era moving from club to club with the same backroom staff. The manager is there to make a decision but it is a collective decision. My ambition and objective was to do exactly what I did as a player and that was to put as much enjoyment back into the game as possible. As free spirited as I was as a player, I did have some discipline and I knew when I had to muck in. I might not have been the best at doing that but I didn't shirk my responsibilities.

As is par for the course, though, I wouldn't be cutting my managerial teeth in any conventional role now I had settled back in England. I was contacted by John McGrane, a very good friend who was part of the Canadian Soccer Association and manager of a club in Hamilton. He told me about a new franchise that was being developed in Nova Scotia called the Nova Scotia Clippers and they were to play in the Canadian Soccer League. I'd taken my Canadian License so agreed to go out there and meet a guy called Stan Brechin who was the owner. I took the role as it was a good chance to prove myself so I left a temporary job at Hyde United which had been recommended to me by Martin Buchan. It was a nice experience but I wanted to go on to a higher level.

The Clippers were so called because it was a sea port. In fact it was the sea port where the survivors of the Titanic were brought back to. The hospitality shown to me by Stan was first class, absolutely sensational. His wife Moira was fantastic and his daughters were really lovely too. The league was sponsored by Umbro and there was a package sorted with the airlines so that the teams would put around $50,000 in a pot and the airlines would fly us around.

There were some good sides in the league, Vancouver, Toronto, and Montreal Supra where, funnily enough, Eddie Firmani was coaching. I was able to get in a couple of Danish and Canadian players. The hotbed for players at that time was in Toronto so we went there for the draft. We were allowed first pick because we were a new franchise. My first choice was a player called Tommy Kouzmanis who had one of the best left foots in Canada. We could trade with other clubs and naturally we got offers for Tommy immediately, some putting up numerous players as a trade, but I refused because I was building a side to compete and win, not just make up the numbers. Tommy wanted to come and work with me which was nice. We also got a couple of players from Toronto and paid for their rent and housing in Nova Scotia.

We had a very good pre-season in North Nova Scotia with fantastic fresh air and it was great preparation. I was determined that we would get off to a good start in the league and I was also playing. The first game was against Vancouver and we drew 1-1 which was a great result that set us up for a game at home against Winnipeg Fury. I scored two goals to record a first win for a professional franchise in Nova Scotia. To keep the cost down, we'd play a couple of games on the road and then come home.

We built a competitive side with good results and playing in a way I felt was what I wanted to see. Unfortunately, Tommy suffered an anterior cruciate ligament injury just a few games into the season which was a big blow. It was the same injury that I'd had so I felt a lot of sympathy. I was enjoying educating his left foot but it was now my left foot that I was depending on again. We did have some good players including a kid called Dino Lopez, who was a centre half, and went on to play for Canada, as did Tommy. Also we had a great goalkeeper in Shel Brodsgaard and

I'd picked up a cracking player called Kevin Wasden, an Indian from Western Canada who sadly died in a car crash back on his reservation in January of 1992.

The Clippers qualified for the play-offs with a few games to spare so I'd done my job. In those play offs we met North York and were beaten 4-0. When we were due to play them in the return game, Stan told me that even if we won we wouldn't be able to afford to fly over to Vancouver but I said that there was no chance of us giving up. Stan insisted that we couldn't afford it, but I said that there was no way any team of mine was going to lie down. As it happened, at half time we were 1-0 up and I'd scored the goal. Stan came in to the dressing room, looked at me, then said that he knew I would do that.

We lost the game and because of the financial situation it was the last game for the franchise too. It was a struggle for Stan who put his money into the team and, bless his heart, did everything he could for it to survive.

I was offered the job at Montreal because Eddie left, but I said I wouldn't leave a sinking ship at Nova Scotia. It's the spirit I've always had, I wanted to stay with the club to the end. I was well loved in Montreal but even when we went over there to play, I thought it was only fair that I put the team out and watched from the sidelines. I wanted them to see my boys and what they could do. Funnily enough, the Canadian Open was on at the time and I got a chance to meet my old pal John Lloyd who introduced me to his wife Chris Evert.

After the Nova Scotia spell, I moved to Tampa where I coached a club called the Countryside Lightning, helping to develop a program for the younger players. We had lots of teams and it was tremendous fun. It was a great insight to coaching in America and how I could put my own experience to good use. We won seven state championships in different age groups in a single year.

North America were looking forward to hosting the 1994 World Cup and as such they were re-launching their national league as the MLS. I went over to Orlando where Ireland were based for the Holland game and had a really good time meeting everyone there after Jack Charlton invited me over to spend a little time with the squad. As someone who had invested so much time and effort into the North American game, I was proud that they finally got to host the World Cup, even though I have to confess I was surprised that it was awarded to a nation that didn't have an existing league at the time. That said, I felt they did a wonderful job of hosting and promoting the tournament. I was there for about three years before deciding it was time to go back to the United Kingdom.

*****

In February of 1998 I got a call from my brother to tell me that Dad was in hospital with heavy congestion and bronchitis on his lungs. I knew it was serious, as they wouldn't have called me to get down there from Manchester if it wasn't. I went to the hospital to see him and sat at the end of the bed and rubbed his feet. Dad looked at me and then the doctor and said, 'This is my Gordon.' I went back north the next day and received a phone call to tell me he'd passed away and I was devastated.

I went down for the funeral in my new car and I was just outside Ealing when somebody crashed into the side of it with me and my family inside. Thankfully, nobody was hurt and we were able to get to the funeral where I insisted on being a pall bearer. I can't believe how much I cried when my dad died. He didn't tend to shower us with love and affection simply because there were so many of us, but he did care for us and always wanted to know how and where we were.

Afterwards, we drove back to Manchester in a naturally sombre mood, and parked up in the driveway, smashed car and all. The next morning my son Sam called to me to ask if I had left the car door open overnight. It had been broken into by a drug dealer from Macclesfield who had stolen things from inside. The police caught him but it's fair to say that it was a dreadful week.

I was doing a programme for Sky Sports in the early New Year of 1999, about eleven months after my Dad passed away. The programme was in Twickenham by the Gillette building where Sky had their offices. I called Mum and asked if it would be okay if I stayed with her. She said it was fine and insisted that she would make me breakfast, after all I'd been the only one that had moved around, as my brothers and sisters had all stayed fairly local.

The following morning I got up to leave, telling Mum that I loved her lots, that I would be working only up the road, and would speak to her soon. She said, 'Don't be afraid to call.' The next day, my brother called to tell me that Mum had a heart attack and died instantly. It absolutely broke my heart, I cried and I cried and even now, thinking about it, it brings tears to my eyes.

Something must have told me that I had to go and stay with her because I didn't often do it. Making the journey back down there again in a matter of days felt so very strange. In the house I looked out of the back window and saw my dad's shed down the garden and I'm certain that Mum died of a broken heart. When she died we had so many people there. The local policemen stood at the top of the road with their hands on their heads as a sign of respect.

*****

Because I was living back in the Manchester area, I was involved with the launch of Manchester United's new television channel MUTV, which was launched at the Red Cafe. The person who set it up was previously the sports editor of *The Sun*. I was invited to go on live television to speak about United on a Friday afternoon and also do some commentating on the youth and reserve games with Steve Bower. It was great to watch young players like Ritchie Wellens, and you could more or less tell which players would go on to make the first team and others that likely wouldn't.

Steve and I used to have a lot of fun sat on a rickety old gantry that had been built especially for us. I loved my time working and watching the younger players in particular but I was also pleased for a lot of the reporters who went on to get jobs with Sky. I still had ambitions of getting back into the game as a coach, or manager, or assistant somewhere and when Brian Kidd left his post as Sir Alex's assistant in 1998, I felt it was the right time to step forward and offer my experience. I was forty four, a good age to get back into it all, I knew the club from my time there and I had experience of the game the world over. I had been around the club working on the television side of things, knew the kids and the players there, so felt that I had good credentials to get the role. I applied for the position by letter and received a reply from Sir Alex thanking me but saying he already had someone in mind. In the end he chose Steve McClaren and that was that. I'm sure Steve was the man he wanted anyway but I still felt as if my reputation as a joker was something that did me no favours, that I was not the right man to handle discipline.

I'd passed my coaching courses with flying colours but I don't think I was being taken seriously when I said I wanted a more significant position. As time went on, I was involved with hospitality at games. I'd do a show on Piccadilly Radio with Malcolm Allison and Gary Owen on a Saturday afternoon and I also worked on Sky and the BBC doing punditry work. There were a number of options for former professionals to get involved in with the growth of Sky and their involvement with the Premier League. My friend Imre Varadi, for example, became an agent. I couldn't do that, but I have to say it's better for agents to be former players.

I have plenty to say about agents because it's hardly a revelation to say that most of them are more interested in money than the career development of their clients, but what really gets me is that so many of them are not football people and the money goes out of the game. A prime example is Paul Stretford, the agent of Wayne Rooney. Stretford started out as a vacuum cleaner salesman before he landed on his feet becoming an agent for Frank Stapleton. More recently he's engineered a big bumper contract for Rooney when the player announced he wanted to leave Manchester United in 2010, only to sign a new deal several days later. Then the summer of 2013 saw a similar saga.

If he was a true representative with Wayne's best interests at heart, in my opinion he'd be more concerned with working with Wayne and the club to ensure his top flight career goes well into his thirties. What's a few more thousand quid on top of the millions the best players earn today when you have the opportunity to become the all-time leading goalscorer of Manchester United?

Footballers have short careers, I know that better than anyone, but how can it be that when they are rewarded so handsomely now with everything catered for, the opportunity to establish themselves as a great isn't as enticing or motivating as a few extra thousand quid.

I agreed to sign for Manchester United without even knowing how much I was being paid, and I didn't need an agent for that. I do want to make the point though that Imre isn't like that. As a former player he knows the drill, and accepting that agents will always have a role in the game, it should be the case that former players get into that side of it a lot more. Like I said, that isn't and wasn't my cup of tea and at the age of forty six, although I enjoyed analysing games and discussing the sport, I really wanted to get back into coaching, and my time in Tampa with younger players and watching the kids play at United was to have an influence on my next career path.

11

Chester

Chester was an experience and one that I do count as valuable. It wasn't the best of experiences, I have to admit, but it was one that I had to go through in order to learn. I went there in 2001 because I met the owner Terry Smith, and he convinced me to be Director of Youth Football at the Deva Stadium. The youth system at Chester was in a state as they couldn't get any funding from Sport England or the FA because they hadn't complied with certain regulations which were very tough. The YTS lads weren't getting paid so I had to come in and restructure the whole of the programme.

The League came in to audit us and said that if we were to get to the rest of our Centre of Excellence money from Sport England, which came to about £65,000, we'd have to do certain things that weren't in place. The criteria was tough and I sat with the Football League and Sport England for about four hours to try and sort everything out. We went through all the pages to discuss what we needed to do at Chester, ensuring that all our coaches had licences and that we kept up with the PFA to make sure we never got our licence revoked.

We had about 250 players, some of the best young kids around. We had some good scouts and the mismanagement had not been from their end. The changes didn't happen overnight though I was sometimes in there until ten o'clock in the evening trying to organise everything. Because Chester had already burnt their bridges with certain local organisations it was very difficult to get things sorted. One of the pre-requisites of the agreement was that we had to get a new training ground for the youth players. Unfortunately, the first team had damaged relationships with colleges and universities so I had to go in to see different people to rebuild those bridges. We rented a local sports facility and had to work through the evening to clean up the parks. Not only did we have to make sure that all our coaches were qualified, but they had to go through in-house training and that was my responsibility.

Because of my involvement I wanted to make sure I knew everything. I was also responsible for the auditing and ensuring that everything was above board so that the YTS kids got paid at the end of the week. A good friend of mine called Charles Osula was the Under sixteen YTS coach and we got everything in place so that when I was eventually rewarded for my hard work and given a promotion to Director of Football, I promoted Charles, or Chas as he was known, into my old position. I wanted to make sure that he would run things in the same way, but we always had difficulties because we were in a bit of a precarious position, and other clubs would be trying to poach our players.

Crewe, Man City, Liverpool, Everton, Tranmere, all of them were trying to pinch our players. The league had certain rules that clubs had to follow, but once they had signed terms that was it, we were helpless. At one point we had fifteen compensation claims against other clubs. The only decent club was Everton who paid us £8,000 for an eleven-year-old, and that money paid for the scholars' wages. When you consider the catchment area we were in, with not only the clubs listed above but Manchester United too, it really was a battle to try and get the best kids and develop them.

We had a great scouting network, in particular there was one very special scout named John who really was fantastic and worth his weight in gold. Players are only worth what someone is willing to pay for them and that fluctuates with their form. We had a vast amount of kids who we believed were the best in the area, and even if we made a conservative estimate of every kid being worth £1,000 to the club plus another thousand for every year they were developed by the club, then that meant we obviously had around at least a quarter of a million pounds in collateral. The compensation clause was set by the league. If a player had been with us for three years and an Arsenal or Liverpool came in, then the fee escalated.

The most cost effective result would be that players from your youth system end up in the first team, and we would really hope that the first team would have three or four players from the youth team while the reserves would have been made entirely of academy products.

The most enjoyable part was of course a Saturday when the games came around and we got to watch the kids go out and play. As part of their development, we wanted to introduce them to the game in a similar vein to the schooling apprentices were used to receiving, but there were certain things the PFA wouldn't let youngsters do as jobs. It was a task and a half. We managed to get our funding from Sport England and I had done a good job turning it around. The youth team of a football club is often like a separate entity and with Chester, the reserve team was scrapped as they couldn't afford to keep it running. Everything with the youth system was sorted as we got our training and games organised and I was satisfied with the job I'd done. As Director of Football I was now in a position where I could look over the whole club but I didn't have any input into the managerial side or the first team, and I had no problem with that. Graham Barrow was manager of the first team and that was fine as I had a good relationship with him.

It was a difficult time for the club as the supporters didn't like the owner even though he was putting all his money in. Terry's father, Gerald, had car dealerships in the States but wasn't prepared to put any more money in to help. I went on holiday to Keith Curle's place in Florida, and there I had a call telling me the manager had been sacked and asking if I'd like to take over. I knew for a fact that if I didn't take the opportunity and a new manager came in, he'd probably employ all his own staff and I'd be gone. Everything had been fine with what I'd done and I'd enjoyed my roles at the club but I knew that in order to stay on I'd have to take the manager's job. I'm still friends with Terry Smith, who has since moved back to North America, but because the fans felt that he wasn't putting enough money into the club they treated him in an awful way. Smith had come in to sort out problems from the previous owners after a very low spell for the club had seen them relegated from the Football League into the Conference. This was at a time when there was talk of ITV Digital putting a major cash investment into the Football League. It would prove to be a disaster for many clubs, but for Chester City, a club attempting to regain its League place, you could see why talk of the deal which was imminent caused panic. The board members were trying desperately to get the club back up with the resources they had available because, as far as they knew, the League clubs were about to benefit from a television cash bonanza and they wanted to be among it. The fans naturally wanted to see their team succeed and perhaps shared in some of the panic that it would prove more difficult if we didn't do it immediately.

The supporters were protesting every week and with me being a friend of Terry's, it only wound them up even further. I could see what they could see, that despite everyone's best efforts, the club was gradually folding, so I did what was the best thing I could do in my power and that was to try and get the team to play some good football again to get the supporters backing the team. Without their money, the club wasn't going to go anywhere. They were protesting about the chairman but without him, who was going to run the club? Where were they going to find the money? It was costing £45,000 a month to run on wages alone.

I had plans to bring in players and make changes and I brought in the Rose boys, Michael and Stephen, from Manchester United to play left back and midfield. I had some good youngsters and the long term plan was to run the club with that healthy tradition as explained before. Naturally they wanted to move up the footballing ladder and that's the kind of situation I inherited, with players who weren't interested in playing for the club because of the mess it was in, youngsters who didn't want to stay there, and supporters who weren't behind us.

I'd done my best to sort the youth team and felt I'd done well, but the situation with the first team was completely different. Terry was under so much pressure and he was hated so much that he wouldn't turn up at the ground anymore. It became so bad that Terry eventually called it a day and a guy called Steve Vaughan came in. He was supposed to be the new owner, the saviour who would revolutionise everything, but it was all a bit of a mess. The club owed Terry so much money for what the family had put in that before Terry actually did leave, he offered me the club for nothing. The club had a debt of £250,000 and I wasn't about to take it on when it was destined to lose around another half a million a year, it was tough enough being manager.

Having seen what Terry had been through, with supporters finding his house and breaking his windows, I didn't want that kind of pressure. Perhaps the biggest mistake that Terry did make was allowing a couple of supporters on to the board. He should have just kept the board as it was, but that decision made things even more difficult for him. We started to have demonstrations and boycotts so we were losing what little revenue we did have. I saw it as my responsibility to look after the players and make sure that we all concentrated on the football as I wanted the club to survive.

Naturally though, I had players who wanted to move with all that was happening, and it didn't help that with only a skeleton staff running the club, I would often receive a phone call when I was taking training telling me that some emergency had cropped up. So I'd have to leave training to Chris Malkin in order to sort something out so that the club didn't collapse. Players would come in and ask to be moved and I couldn't bring anyone in until they had been signed by another club, but the problem was that they were on such good wages nobody else would touch them.

With morale low, the team wasn't performing either, which meant that they were even less appealing to potential buyers. I was willing to let anyone leave if they wanted, but we didn't have the money to just pay them off. I was honest and upfront with them, saying that if they produced I would be able to help them leave the club.

Mark Wright was interested in our goalkeeper Wayne Brown but wanted to pay on the never never and that was no good to us. We would get clubs taking our players on trials but sending them back because they hadn't impressed enough. I'd had no conventional apprenticeship on my path to becoming a player and if this was my apprenticeship, my baptism in to what club management was all about, I was definitely doing it the hard way.

We were training on Chester racecourse, but then when we couldn't pay our bill, we were kicked off. The only money we had in the bank was for the youth system which I'd worked so hard to set up. Things had become farcical but they were about to take a more surreal turn.

I went into the chairman's office one day, he wasn't there anymore and had left it in a mess, and I saw a safe. I got the keys from the secretary and we opened it up to see eight little cloth bags which the chairman must have missed. The bags were full of pound coins collected from the proceeds of match programmes. I needed £1,200 for the electricity bill and £1,500 for the gas, otherwise they were going to turn off the power and we wouldn't have been able to play any home games. I was able to go down and pay the bills in pound coins. The cash in the safe had come to around £8,000 so after I paid the utilities with it I had to pay the YTS boys and the Centre of Excellence coaches.

I'd get cheques from the chairman on a Friday to pay the players wages and I lost count of the number of times I got calls from the bank at three or four in the afternoon to tell me the cheques had bounced. How was I supposed to get anything out of them? I went to the bank to discuss it with them and they talked with the chairman. We were flat broke and the chairman said that we should use the money from the youth system. I protested, saying that we'd worked hard enough to keep it going for a couple of years, but the chairman had the final word and so I ended up taking £25,000 from that pot to go and pay the players wages in cash on the Saturday to convince them to play.

It was hardly surprising that our form at the start of the 2001/02 season was inconsistent. We lost our first two games but then won our next two against Hayes and at home to Nuneaton. A loss at Barnet was followed by two draws, at home to Telford and away to Farnborough Town. On the eve of our home game against Stalybridge, some guys came with chains to lock up the gates saying they were going to close the ground because we owed the council so I left a message for the chairman. Whenever he did make a rare appearance at the ground, he'd do it overnight so he wasn't hounded or lynched, and he'd leave me little notes in his office saying we needed to sell here or there. In his absence, I'd become the figure of hate for the supporters so I knew exactly how he felt. During one game, I was spat on by someone and we were winning!

My son Sam was in the Chester squad and was also getting criticism. It was unfair as he had done his YTS at Crewe Alexandra, one of the best academies you can get. As a manager I couldn't protect him all of the time and of course, I'm his father so I have my own views. I thought he was a cracking player yet he was getting it in the neck because of his connection to me. I have no problem with anyone having a go at me, they can do it all they like, I can handle it, but start on my family and that's something completely different and uncalled for.

I had plenty of sympathy for the fans and I was working myself to the bone under extreme pressure to try and make things right. It's human nature though when things start to turn personal against you that you begin to lose a bit of that sympathy. I would never say that I came to resent the Chester City supporters, I understood that in difficult times the manager is not always going to be popular, but the level of abuse being aimed at Sam was difficult to stomach.

I was not going to be one to simply walk away. I had ideas and philosophies that I firmly believed in. The groundsman came out and said that he could see what I was trying to do in turning the club around but we had a small section of morons who were hell-bent on destroying the club. Ahead of a midweek away game at Leigh, unbeknown to me, the chairman had sent an email around all the other clubs saying that all of our players were up for sale. Some players from other clubs found out and told some of ours. We got to the stadium at about 6pm and one of the players showed me the email. I could not believe it. I had to put a team out that knew they were being offered around. I was honest and told them I didn't know anything about it, but the players responded by asking how could they play knowing the situation.

They had been let down, but I felt I had been too. I said to them, 'Guys, I'm not telling you this to make everything rosy.

I know a lot of you don't want to be here and I know you don't like what's happening. I want new players in but there's a way of doing it. I can give you some advice, take it or leave it. The best and maybe the only way you have of leaving this club is to go and perform out there on the field. I will make a promise to you that if someone comes in for you, I will let you go. That field out there is your shop window.' We lost 3-0 in front of about 500 people. Surprisingly, one of the players came to me afterwards and asked for a new contract. That was fine, but then he said he wanted an agents fee so I told him he could have the contract without the agents fee.

When we heard that Steve Vaughan was coming in, he said he'd like me to stay on as coach. Nothing changed under him as I didn't have any money to bring anyone in. I had players waiting who had agreed to sign, such as Simon Davies, who would go on to manage the club in 2008. But the same problems remained and it was having a direct impact on our form. That loss at Leigh RMI was the second of six consecutive losses and maybe Steve saw things as being at crisis point and so he decided to bring in Steve Mungall who was reportedly going to be the new manager while I returned to be the Director of Football. Unfortunately it was a façade and my role never changed, it was just bullshit to try and put the fans off. I wouldn't have had any problem with it if Steve Vaughan had said he wanted me to leave the job but as I understood it, Steve Mungall was brought in as my assistant. Perhaps the chairman had a point about deflecting the attention as we won against Hereford on October 9th to end the bad run we'd been on.

I'd had enough by that point and decided to leave. There was too much pressure on me to do too many jobs and the only thing for certain was that I was going to get it in the neck because of how the team were performing on the pitch, no matter how well I did in a particular role. The club was a mess, the players weren't interested and the supporters were crossing the line. I said to the chairman that I felt it would be best if we shook hands and called it a day, he agreed and Steve Mungall took over. I released a statement wishing the club the very best so now the supporters could get past all the nonsense and back to supporting their club.

And Chester was a fantastic club with a great tradition, after all I remember making my England youth debut there.

I got on quite well with Steve Vaughan who had decent ideas for the club to get them back into the league. Sam's contract was paid up by the chairman. I certainly wasn't going to leave him there to put up with anymore of the shit that he had dealt with. I was broken-hearted that it had happened to him and the experience really shook him up and put him off playing. Sam hadn't done badly. He scored the only goal in a game against Nuneaton and they still booed him. There were accusations of nepotism which I found unfair. I love my son dearly and want him to achieve the best he can in life but I felt then and I still feel now that with Sam's background in the game, he was a pretty good catch for Chester. In fact, I felt it was a better move for Chester at the time than it was for Sam.

It's difficult for any player to succeed when the people who are supposed to be behind you are trying their best to bring you down. It would have to be an incredibly thick-skinned or ignorant person or professional to be able to perform to their best in atmospheres where everyone is on your back, almost wishing you to fail. I guess with Chester being close to Liverpool, there was a strong affinity with that club and against Manchester United so maybe my history didn't do me any favours either.

I received a letter about six years later from Wayne Brown, my goalkeeper at Chester. He had been a troublemaker at the club at the time but apologised, saying he thought my training systems had been great. What do you say? I just responded saying thanks, and wished him all the best. Dean Spinks said I was bringing in new ideas and changes that were good but that the club and players weren't exactly ready for them. Because the club weren't winning games the fans weren't patient, and that meant we couldn't put any long term plans in place that would receive support. My primary goal was just to make sure the club survived and I don't think I was wrong in doing that.

My bridges had been burned with management but despite the way everything had turned out at Chester in the end, the time I'd spent working with the kids had inspired me to want to develop youngsters. I'd looked at it and thought and felt that the biggest impression I could leave was to develop and help bring through the players of tomorrow.

I'd spent some time training kids in Macclesfield. I'd seen kids come through in the professional and semi-professional world and I felt that the best chance I had of making a difference was to get in at a time and a level before they started developing bad habits. The thought of making a difference like that appealed to me tremendously as it's an ongoing part of the game. Some things can't be taught, but what you're doing is dealing with the next generation of players, and getting to them at a stage before they are weighed down with the thoughts of tactics or the merciless pursuit of victory. I wanted to instill the desire to entertain and enjoy, give them the opportunity to express themselves, explore the game, show their initiative. You need to take your experience whether good or bad, and turn it into a positive. In one way or another, I have done that ever since I've been involved in the development of youngsters. My next full-time position would be out of the game but still involved with kids, and it would turn out to be one of the most rewarding times of my life.

Before that, however, I was approached about an opportunity in Scotland.

*****

Stenhousemuir were making strides to become the only club, aside from Rangers, to have a proper youth academy and I was approached by journalist Alasdair Ross and John Bagnall, who was in construction and who was to put some money into the club. We made plans to set up the academy and follow the kind of blueprint I'd done at Chester in the youth system. We had found premises and begun planning. The people were fantastic up there, as was the club itself, but there was a cash flow problem within the organisation and when they couldn't quite get their own funds together the project couldn't come together.

It was a shame as the Scottish FA had become involved and Alasdair was working hard on getting funds from them as well, but it really was just a case of the money not being put together by the club. I was really excited about it, I knew there were good players in Scotland and I was looking forward to being the 'football man' in the project and we tried all we could to get it off the ground as I really believed in it. The talent is there and if an independent academy could have been set up then it could probably have worked. It was a shame all round really, Alasdair was the brains behind the operation and it was a great idea, but sadly he died from cancer not long after that.

Those dark days at Chester had provoked a period of reflection. I had to evaluate what I was most passionate about and the one thing that had survived was my enjoyment of the development of young people. I won't say that I fell out of love with the game but for a while I avoided any news of any move back into management.

I like to believe I can deal with most things levelled at me but the problem I had was that I'd done a lot of work at Chester, a lot of work I believed to be very good, and not only had I not got the credit for it but I'd been subjected to disgusting abuse from supporters and my family had been affected. If that was management in the current climate, others were welcome to it. I was only interested in contributing and trying to make a difference. I wasn't really bothered about not getting credit for the work I'd done, but to receive abuse for things that were beyond my control was beyond the pale. In time I got over it and I know that not every managerial opportunity is wrought with those kind of problems, but in the short term I suppose it would be fair to say that I was glad to have a short break from the game.

I became a lecturer of sport and recreation at Macclesfield College where I looked after special needs children on a Monday. The best time I had working there was with that class on a Monday afternoon, I still remember all of them now. I went to the College to see the Principal and he said he wanted to get a greater connection with people and asked me to join. I didn't want to be a teacher, so being a lecturer was great.

Playing in front of 100,000 people was nothing compared to Monday afternoons spent in the gym with my students. I coached the College team, and would coach values and ethics for NVQ students, teaching them how to plan and organise a training session, including the administration side. I still enjoyed my punditry in the media and enjoyed doing work on the television and a little bit of after dinner speaking. My role at the College moved from part-time to full-time and it was really great. I think my proudest moment came when I took them to Old Trafford on the stadium tour. The teaching assistants, Alan and Edith, were fantastic help. The next week we received pictures that the students had taken and put them all over the college. I gave a signed shirt to one of the students, Gareth, who was twenty one and a real diamond and he never took it off! Gareth had a tendency to go to the toilet and be gone all day but one time he went out and came back in to the room, approaching another student, Lisa. He got down on one knee, asking her to marry him and we were all sat there gobsmacked, wondering what she would say, until she finally responded by telling him to stop being so bloody stupid! Oh, we were in hysterics!

It was all good fun but there's talking about the game and there's being involved in it, and I still had a great passion for football that I'd managed to find once again, so much so that I wanted to remain actively involved. I had the next steps in my life which I wanted, and had to do, but because it meant moving back to America, it naturally meant leaving the College and that was a sad day. Everyone, including myself, was very emotional when I went in to tell them I was leaving. I gave Chas Osula my job. I could have stayed there, teaching at college and being involved with United both talking about them and getting to go and watch them, but events in my son's life meant that I was destined to move back to North America.

12

Lone Star

It might be fair to say that the Chester City spell and the Stenhousemuir experience were a pretty close parallel to my time at Derby County and QPR in that I'd tried to re-invigorate my career but for whatever reason it hadn't quite worked out. The first time, I'd gone to America and got back on track over there and that was to happen again. So I suppose if you were looking from the outside you might say that I made a second clean break across the Atlantic and started over again.

It's not that I was looking for fresh starts all the time though. I would have been quite content to have continued at the College together with bits and pieces for United's television channel. We'd carved out a nice little life in Tytherington in the UK where everyone knew us. And I'd probably settled more in the Macclesfield area than anywhere else I'd lived. In the time we were there we saw a lot of young people grow up and become young adults, getting married and having children, and I suppose when you think of it like that it has a settling effect on you personally. I lived around the corner from Joe Corrigan and I opened up the local sports club with him. Sam had gone to school in Tytherington and a lot of his friends were there too. But after what happened at Chester, Sam decided to try his luck in the States, and so he went to Texas.

We would go and visit him as often as we could and we were clocking up a lot of air miles. Claire was working for the Emirates Airline at Manchester Airport and one day she said she was wondering if we might be able to get our green card back and move out to the States. A close friend of mine, Jeff Coleman, asked me to go over there to coach as there were loads of jobs and he knew we would love it. I would stay with Jeff in his lovely house in Dallas when I visited Sam, so I knew the State well and after some consideration, Claire and I decided that we'd try get our green card back. Claire was desperately missing Sam who was on his own.

One of the saddest things that I've ever had to do was say goodbye to Sam at the end of visiting him. We'd more or less decided to make the move anyway, but what made our minds up was learning that Sam had been involved in an incident at a store. He had been held up at gunpoint by someone who wanted his money. He was a college student with little money but he gave him what little he had and the thief got away. Being four thousand miles away we felt helpless so that was that, we knew we had to get out there.

We learned that because of my status, we could get a green card so we sold our house and moved into a friend's house in Wilmslow while Claire picked out a house in McKinney, Texas which looked very similar to a UK style house. It was a lovely five bedroom and four bathroom house which we bought for the same price as we sold our smaller house in England.

Jeff dabbled in commercial real estate so he did the closing for us, but when we first moved into the house we had nothing as it was all in storage. The only thing I'd seen of the house was pictures that Claire sent me. She had fallen in love with it and had already planned what she wanted to do with it. When I first got there, she told me not to look at the wallpaper, just walk through and look at the pool. But it was great because I knew Claire felt at home, and that was perfect for me knowing she has a magic touch with houses. We bought a television and a bed and we arranged it so we would have the downstairs of the house and Sam could have the upstairs. Over time, his girlfriend Kiley moved in too.

I was given a little bit of coaching work to begin with at the Texas Spurs, later to become Texas Football Club, but before long I was given full responsibility. The problem was that the club was being micro-managed and that didn't sit well with me. They were doing it their own way and I'd forgotten more than most of them knew about the game. So I decided to set up my own little club and called them United FC. We played in red and white, had half-a-dozen teams there, and were sponsored by Umbro. It was a nice little business that I hoped I could pass on to Sam later on so he could make a good living from it, and not have to worry about listening to people who don't know what they're talking about.

Claire did the books and made sure all the taxes and ordering systems were in place. For nearly seven years we traded with teams and set up camps. The intention was to develop a centre of excellence but the problem we had was that many coaches in North America thought as soon as they had kicked a ball that they knew the game inside out. We also had the opposite problem with coaches coming from Europe who thought just because they had kicked a ball they could teach the game. Some of them didn't even have licenses!

I had the UEFA A license, the best I could get, but they said it wasn't recognised by the United States. Now that wouldn't be so bad if I didn't encounter instances of people blatantly lying about their past. One guy said he'd played for Newcastle, another said he'd played 350 professional games but I doubt he played fifty.

It was no secret that in setting up the club with the name and colours of Manchester United I would do my best to steer any talented prospects to my old club, but the most important thing to me was that we developed the young players and made them into potential professionals for the good of the North American game. I'd been involved in the game in the country since 1975 and I had a passion to see it succeed.

Unfortunately it became very political and after seven years of doing it, I'd had enough of all the rubbish that went with it. Running United FC was fine, but when we went to tournaments and met with other clubs, you'd get to meet the people who ran them and it just felt like a money-making machine rather than having a sincere interest in the development of the youngsters.

United FC wasn't run with the most expensive facilities but it cost around $2,500 per player per season to run. You would have to pay for uniforms and tournament entry fees on top of that, and the system was such that camps were obligatory and the parents had to pay for them out of their own pocket. That didn't feel right to me. I felt that a system could be set up where it would still be paid but you didn't have to rob people to do it. I wouldn't charge anywhere near the same prices as other clubs. For what they were paying though, they were getting a professional.

My primary desire was to bring great players through, but it would upset me when a kid would have to stop attending because their parents couldn't afford it. More often than not I'd just keep taking the kid anyway without pay as money shouldn't be an object when it comes to developing a young player. The government set up a development programme but that still came with a fee. How can you have an elitist system like that, potentially punishing your better prospects?

I was seeing things I didn't like. There were so-called managers who would take their teams to camps or tournaments and if they flew, the kids would be in economy while the manager would be in first class. That's taking advantage and how can you do that when every spare cent, should be put back into helping the kids develop?

Everything was dollar and status. Added to that, the entire development system in North American sports is much different to how it is in the UK as they have the National Collegiate Athletic Association which they have go to through and then there is also the draft pick. There needs to be some kind of flexibility with the NCAA so that a culture of excellence can start earlier, around the age of nine, ten or eleven in the same way that it is everywhere else. But in the USA there is standardisation, a belief that putting it across the same development programme as their other major sports is what will be best and what will eventually help the popularity of the game. Unfortunately with this mindset they are ignoring all the developments that have happened across the rest of the world. It's as if they are trying to re-invent the wheel sometimes.

Since 1975 there has been progress but it hasn't been helped at times by what has seemed a constant resistance to FIFA regulations or conforming with what is universally accepted as the standard way to run the game. It's no coincidence that the game has become more popular as they've tampered with it less.

There was so much in the way of politics that it had an impact on what should have been the enjoyable side, just coaching the kids. In addition to all of this, the weather was extreme and being in such heat morning, noon and night, took its toll on me. I'd come home very tired at nights and still people would ask me how I could complain. Well, each to their own.

By this point, Sam and Kiley had moved out after being married for about four years. They were married in McKinney. Kiley is very educated, a fashion designer and a colour specialist for Chico's and as such she was a wanted commodity and received a job offer in Fort Myers, Florida. Sam was the only reason we were in Texas and the only thing that was holding us there, so Claire and I made the decision to wind up United FC and join them in Florida. As for the future of the entire project? Who knows.

It could well be that I decide to do that again in the next few years. I've got the experience of having done it once, and I've got experience of coaching in the Florida climate, but what I wanted to look at was being involved at a higher level. Instead of constantly banging my head against the system, I wanted to try and change the system. I knew that in closing United FC I wouldn't have the aggravation I had, plus it was a hassle for Claire who had to handle so much on the administration side and that wasn't easy for her. At the end of the day, part of my desire for establishing the club in the first place was to create a business and a legacy for Sam to take over, and without him being there I didn't have the same motivation when it came to tackling the red tape. It's something that I would consider in the future, but I'd hope that if and when that time comes, it would be in an environment where there aren't the same kind of obstacles.

*****

With all of my experience and knowing I was staying in North America, the logical next step was to take up coaching youngsters in a situation where I wouldn't be constantly trying to fight for the changes I felt were needed, or perhaps act as an advisor for clubs looking to improve their youth development.

My old friend Joe Raduka got in touch to discuss a couple of situations in Ohio, so I decided to work as a technical advisor for several clubs. I'd known the directors of the respective clubs for a while and as soon as they knew that I was ending my work with United FC they offered me a role. I said it was fine, but wanted to make it clear that I would be based most of the time in Florida but would need digs in Cleveland.

It's not all bad as there are a number of coaches who do want to honestly learn, and hopefully we're all on the right track to building for a better future for the North American game. I hear quite often the phrase, 'We've come a long way in ten years.' Yeah, but so has the rest of the world!

The only way to do it is to jump in the deep end and swim with the big boys to see how it goes. The talent is definitely there, and it is still respectively cheap, but the problems that have gone on in the past and the problems that still exist at youth level will continue to be handicaps to the progression. I've been involved with the game in the United States, on and off, for almost forty years, but there are still some odd little things you come across from time to time. Those guys who lied about their background for instance when they get found out it damages the credibility of all of us. It might surprise a few back home, but several times I've had to send people to my Wikipedia page.

It's not all politics. As I said, there are some coaches who want to learn, and they will be the coaches that establish the culture of excellence for tomorrow. One such coach is Chad Deering, an experienced player and coach who really understands the game and is great to bounce ideas off. He's the kind of coach that if you were to get a position in the North American game, you'd have him by your side in a heartbeat. Look at baseball, look at New York Yankees – it is a huge entity with a culture of excellence. Compare that with the soccer team New York Red Bulls – do they have one? No they don't because if it doesn't work, they fold it up and go somewhere else.

You cannot create such a culture if you don't have a stable environment to cultivate it and you also have to give it time. Time to stumble, time to blossom, but time. You cannot put 150 years of history in a microwave and expect to have the same kind of feel as you get in the British game.

People forget that the American approach to sports is different to England or Europe. All the major sports in North America are governed by coaches, with everything boiling down to statistics and set plays and following instructions. Football – soccer – is down to a player once he's on a field, to play ninety minutes. Yes he'll follow tactics, yes he'll follow instructions, but the beauty of the game is in the unexpected and if that's the one thing you're trying to control then it's no surprise that you don't see it enjoyed on a wider scale. You can't simply change your player every time the ball goes out of play.

A football team is made up of eleven individuals, a successful football team is made up of eleven that are good at what they do and whose skills complement each other. The change will occur over time but it's a change that does need to happen. I view my own role in this as important and I take it seriously, and if I can give advice from the benefit of my experiences in the North American game then I will do so. What's the point of taking these roles and having the responsibility and opportunity if you don't take advantage of it and say something when it needs to be said? Nothing will change otherwise.

As you can tell, I'm so passionate about the development of tomorrow's stars and it's something that I've been around my entire life. When I was given the chance to play for Millwall I was picked from non-league football and that's the kind of thing that the system would probably not allow in the States. You can imagine how frustrating it is trying so hard to make a fundamental change and not getting anywhere with the bureaucracy, and then going back to the UK where I learned the game and not being taken seriously at times. Maybe the game has changed so much that people take themselves too seriously and view their own roles like that too.

I've always said that football is a simple game complicated by coaches. I look at my own role sometimes and wonder if I'm better off doing what I'm doing. I have had ambitions to work with more senior players and it's something I feel I'm still capable of doing, but for the last few years the majority of my time has been spent trying to prepare for a better tomorrow with younger players, and perhaps that could be the best way of making a difference.

There are many things that I don't like about the modern game although I think English football is still the best there is, but when I see statistics like the one that says less than thirty-three per cent of players in the Premier League can play for England it worries me. The players are there and some are getting chances, but there has to be a greater change in emphasis in order to get the national team performing at major tournaments. The focus has been on results and qualification as the be-all and end-all but that's not the bottom line. I don't like the fact that England and the FA have so often tried to imitate rather than carve their own path. They observe the success of Spain and try and build a team with smaller, technical players. They were aware of the success of African teams shortly after the turn of the century and tried to create athletes. It's all based on what is flavour of the month but what is forgotten is that it took those countries years to develop that style from grass roots level and that is why it is so successful.

Spain had a long period of underperformance as they built their incredibly successful team of the last decade, and you can see the same in Germany. Following that 5-1 win for England in Munich in 2001, the German FA decided to make drastic changes to the way they developed youngsters. And by God, they are now seeing the rewards for it, both in their national team and domestic teams. People often wondered what kind of style could overcome Barcelona but Bayern Munich dismantled them in the Champions League playing in a traditional, efficient German manner that was exciting to watch.

There are certainly lessons to be learned from the way that other nations do things but the key lesson is to stay true to your own identity because every dog will have its day. Football is cyclical, some teams have good periods and some teams have bad periods and that is simply something that has to be accepted. Manchester United's period of success under Sir Alex Ferguson was a freak, you cannot expect a quarter of a century at the top of the tree. If you can have a decade of contending at the top then you can consider yourself very successful. In order for England to do that, they have to give themselves the best possible chance and only having one in three players to pick from in Premier

League teams is not doing that.

Incidentally, and it probably won't come as a surprise, but I've always felt it's important for the top English teams to have British managers. I was very happy when United went for David Moyes, I felt that sent a good message through the game. Unfortunately it didn't quite go to plan under David at Old Trafford. I've got mixed feelings about the club hiring its first foreign manager in Louis Van Gaal but, with my thoughts on Dutch football already stated, I hope he can bring back an entertaining brand of football to the club.

The influx of foreign players has also influenced behavioural changes in the British game and that's something that I'm not fond of. Whether the impact that has had is irreversible I don't know, but what I do know is that I have the capacity to try and make a difference and I will always do that. The way I can do that at the moment is to try and influence the behaviour of tomorrow's players, to teach them to enjoy themselves, to express themselves and to try not to cheat a fellow player. For the last few years I've been doing that to hopefully guide youngsters in the North American game in the right direction but it's a universal philosophy that should be taught to kids worldwide.

It can get frustrating talking about all the political side of it but then the beauty is that I can talk about football as a game and in a way that never changes. The basic rules have never changed, the principle of the game is to score more goals than your opponent. I'm sure that doesn't need to be spelled out to anyone reading, yet I'm saying it because sometimes I'm not sure if even those inside the game appreciate how different things are in the modern game to how they were in the late 1970s. You can read or hear people talking about Lionel Messi as if it's a foregone conclusion that he is already the best of all time, but to me there will always be a question mark.

Maybe the only reason I envy the players of today is because of the surfaces they get to play on. They are immaculate, even the training fields, and lower division pitches can be like bowling greens. I would have loved to have played on them, and when thinking about what the likes of George Best or Pele could have done on today's pitches, I can't help but think that's the time you'd see a real player. Surely everyone has seen footage of George evading tackles from some of the roughest players in an era where there was no protection, and yet still be magic. For those reasons, I feel that you could pluck any number of gifted players at their peak from an older generation and put them into today's game and they would be even better. I don't like clichés but I'm sure even Lionel Messi would find it difficult to deal with the over-zealous attention of Chopper Harris and the lenient eyes of a referee on a field that resembles a farmyard.

At the time, though, we didn't know any better and I just loved playing no matter what the conditions. I don't think I've mentioned it up until now but I wore Adidas boots. I'd often find myself messing about with them as soon as I'd seen the state of the pitch. Some surfaces looked great before anyone walked on it, but after about five minutes of playing it'd cut up. I'd always wear brand new leather studs as they're really good at holding the ground. I'd always put Vaseline on them as well, which was a tip given to me by Mike Summerbee. I was very lucky that the boots would grip and I can remember a game at Chelsea where I was gliding across where everyone else was slipping. I'd never go on to a wet pitch without my leather studs, and I'd only use rubber studs on very dry surfaces.

When wearing the leather studs I'd always scuff them a bit as I was running out so that a bit of the nail was coming out. I'd never kick anyone, and I'd never dream of hurting an opponent or have any intention to do so, I think it was mostly about protection. I needed it, too, because I didn't wear shin guards or any protection on my shins. I was susceptible to kicks as a result but I always reasoned that I could be quicker, faster and smarter than my opponent so much that it wouldn't be a problem. I played most of my career without them as I found that they hindered me to be quite honest. There were wrap-around ones which went around your ankle and with them your leg could barely breathe, it was like playing in a sleeping bag. They were introduced in the 1974 World Cup and so they were the thing to wear, but didn't last long with me. Another problem with the regular shinpads was that you'd have to try and keep them in place, and tying them would cut off the circulation as well, leading to cramp. I just couldn't be comfortable with them, so for better or worse, I decided to go without. I suppose it was just as well that I had a good relationship with referees just in case. I'd shout, and rant and rave as much as anyone but importantly they knew I just loved the game, I wasn't out to con the referee, cheat an opponent, or kick anyone. It was ironic that I'd get sent off twice in my adult career and neither was for a dirty challenge.

I'm wandering away from the point, I suppose. So where was I? Oh yes, the latest stage of my career in North America and what the future holds.

I still have ambitions and I give my all in everything I do. Despite being away from my family when I'm coaching around North America I do enjoy still enjoy it. Though I've been doing it for such a long time, it is interesting to see different places and always nice to meet new people.

In Cleveland, in an evening after training I'd go to a local bar. They'd have karaoke nights and one of the regulars who loved these nights was a ninety-two year-old guy called Cowboy Mike. I loved talking to him. He told me he used to ride horses around when it was just fields where we were eating, but his last horse had died thirty two years ago. Mike was brilliant, he was a bit slow getting up on stage to sing and would walk the wrong way off of it but he was in charge of all his faculties. He was absolutely fascinating as at his age he'd seen the wars and lost friends in them.

We were sat in the bar one night with Mike and a couple who had driven from Wyoming were passing through and just stopped off to get something to eat. The guy was an eye doctor and his wife's family name was Hill. I knew we'd had some of our family come out to America at some point and when we discussed where she was from and her family's background in London, we ended up convinced that we must be related. That was Cowboy Mike, bringing everyone together and he was up there singing 'A Boy Named Sue', the song made popular by Johnny Cash. The country was declared a Republic in 1776, so he's been alive for about a third of the time that North America has been officially recognised which is incredible. The stories he told about the introduction of technology and the building of the highways and skyscrapers, really put things into perspective. It also shows you what a small world it is and how anything can happen. Lord knows if that lady and I were related, but what are the chances of two Hill's from the same area in England bumping into each other in an area of North America that's not exactly remote, but at the same time, not renowned as a tourist destination?

When I'm away coaching, I obviously have a lot of free time so I like to take the opportunity to indulge in another of my childhood loves and go fishing. In Cleveland there were some beautiful spots to do just that, as there were in Boston when I spent a short time coaching in the early Autumn of 2013 but just as they say 'there's no place like home,' for me, Palm Harbor in Florida is now home and really is the best place to relax. I can fish to my heart's content down there too.

Due to my being away, Claire had to sort the house out, but as always she's done a smashing job of it. I didn't grow fond of the cross country driving as twenty hours on the road can take it out of you, even if you are seeing some of the most magnificent countryside, so I decided after I finished my coaching in Cleveland that I would only take flights from that point. Flights do take it out of you but not as much as driving.

Every year I manage to get back over to England and often stay at Mottram Hall. The visits usually coincide with a tour with groups of American players I coach. They come over to enjoy the English culture and see the style of play, and no such visit would be complete without returning to Old Trafford.

My association with Manchester United is a huge part of my life and I still get an incredible feeling whenever I return. The bricks and mortar might change, as might the actual look and shape of the stadium, but when I go out to see the pitch, I can still remember bombing up and down that left hand side in front of all those magnificent supporters. I like to walk down the old tunnel that so many greats walked down before me.

You might think that stadiums need to be filled with people to create an atmosphere but there is a great one every time I'm at Old Trafford as it's bursting with memories and wonderful people who remain at the club from my time there. I feel fortunate that I've managed to maintain that good relationship with the club and it's funny, but I probably got on better with a few of my team-mates after I left! Living where I do though, the opportunity to meet up with them hasn't popped up often in recent years.

Martin Buchan is a prime example of someone I get on with better after retiring, and in his role with the PFA, he came to my aid when I was having a problem with my knee. A few years ago on the recommendation of the PFA, I went to see a doctor who had worked with the Arsenal team and performed surgery on Robin van Persie's ankle. I was his ten o'clock appointment and he told me that his eleven o'clock was none other than Stevie Coppell – what were the chances? It was lovely to see Stevie and I gave him a big hug. Like me, Stevie was robbed of his peak by a knee injury. I joked that we ought to go into the doctor's office and see what price he'd give us for a job lot.

Recently I was getting close with Brian Greenhoff again when he was tragically passed away in May 2013. Brian had sent me copies of pictures of his FA Cup medal, given I hadn't seen most of my mementoes from my United days, and we were looking forward to meeting up together in the summer of 2013. He was no age, just sixty, and his passing reminded me of the fragility of life. When you get that sort of reminder it makes you appreciate what you have and your memories, and I will treasure the times with Brian and all my other team-mates when we were part of a United side that people recall with fondness. Whether that's to do with the romance of not knowing what our collective potential could have been I don't know, but in the rich history of the club it's definitely not a bad position to assume. In the context of lost potential, we are in rich company.

Death is something we have to deal with, and it happens to us all, but some years are worse than others. 2013, the year in which I decided to write my life story, was a bad one. Brian's death shook me because he was about the same age as me and he should have had plenty of his life still in front of him, and then Jack Crompton passed away not long after. As I was finishing my book I was struck by another blow when I learned of the passing of Bill Foulkes. Jack had lived a long and fulfilled life and maybe it was just his time and Bill had been unwell for a while but it still provoked a significantly poignant moment as I finished writing my memoirs to hear that the man who had probably proved pivotal to my career in many ways had sadly died. Bill had a great life, achieved many incredible things and will be remembered as he should by thousands – and I can consider myself fortunate and privileged to have known him.

Tony Gubba, the sports commentator, was another from the footballing community who left us in that year and I remember him with much fondness. We're all going the same way but it still stuns you that one day you can hear someone talking and the next their obituaries are being written. These losses were difficult to stomach, as too was the death of Adam Broadbent, the son of the neighbours of mine, Edna and Chris who I spoke about much earlier in my story. They ran a jeans factory in Manchester back when I used to play for United. I'd watched him grow up and get married and settle down with his family and then, in 2013, I learned that he'd had cancer and died. It was incredibly tragic and for parents to outlive their child should not happen.

*****

I never had a team growing up that I really supported but I had a fondness for United that had started with watching the team in the 1960s and the fact my brother Sid supported them. When you sign for United then more often than not, your name will always be associated with them first and foremost no matter who else you play for. That's the way that it's always been and, I suppose, always will be.

It's an honour to be referred to as 'Manchester United's Gordon Hill' especially considering that it was only around two and a half years I spent there. It's funny, because I spent just as long at Millwall and the spell I had in Chicago was nearly as long, too, when you count both times. All had a major influence in my career. Millwall gave me my chance and I will always hold a special place for them and without Chicago and the help of Bill, I might never have gone to Manchester. All three clubs gave me something beyond football.

I adored my time down on the Cold Blow Lane, mixing with supporters and really feeling like I was one of them. Millwall fans have a reputation that is sometimes unfair but, as a former player, the way they have affection for you is a feeling like no other. Chicago was my first taste of America and what an introduction. I was very fond of the Chicago Sting and was very sad when it became another victim of the financial crisis in the North American game.

To go back to my earlier point about a culture of excellence in the game in the States, one thing that would be very welcome in my opinion is that if a franchise or a club is 'reborn', they should try and remain faithful to the heritage of the game. There's the Chicago Fire, and for me it would have been nice if they had kept the Sting name instead. It builds a legacy instead of a pattern where the attitude almost seemed like 'That didn't work, knock it down and start again.' I have to say though, even if they had brought the Sting back, they could have kept those horrid yellow kits!

Maybe it was only after returning to the club just to play those training matches in 1985 that I felt that United was 'my club', and that I've felt like that since. I'll always support them and want them to win, I always get asked about playing for the club wherever I go. Admittedly, there may have been a short spell after I left where I had mixed feelings. I could never put it in to words but then I heard Brian's feelings after he had left United and even though we had both got a deep love for the club, there was a time when we didn't want them to succeed under Dave Sexton. It wasn't personal against Dave but it was something that both Brian and myself had been forced to feel because of, effectively being pushed out of the club. Sure, I had sympathy for my former team-mates in 1979 after they suffered heartbreak in the Cup Final when Alan Sunderland scored the goal that beat us.

See, no matter what, it was always 'us' and that just goes to show that maybe that was the hold the club had over me. I loved United, I was United. And, after my second spell in the States when I came back and did a little bit of training with the club in 1985, it was almost as if I'd never been away. I was at the Cup Final in 1985 when Big Norman curled that beauty into the Everton goal and no-one was more thrilled than I was.

Football, like life, can give you every single emotion. Pride is one, and I was the proudest man at the Millennium Stadium in Cardiff in 2004 when United faced Millwall in the FA Cup Final. I was sat with both sets of fans around me and I was asked who I wanted to win. I replied simply that I didn't care. I only wanted to enjoy the occasion. It's a cliché to say that there were no losers but for Millwall, just getting to the final was as big an achievement as it was for United to win it. I could not have been happier on the day, and I was also delighted that the Lions maintained their Championship status in the 2013/14 season and hope one day they can gain promotion to the Premier League.

I don't mean to be condescending and I know any Millwall fans reading this will know that I'm not, but historically, their level has been in the top half of the Second Division or equivalent and there is nothing wrong with that. Everyone wants to punch above their weight and prove how good they can be but they also know who they are and their identity, and that's part of why I love the club so much. Naturally though, with the size of United and my work there in the nineties, most of my involvement when it comes to being asked about my former clubs is about them. Their success in that decade was something wonderful to witness close hand and I was so pleased for the supporters. When you're part of the fabric and the history of such a club, it's part and parcel that you would hold the side you played for with a little favour.

There were no airs or graces, even the top stars in that side would be aware of you and know your role in the history of the club. I don't know if that could be said of today's players being made instant millionaires as soon as they make the team, but if there's one thing I'm certain of it's that the club itself tries to make sure the players are still aware of it.

A couple of years ago, on one of my summer trips, I was at Mottram Hall sat having a drink and observing a player in the distance who was being put through his paces by a personal trainer. Later on he was introduced to me as Tom Cleverley, and on being told who I was, Tom said it was a pleasure to meet me and that he knew all about me. The only advice I could offer him on that occasion was simply to make the most of the precious opportunity he had. I was pleased to see Tom taken on a pre-season tour to America shortly after where he scored a great goal, and it was also good to see him break through and be given his chance in the first team. If he shows the same kind of dedication to his personal development as he seemed to that day, then he could have a great future. I'm not sure all of the younger players in this generation can be said to have a lot of time for players from the 1970s, maybe because they're not aware, or perhaps for other reasons.

As they grow and realise that football gives you two careers, and that people can quickly forget about you once you're not playing, then they may change the way they think. I'd learned the hard way when I was injured, that if you're not playing, people won't want to know you, but I had the pride to battle back and the determination to be involved with the game once I'd finished playing. As I said, you have two careers, three if like Tommy Docherty you've got a lot to say! Player, coach/manager and pundit. Normally, moving into punditry means you're not involved with coaching or managing, but I've done all three and feel that I've plenty to offer on the coaching or managing side.

These are my memoirs and not a CV so I'm not going to lay out all of my ideas and besides, anything would be dependent on the role, the club and the resources available. There are some things that aren't rocket science and yet time and time again I see clubs ignoring what I feel are obvious things that would help. The last generation in particular has seen an over reliance on statistics and science and for me it's no surprise that success stories are mostly those that stay true to the heritage and basic principles of the game. Barcelona's recent team with Iniesta and Messi is loved by purists but they were beaten convincingly in 2013, by a very German Bayern Munich team. It's probably worth a mention that Van Gaal is the man widely credited with the creation of the modern Barcelona and Bayern, so my concerns about a foreign manager at Man United are allayed by the track record of the man in question.

Bayern have returned to the forefront of the European game by remaining true to their own principles and sometimes it genuinely confuses me to see clubs not taking advantage of some simple principles that would improve their chances. First and foremost, I've always said that as a manager I would ensure I have a coach available to specialise in every position. You see that for goalkeepers, and it should be the same for outfield positions too. You can have the most experienced defender as your manager or first team coach and that's all well and good, but what can he tell your world class striker to help him improve? For me it should be a priority to have the best available coach you could attract to specialise in every position, and ensure they are appropriate for the division they'll be coaching in as well. It's simply a matter of logic that an experienced striker can give a greater insight into the art of finishing, or the right runs to make.

Something I don't see a lot of in the game that I'd like to see is that professional sneakiness, and I don't mean cheating an opponent, I mean in the same way that we had it in our team in 1977. It was a craft that the Brazilians mastered, the stealing of a football from an opponents toes, a bit like the Artful Dodger from Oliver Twist! I know there are so many people who bemoan the lack of natural wingers in the game because of the number of times they tell me, and I'd love to be able to give back the benefit of my experience and knowledge.

I'm happy and fulfilled in the work that I do as I love the game so much, but I've not yet given up on being involved again in the senior game at some level. I'm open minded about what capacity that will be. I've been involved in youth development for so long that maybe that would be something I could do at a professional club, while I still feel I've got a lot to offer as a senior coach or even a manager. Opportunities often present themselves and I assess them as they come, and as long as a proposal looks interesting and worthwhile, then it's something that I consider. One thing is for certain, I have plenty left in the tank to give to the game.

13

Home is Always Where the Heart is

My whole life and demeanour changed from the day I met Claire. Yes, I can still make rash decisions, yes I'm still flamboyant, and Claire will tell you that she's heard all my jokes fifty million times. She won't come to functions with me any more because she's been there and seen it all. She knows me better than anyone, she's my best friend, wife and lover. We've been through highs and lows together and I would not change her for the world. When I met her I was in such a tough place. It's said in football that it's hard for a player to keep moving while the family gets left behind. Claire has made sure that we have always had a great structure, we've always remained together and she deserves all the credit for that. I've gone out to provide, she has worked too, but she has done so much to keep everything together as well. I'm not one to overstate things, she has been wonderful and has always made sure we had a strong family unit and a stable home life for Sam.

We've been together for over thirty years and I have absolutely no regrets about anything other than I wish I could have met her earlier so that she could have seen me playing for Manchester United. You can't change what's been though. They say everything happens for a reason and she rescued me from a life where everything wasn't looking so great. I could have easily gone down the road of drinking and gone off the rails. I've seen it happen to too many people. You could say that Claire rescued me and made me realise that even though things were bad, I had a life to live.

As I write this part of the book, I'm in Cleveland, while Claire is in Florida and every single day I miss her terribly. Knowing that she's next to me, knowing that we're having a cup of tea, that's the kind of comfort I like as I'm a traditionalist, an old fashioned kind of guy. I've never been a womaniser, and I love Claire with all my heart and of course, she gave me my boy Sam. I love my daughter Kerry dearly. Missing out on so much of her growing up made me treasure Sam and every moment spent with him. I would never hesitate to give him anything and if he needed a heart he could have mine.

Kerry has two children who I adore called Cameron and Grace, and in July of 2013, Sam and his wife Kiley gave me a beautiful granddaughter named Gabriella who really is the apple of my eye. Claire and I love spending time with them but we also like to make sure we give them enough space to live their own lives. I think that comes from my own childhood where we had such a big family that Mum and Dad never really interfered in our personal business. They'd help and give advice but they also knew we had each other. I always make sure I tell my brothers and sisters that I love them and there's no shame in telling them that.

There's a photo of our parents fiftieth wedding anniversary with all the grandchildren at the time and it really brings a tear to my eye. It reminds me of where we came from, the times we didn't have a pot to piss in, but we had a strong family bond. I'm very conscious of letting them all know how much they mean to me, and I don't want to leave this planet without them all knowing how much I love them.

I spoke briefly about my relationship with my brothers and sisters at the start of my memoirs and I want to re-visit that now to talk about how things are now and how things change. Only when you look back are you really able to say why things happened or why you turned out a certain way. We were close, yes we'd fight and bicker, but that's normal in any family, let alone one the size of the Hill family.

We were very much part of the community and involved with

209

all the other families in the neighbourhood and so, as brothers and sisters, we all had our own friends and mixed in our own set of friends. There'd be a knock on the door in the morning and because there were so many of us, we would never know who it was for, and so one by one we'd all go and do our own thing. There were big families all around and it would be a case of doing something with my brothers now and then, and more often than not, that would be playing football. We didn't live in each others pockets. You grow up, and with all the changes and events that happen in life, you grow a different closeness. I still have many of the same friendships as I did when I was a kid, and I still remember my childhood days with much fondness.

The environment in which I grew up certainly influenced the way I would be later on, playing with my brothers' mates at football I had to learn to get along with all kinds of different people, and we knew so many people that it always helped me to be as social as possible. I'll talk to anyone for a conversation and I've always been the same. I try to be as friendly as possible and I think that's something that I learned from mum. Of the many things I learned from her and the values my parents taught me, that was one of the most valuable as it stood me in good stead for later life. There are many players of great talent who simply shrank under the pressure of playing for Manchester United but I think my childhood, the way I was always active and always with friends, helped me settle in so quickly. To be honest, the fact that United were such a family club helped as well. The atmosphere there was brilliant and as I've said a few times it was something that I really felt a part of.

It's a bit ironic that I felt so welcome at United with that kind of atmosphere as the first few weeks I was there, I spent so much time alone for probably the first time in my life. You get used to it and yes, I knew the players, but we rarely socialised together and it was the first time I'd been apart from everyone I'd known and grown up with, so I had to grow to enjoy my own company. Quite the contrast, isn't it, from being surrounded with lots and lots of people and then being on your own, yet that's something that has been a part of my life ever since. I learned to manage on my own, and that's why I can work away from time to time, but

I don't like it for too long.

After Jackie moved up and we lived in Buxworth, that was the first time I really had an opportunity to see the countryside and I fell in love with it. When I started seeing Claire, and she brought Cleo with her, I absolutely loved going out into the fields. When Cleo sadly died, we made a decision that we would get another English Sheepdog and also name her Cleo. In fact, we only broke that trend once, when we named one of them Flossy, and for whatever reason she just didn't settle with us. She needed to be outdoors more. The Cleo that we currently have has been with us since we went to Texas, she's our fourth, and I absolutely adore her. She's a great football player and her right paw is maybe better than my right foot!

Our family have always been great dog lovers. When I was a kid, we had a dog called Kurt which my brother David brought home, and we had a labrador called Blackie. I got a dog, but really it was a mongrel called Sandy, but then when I moved to the States for the first time for those few months in 1976, mum took Sandy in. She looked after all the grandkids and all the dogs, it was like the RSPCA sometimes. The dogs loved her too, they wouldn't leave her side, even animals knew what a wonderful person she was. Thinking about her now makes me miss her terribly, I wish I could talk to her every day just to tell her what I'm doing or get her advice on something. Or even just to tell her I love her. Because, when you strip everything away, and take away the career, I'm just a man who loves and lives for his family.

I played football because I was gifted and fortunate to get the chances I did, but I also did it because I love the game. I never cheated and have always behaved in an honest manner, just loving being associated with the game at its purest level. I never sought to get any recognition, personal acclaim or superstardom. Yes I could be flash on the field but it was always to try and score a goal, never to embarrass a fellow player. Of course I really enjoyed my time at United and playing for England was unbelievable but I also enjoyed my time at Northwich Victoria and reconnecting with the very root of the game. In today's game you look around and wonder if the players even enjoy the game. Too many have been bred as money-making athletes. I absolutely loved playing as a kid and playing in properly organised games with the nets up. When you get back to the basics, how can you not enjoy a game of football at any level if two sets of players are trying to win but also trying to entertain while doing so? It would be fair to say that I've had a love affair with football, football as a game and not just a source of income. That was simply an added bonus.

The real riches I got from the game were the friendships I have made and the chance to see as much of the world as I've been able to. To be honest, it's probably only with sitting down and writing my memories that I come to terms with everything I've been able to see and do. Like I've explained, I have burning ambitions in the game and still feel like I have plenty to contribute. I'm always asked about whether I would like to return to the United Kingdom, and should the right opportunity arise, I would, but until that point, I'll settle for the palm trees in Florida.

I'm not one to go looking for compliments but I cannot deny that it is always really nice and flattering to hear good things said to me. When I was told Bill Foulkes had recommended me to United – wow, how great an honour. When the great Jimmy Murphy, possibly the greatest identifier of talent in British football history, said that the club must sign me, there are just no words which do justice to how that made me feel then and how proud it still makes me feel today. However, nothing can compare to my wife, son, daughter and family telling me they love me, or the feeling I get when I see my grandchildren smile. What a feeling – heaven.

Appendix

Gordon Hill
Professional Record

Millwall 1972/73

DATE	COMP	OPPONENT	SCORE	GOALS
24 Apr 1973	D2	CARLISLE UTD (A)	W1-0	

Millwall 1973/74

DATE	COMP	OPPONENT	SCORE	GOALS
8 Sep 1973	D2	BLACKPOOL (A)	L0-1	
11 Sep 1973	D2	PRESTON (A)	L0-2	
15 Sep 1973	D2	HULL CITY (H)	W3-0	
17 Sep 1973	D2	SHEFF WED (H)	W1-0	
22 Sep 1973	D2	SWINDON TOWN (A)	W3-1	
29 Sep 1973	D2	CARLISLE UTD (H)	L1-2	
10 Oct 1973	LC2	NOTTINGHAM FOREST (H)	D0-0	
13 Oct 1973	D2	BRISTOL CITY (H)	L0-2	
16 Oct 1973	LC2 R	NOTTINGHAM FOREST (A)	W3-1	1
20 Oct 1973	D2	BOLTON (A)	W1-0	
22 Oct 1973	D2	PRESTON (H)	W5-1	
27 Oct 1973	D2	MIDDLESBROUGH (H)	L0-1	
31 Oct 1973	LC3	BOLTON (H)	D1-1	
3 Nov 1973	D2	NOTTS COUNTY (A)	D3-3	1
6 Nov 1973	LC3 R	BOLTON (A)	W2-1	
10 Nov 1973	D2	CARDIFF CITY (H)	W2-0	1

17 Nov 1973	D2	CRYSTAL PALACE (A)	D1-1	
21 Nov 1973	LC4	LUTON TOWN (H)	W3-1	
24 Nov 1973	D2	LEYTON ORIENT (H)	L0-1	
8 Dec 1973	D2	LUTON TOWN (H)	L0-1	
15 Dec 1973	D2	SUNDERLAND (H)	W2-1	1
19 Dec 1973	LC5	NORWICH CITY (H)	D1-1	
22 Dec 1973	D2	CARLISLE UTD (A)	D1-1	
29 Dec 1973	D2	BLACKPOOL (H)	D2-2	
1 Jan 1974	D2	ASTON VILLA (A)	D0-0	
5 Jan 1974	FAC3	SCUNTHORPE (H)	D1-1	
8 Jan 1974	FAC3 R	SCUNTHORPE (A)	L0-1	
12 Jan 1974	D2	HULL CITY (A)	D1-1	
20 Jan 1974	D2	FULHAM (H)	W1-0	
26 Jan 1974	D2	OXFORD (A)	W3-0	2
2 Feb 1974	D2	SUNDERLAND (A)	L0-4	
16 Feb 1974	D2	SWINDON TOWN (H)	W3-0	
23 Feb 1974	D2	NOTTINGHAM FOREST (H)	D0-0	
26 Feb 1974	D2	BRISTOL CITY (A)	L2-5	1
2 Mar 1974	D2	PORTSMOUTH (A)	D0-0	
9 Mar 1974	D2	MIDDLESBROUGH (A)	L1-2	
16 Mar 1974	D2	BOLTON (H)	W2-1	
23 Mar 1974	D2	CARDIFF CITY (A)	W3-1	1
30 Mar 1974	D2	NOTTS COUNTY (H)	D0-0	
6 Apr 1974	D2	LEYTON ORIENT (A)	D1-1	
12 Apr 1974	D2	WEST BROM (H)	W1-0	
13 Apr 1974	D2	CRYSTAL PALACE (H)	W3-2	
17 Apr 1974	D2	WEST BROM (A)	D1-1	
20 Apr 1974	D2	LUTON TOWN (A)	L0-3	
27 Apr 1974	D2	OXFORD (H)	D0-0	

Millwall 1974/75

DATE	COMP	OPPONENT	SCORE	GOALS
17 Aug 1974	D2	SUNDERLAND (H)	L1-4	
19 Aug 1974	D2	NOTTINGHAM FOREST (H)	W3-0	2
24 Aug 1974	D2	MANCHESTER UNITED (A)	L0-4	
27 Aug 1974	D2	NOTTINGHAM FOREST (A)	L1-2	
31 Aug 1974	D2	FULHAM (H)	W2-0	

2 Sep 1974	LC2	WEST BROM (A)	L0-1	
7 Sep 1974	D2	BLACKPOOL (A)	L0-1	
14 Sep 1974	D2	OXFORD UNITED (H)	D0-0	
16 Sep 1974	D2	MANCHESTER UNITED (H)	L0-1	
21 Sep 1974	D2	ASTON VILLA (A)	L0-3	
24 Sep 1974	D2	HULL CITY (A)	D1-1	1
28 Sep 1974	D2	BRISTOL CITY (H)	W1-0	
5 Oct 1974	D2	NORWICH CITY (A)	L0-2	
19 Oct 1974	D2	BRISTOL ROVERS (A)	L0-2	
26 Oct 1974	D2	WEST BROM (H)	D2-2	
2 Nov 1974	D2	OLDHAM (A)	D1-1	
9 Nov 1974	D2	BOLTON (H)	D1-1	1
16 Nov 1974	D2	YORK CITY (A)	L1-2	
30 Nov 1974	D2	NOTTS COUNTY (A)	L1-2	
7 Dec 1974	D2	LEYTON ORIENT (H)	D1-1	
14 Dec 1974	D2	SUNDERLAND (A)	L0-2	
26 Dec 1974	D2	OXFORD UNITED (A)	L1-3	1
28 Dec 1974	D2	PORTSMOUTH (H)	D0-0	
4 Jan 1975	FAC3	BURY (A)	D2-2	1
7 Jan 1975	FAC3 R	BURY (H)	D1-1	
11 Jan 1975	D2	LEYTON ORIENT (A)	L1-2	
13 Jan 1975	FAC3 R2	BURY (THE HAWTHORNS)	L0-2	
18 Jan 1975	D2	NOTTS COUNTY (H)	W3-0	
8 Feb 1975	D2	OLDHAM ATHLETIC (H)	D0-0	
14 Feb 1975	D2	CARDIFF CITY (A)	W1-0	
29 Mar 1975	D2	SHEFF WED (A)	W1-0	
31 Mar 1975	D2	PORTSMOUTH (A)	L0-1	
1 Apr 1975	D2	ASTON VILLA (H)	L1-3	
18 Apr 1975	D2	SOUTHAMPTON (A)	L2-3	
26 Apr 1975	D2	BRISTOL ROVERS (H)	D1-1	

Millwall 1975/76

DATE	COMP	OPPONENT	SCORE	GOALS
23 Aug 1975	D3	WREXHAM (H)	W2-1	1
25 Aug 1975	LC1	SWINDON TOWN (H)	L0-1	
30 Aug 1975	D3	PRESTON (A)	L1-2	1
6 Sep 1975	D3	HEREFORD TOWN (H)	W1-0	1

13 Sep 1975	D3	GRIMSBY TOWN (A)	L1-2	
20 Sep 1975	D3	SOUTHEND UTD (H)	W2-1	2
24 Sep 1975	D3	ALDERSHOT TOWN (A)	D1-1	
27 Sep 1975	D3	BURY (A)	L0-2	
4 Oct 1975	D3	MANSFIELD TOWN (H)	W1-0	
11 Oct 1975	D3	SHEFF WED (A)	L1-4	
18 Oct 1975	D3	ROTHERHAM (H)	W3-1	1
21 Oct 1975	D3	WALSALL (A)	D1-1	
25 Oct 1975	D3	CHESTERFIELD (A)	D2-2	1
1 Nov 1975	D3	COLCHESTER UTD (H)	D1-1	1
4 Nov 1975	D3	SHREWSBURY TOWN (H)	D0-0	
8 Nov 1975	D3	CHESTER CITY (A)	L1-3	

Manchester United 1975/1976

DATE	COMP	OPPONENT	SCORE	GOALS
15 Nov 1975	D1	ASTON VILLA (H)	W2-0	
22 Nov 1975	D1	ARSENAL (A)	L1-3	
29 Nov 1975	D1	NEWCASTLE (H)	W1-0	
6 Dec 1975	D1	MIDDLESBROUGH (A)	D0-0	
13 Dec 1975	D1	SHEFFIELD UTD (A)	W4-1	1
20 Dec 1975	D1	WOLVES (H)	W1-0	1
23 Dec 1975	D1	EVERTON (A)	D1-1	
27 Dec 1975	D1	BURNLEY (H)	W2-1	
3 Jan 1976	FAC3	OXFORD UNITED (H)	W2-1	
10 Jan 1976	D1	QPR (H)	W2-1	1
17 Jan 1976	D1	TOTTENHAM HOTSPUR (A)	D1-1	1
24 Jan 1976	FAC4	PETERBOROUGH (H)	W3-1	1
31 Jan 1976	D1	BIRMINGHAM CITY (H)	W3-1	
7 Feb 1976	D1	COVENTRY CITY (A)	D1-1	
14 Feb 1976	FAC5	LEICESTER CITY (A)	W2-1	
18 Feb 1976	D1	LIVERPOOL (H)	D0-0	
21 Feb 1976	D1	ASTON VILLA (A)	L1-2	
25 Feb 1976	D1	DERBY COUNTY (H)	D1-1	
28 Feb 1976	D1	WEST HAM UTD (H)	W4-0	
6 Mar 1976	FAC6	WOLVES (H)	D1-1	
9 Mar 1976	FAC6 R	WOLVES (A)	W3-2	
13 Mar 1976	D1	LEEDS UTD (H)	W3-2	

16 Mar 1976	D1	NORWICH CITY (A)	D1-1	1
20 Mar 1976	D1	NEWCASTLE (A)	W4-3	
27 Mar 1976	D1	MIDDLESBROUGH (H)	W3-0	1
3 Apr 1976	FAC SF	DERBY COUNTY (Hillsborough)	W2-0	2
10 Apr 1976	D1	IPSWICH (A)	L0-3	
17 Apr 1976	D1	EVERTON (H)	W2-1	
19 Apr 1976	D1	BURNLEY (A)	W1-0	
21 Apr 1976	D1	STOKE CITY (H)	L0-1	
25 Apr 1976	D1	LEICESTER CITY (A)	L1-2	
1 May 1976	FAC F	SOUTHAMPTON (Wembley)	L0-1	
4 Mar 1976	D1	MANCHESTER CITY (H)	W2-0	1

Manchester United 1976/77

DATE	COMP	OPPONENT	SCORE	GOALS
21 Aug 1976	D1	BIRMINGHAM CITY (H)	D2-2	
24 Aug 1976	D1	COVENTRY CITY (A)	W2-0	1
28 Aug 1976	D1	DERBY COUNTY (A)	D0-0	
1 Sep 1976	LC2	TRANMERE ROVERS (H)	W5-0	1
4 Sep 1976	D1	TOTTENHAM HOTSPUR (H)	L2-3	
11 Sep 1976	D1	NEWCASTLE UTD (A)	D2-2	
15 Sep 1976	UEFA CUP 1 Leg 1	AJAX (A)	L0-1	
18 Sep 1976	D1	MIDDLESBROUGH (H)	W2-0	
22 Sep 1976	LC3	SUNDERLAND (H)	D2-2	
25 Sep 1976	D1	MANCHESTER CITY (A)	W3-1	
29 Sep 1976	UEFA CUP 1 Leg 2	AJAX (H)	W2-0	
2 Oct 1976	D1	LEEDS UNITED (A)	W2-0	
4 Oct 1976	LC3 R	SUNDERLAND (A)	D2-2	
6 Oct 1976	LC3 R2	SUNDERLAND (H)	W1-0	
16 Oct 1976	D1	WEST BROM (A)	L0-4	
20 Oct 1976	UEFA CUP 2 Leg 1	JUVENTUS (H)	W1-0	1
23 Oct 1976	D1	NORWICH CITY (H)	D2-2	
27 Oct 1976	LC4	NEWCASTLE UTD (H)	W7-2	3
30 Oct 1976	D1	IPSWICH TOWN (H)	L0-1	
3 Nov 1976	UEFA CUP 1 Leg 2	JUVENTUS (A)	L0-3	
6 Nov 1976	D1	ASTON VILLA (A)	L2-3	1
10 Nov 1976	D1	SUNDERLAND (H)	D3-3	1
20 Nov 1976	D1	LEICESTER CITY (A)	D1-1	

27 Nov 1976	D1	WEST HAM UTD (H)	L0-2	
1 Dec 1976	LC QF	EVERTON (H)	L0-3	
18 Dec 1976	D1	ARSENAL (A)	L1-3	
27 Dec 1976	D1	EVERTON (H)	W4-0	1
1 Jan 1977	D1	ASTON VILLA (H)	W2-0	
3 Jan 1977	D1	IPSWICH TOWN (A)	L1-2	
8 Jan 1977	FAC3	WALSALL (H)	W1-0	1
15 Jan 1977	D1	COVENTRY CITY (H)	W2-0	
19 Jan 1977	D1	BRISTOL CITY (H)	W2-1	
22 Jan 1977	D1	BIRMINGHAM CITY (A)	W3-2	
29 Jan 1977	FAC4	QPR (H)	W1-0	
12 Feb 1977	D1	TOTTENHAM HOTSPUR (A)	W3-1	1
16 Feb 1977	D1	LIVERPOOL (H)	D0-0	
19 Feb 1977	D1	NEWCASTLE UTD (H)	W3-1	
26 Feb 1977	FAC5	SOUTHAMPTON (A)	D2-2	1
5 Mar 1977	D1	MANCHESTER CITY (H)	W3-1	1
8 Mar 1977	FAC5 R	SOUTHAMPTON (H)	W2-1	
12 Mar 1977	D1	LEEDS UNITED (H)	W1-0	
19 Mar 1977	FAC6	ASTON VILLA (H)	W2-1	
23 Mar 1977	D1	WEST BROM (H)	D2-2	1
2 Apr 1977	D1	NORWICH CITY (A)	L1-2	
5 Apr 1977	D1	EVERTON (A)	W2-1	2
9 Apr 1977	D1	STOKE CITY (H)	W3-0	
11 Apr 1977	D1	SUNDERLAND (A)	L1-2	1
16 Apr 1977	D1	LEICESTER CITY (H)	D1-1	
23 Apr 1977	FAC SF	LEEDS UNITED (Hillsborough)	W2-1	
26 Apr 1977	D1	MIDDLESBROUGH (A)	L0-3	
30 Apr 1977	D1	QPR (H)	W1-0	
3 May 1977	D1	LIVERPOOL (A)	L0-1	
11 May 1977	D1	STOKE CITY (A)	D3-3	2
14 May 1977	D1	ARSENAL (H)	W3-2	1
16 May 1977	D1	WEST HAM UTD (A)	L2-4	1
21 May 1977	FAC FINAL	LIVERPOOL (Wembley)	W2-1	

Manchester United 1977/78

DATE	COMP	OPPONENT	SCORE	GOALS
13 Aug 1977	CH SHIELD	LIVERPOOL (Wembley)	D0-0	

20 Aug 1977	D1	BIRMINGHAM CITY (A)	W4-1	1
24 Aug 1977	D1	COVENTRY CITY (H)	W2-1	1
27 Aug 1977	D1	IPSWICH TOWN (H)	D0-0	
30 Aug 1977	LC2	ARSENAL (A)	L2-3	
3 Sep 1977	D1	DERBY COUNTY (A)	W1-0	
10 Sep 1977	D1	MANCHESTER CITY (A)	L1-3	
14 Sep 1977	ECWC R1 L1	ST. ETIENNE (A)	D1-1	1
17 Sep 1977	D1	CHELSEA (H)	L0-1	
24 Sep 1977	D1	LEEDS UNITED (A)	D1-1	1
1 Oct 1977	D1	LIVERPOOL (H)	W2-0	
5 Oct 1977	ECWC R1 L2	ST. ETIENNE (Plymouth)	W2-0	
8 Oct 1977	D1	MIDDLESBROUGH (A)	L1-2	
15 Oct 1977	D1	NEWCASTLE UNITED (H)	W3-2	
19 Oct 1977	ECWC R2 L1	PORTO (A)	L0-4	
22 Oct 1977	D1	WEST BROM (A)	L0-4	
29 Oct 1977	D1	ASTON VILLA (A)	L1-2	
2 Nov 1977	ECWC R2 L2	PORTO (H)	W5-2	
5 Nov 1977	D1	ARSENAL (H)	L1-2	1
12 Nov 1977	D1	NOTTINGHAM FOREST (A)	L1-2	
19 Nov 1977	D1	NORWICH CITY (H)	W1-0	
26 Nov 1977	D1	QPR (A)	D2-2	2
3 Dec 1977	D1	WOLVES (H)	W3-1	
10 Dec 1977	D1	WEST HAM UTD (A)	L1-2	
17 Dec 1977	D1	NOTTINGHAM FOREST (H)	L0-4	
26 Dec 1977	D1	EVERTON (A)	W6-2	1
27 Dec 1977	D1	LEICESTER CITY (H)	W3-1	1
31 Dec 1977	D1	COVENTRY CITY (A)	L0-3	
2 Jan 1978	D1	BIRMINGHAM CITY (H)	L1-2	
11 Jan 1978	FAC3	CARLISLE UNITED (H)	W4-2	
14 Jan 1978	D1	IPSWICH TOWN (A)	W2-1	
21 Jan 1978	D1	DERBY COUNTY (H)	W4-0	2
28 Jan 1978	FAC4	WEST BROM (H)	D1-1	
1 Feb 1978	FAC4 R	WEST BROM (A)	L2-3	1
8 Feb 1976	D1	BRISTOL CITY (H)	D1-1	1
11 Feb 1978	D1	CHELSEA (A)	D2-2	1
25 Feb 1978	D1	LIVERPOOL (A)	L1-3	
1 Mar 1978	D1	LEEDS UNITED (H)	L0-1	
4 Mar 1978	D1	MIDDLESBROUGH (H)	D0-0	

11 Mar 1978	D1	NEWCASTLE UNITED (A)	D2-2	1
15 Mar 1978	D1	MANCHESTER CITY (H)	D2-2	2
18 Mar 1978	D1	WEST BROM (H)	D1-1	
25 Mar 1978	D1	LEICESTER CITY (A)	W3-2	1
27 Mar 1978	D1	EVERTON (H)	L1-2	1
1 Apr 1978	D1	ARSENAL (A)	L1-3	

Derby County 1977/78

DATE	COMP	OPPONENT	SCORE	GOALS
9 May 1978	D1	ARSENAL (H)	W3-0	1

Derby County 1978/79

DATE	COMP	OPPONENT	SCORE	GOALS
19 Aug 1978	D1	MANCHESTER CITY (H)	D1-1	
22 Aug 1978	D1	EVERTON (A)	L1-2	
26 Aug 1978	D1	BIRMINGHAM CITY (A)	D1-1	
30 Aug 1978	LC 2	LEICESTER CITY (A)	W0-1	1
28 Oct 1978	D1	LEEDS UTD (A)	L0-4	
4 Nov 1978	D1	WOLVES (H)	W4-1	1
11 Nov 1978	D1	MANCHESTER CITY (A)	W2-1	
18 Nov 1978	D1	BIRMINGHAM CITY (H)	W2-1	
21 Nov 1978	D1	COVENTRY CITY (A)	L2-4	
2 Dec 1978	D1	BRISTOL CITY (A)	L0-1	
9 Dec 1978	D1	MANCHESTER UNITED (H)	L1-3	
16 Dec 1978	D1	ARSENAL (A)	L0-2	
23 Dec 1978	D1	ASTON VILLA (H)	D0-0	
16 Jan 1979	FAC3	PRESTON NORTH END	L0-3	
31 Mar 1979	D1	QPR (A)	D2-2	

Derby County 1979/80

DATE	COMP	OPPONENT	SCORE	GOALS
18 Aug 1979	D1	WEST BROM (A)	D0-0	
22 Aug 1979	D1	WOLVES (H)	L0-1	
25 Aug 1979	D1	EVERTON (H)	L0-1	

29 Aug 1979	LC 2 LEG 1	MIDDLESBROUGH (H)	L0-1	
1 Sep 1979	D1	CRYSTAL PALACE (A)	L0-4	
8 Sep 1979	D1	ARSENAL (H)	W3-2	
15 Sep 1979	D1	MANCHESTER UNITED (A)	L0-1	
27 Oct 1979	D1	STOKE CITY (A)	L2-3	2
3 Nov 1979	D1	WEST BROM (H)	W2-1	1
17 Nov 1979	D1	IPSWICH TOWN (H)	L0-1	

QPR 1979/80

DATE	COMP	OPPONENT	SCORE	GOALS
1 Dec 1979	D2	CAMBRIDGE UTD (A)	L1-2	
8 Dec 1979	D2	WREXHAM (H)	D2-2	
15 Dec 1979	D2	NEWCASTLE UTD (A)	L2-4	
27 Dec 1979	D2	LEICESTER CITY (A)	L0-2	
1 Jan 1980	D2	BIRMINGHAM CITY (A)	L1-2	
5 Jan 1980	FAC3	WATFORD (H)	L1-2	
8 Mar 1980	D2	BURNLEY (A)	W3-0	
14 Mar 1980	D2	WATFORD (H)	D1-1	
26 Apr 1980	D2	NEWCASTLE UTD (H)	W2-1	
3 May 1980	D2	WREXHAM (A)	W3-1	

QPR 1980/81

DATE	COMP	OPPONENT	SCORE	GOALS
16 Aug 1980	D2	OLDHAM ATHLETIC (A)	L0-1	
19 Aug 1980	D2	BRISTOL ROVERS (H)	W4-0	
3 Sep 1980	LC 2	DERBY COUNTY (A)	D0-0	
6 Sep 1980	D2	NOTTS COUNTY (A)	L1-2	1
13 Sep 1980	D2	NEWCASTLE UTD (H)	D1-2	
20 Sep 1980	D2	SHEFFIELD WEDNESDAY (A)	L0-1	

Gordon Hill League Career

SEASON	CLUB	COMP	APPS	GOALS
72/73	MILLWALL	DIV TWO	1	0
73/74	MILLWALL	DIV TWO	39	7
74/75	MILLWALL	DIV TWO	38	6

1975	CHICAGO STING (LOAN)	NASL	21	16
75/76	MILLWALL	DIV THREE	16	8
75/76	MANCHESTER UNITED	DIV ONE	26	7
76/77	MANCHESTER UNITED	DIV ONE	39	15
77/78	MANCHESTER UNITED	DIV ONE	36	17
77/78	DERBY COUNTY	DIV ONE	1	1
78/79	DERBY COUNTY	DIV ONE	13	1
79/80	DERBY COUNTY	DIV ONE	9	3
79/80	QPR	DIV TWO	9	0
80/81	QPR	DIV TWO	5	1
81/82	MONTREAL MANIC	NASL	36	18
1982	CHICAGO STING	NASL	26	9
1983	INTER MONTREAL	CPSL	7	6
85/86	FC TWENTE	EREDIVISIE	19	4
1986	HJK HELSINKI	VEIKKAUSLIGA	2	2
		TOTAL	**343**	**121**

Gordon Hill Indoor Record

YEAR	TEAM	APPS	GOALS
82/83	CHICAGO STING	11	10
82/83	NEW YORK ARROWS	22	10
82/83	SAN JOSE EARTHQUAKES	4	2
83/84	KANSAS CITY COMETS	41	46
84/85	KANSAS CITY COMETS	9	4
84/85	TACOMA STARS	19	11
	TOTAL	**106**	**83**